Congressmen
and the Electorate

Congressmen
and the Electorate

ELECTIONS FOR THE U.S. HOUSE AND THE PRESIDENT, 1920-1964

MILTON C. CUMMINGS, JR.

THE FREE PRESS, NEW YORK
COLLIER-MACMILLAN LIMITED, LONDON

To the memory
of my father

Preface

The book that follows is a study of elections for the United States House of Representatives and of the interrelationship between the vote for President and the vote for Congressmen in presidential election years. It rests primarily on an analysis of the general election results for President and for Congressmen in the 12 presidential years between 1920 and 1964. A substantial part of the book explores the extent of the similarity and the differences between the congressional and presidential electoral support polled by each of the major parties. In these sections some of the factors that have been associated with split-ticket voting at the national level are also examined. The other major concern of the book is with some of the longer term trends in partisan strength at the congressional level that have been manifesting themselves since 1920; for it is these trends that have been reshaping the character of American congressional electoral politics over the last generation and a half.

Several considerations prompted my interest in congressional elections. First there was the obvious intrinsic importance of the process by which our federal legislators are chosen. Although there is a substantial and growing literature on congressional elections, students of American politics have tended to devote more attention to the election of the President than to elections for Congress. For one with an interest in the electoral process more generally, there was also the hope that by studying both presidential and congressional elections together, insights might be obtained that the study of presidential elections alone would fail to provide. Finally I was curious about the light which congressional elections might shed on American politics more generally, and about the consequences that some of the peculiar features of congressional elections —and their relation to the voting for President—have for the functioning of the American political system as a whole.

There are several aspects of congressional elections which are not treated in this book. Although both topics would merit detailed additional study, midterm elections are touched on only incidentally, and the book contains no systematic analyses of congressional primaries. The analysis that follows is based mainly on general election returns for all House contests from 1920–1964, and on the presidential returns from individual House districts for about four fifths of the districts from 1920–1944 and for virtually all districts from 1948–1964.

Many people provided help and encouragement during the course of this study. I am particularly grateful to the Social Science Research Council for grants on two occasions that enabled me to devote more time to the research. I am also deeply indebted to Dr. Ruth C. Silva, of The Pennsylvania State University, who very graciously allowed me to make use of her extensive collection of presidential election statistics, broken down for individual House districts, for the period 1920–1948. Without her generous help, many of the kinds of analyses that follow would not have been possible. Like most scholars in the field of American elections, I also owe a debt of gratitude to Richard M. Scammon. On more than one occasion he provided words of encouragement and data when it appeared that the election returns I was seeking could not be found anywhere else.

In a very real sense, I am also indebted to a large number of my fellow scholars in the field of American elections and the Congress, both through their writings and through frequent conversations with a number of them. There are, however, several individuals to whom I would especially like to express my thanks: to David E. Butler, Dale Jorgenson, and Nelson W. Polsby, who read substantial parts of the manuscript and gave me the benefit of their criticisms; to The Honorable William H. Avery, then a member of the House of Representatives and now Governor of Kansas, who provided me with a place to work on Capitol Hill; to Barbara Busch, a production editor of exceptional helpfulness at The Free Press; to my mother, Lela B. Cummings, who did extensive work on the election returns for 1960 and 1964; to Exa Murray, who typed the manuscript; and to Luella Gettys Key, who read the draft chapters and did what she could to get me to improve the way I presented my material. I am sure that no one will dispute me when I hasten to add that I, not they, are responsible for the book's shortcomings.

While I was working and writing on House elections, I also bene-fitted greatly from informal discussions about their electoral prob-lems with a number of members of the House of Representatives. No other leadership group in American society places their record before those whom they serve for their approval or rejection in more clearcut fashion than do our Congressmen; and it is, of course, their willingness to do this every two years since the late 18th century that helps make our democratic political system possible.

Like many other American political scientists, I also owe a special and profound debt of gratitude to the late V. O. Key, Jr. It was he who initially encouraged me to work on congressional elections, and he read and commented on many of the original analyses of House elections that I made as one of his graduate students working on a dissertation at Harvard University. As all who had the privi-lege of working with him remember, it was an experience to be treasured.

Finally, most authors will know how real a debt is being expressed when I say that I am endlessly grateful to my wife, Nancy, and to my sons, Christopher and Jonathan. She helped me throughout—as thoughtful critic, editor, and research assistant; and they did their part by doing without their father on too many evenings to remem-ber in order that this book might be done.

Contents

❦

List of Tables

List of Figures

»xvi«

Congressmen
and the Electorate

CHAPTER I

Presidents, Congressmen,

and the National Party Ticket

The dissimilarity in the ingredients which will compose the national government, and still more in the manner in which they will be brought into action in its various branches, must form a powerful obstacle to a concert of views in any partial scheme of elections. There is sufficient diversity in the state of property, in the genius, manners, and habits of the people of the different parts of the Union, to occasion a material diversity of disposition in their representatives towards the different ranks and conditions in society. And though an intimate intercourse under the same government will promote a gradual assimilation in some of these respects, yet there are causes, as well physical as moral, which may, in a greater or less degree, permanently nourish different propensities and inclinations in this respect. But the circumstance which will be likely to have the greatest influence in the matter, will be the dissimilar modes of constituting the several component parts of the government. The House of Representatives being to be elected immediately by the people, the Senate by the State legislatures, the President by electors chosen for that purpose by the people, there would be little probability of a common interest to cement these different branches in a predilection for any particular class of electors.

—*The Federalist,* Number 60
Alexander Hamilton

In accounts of American politics, no feature of the nation's constitutional system has received more attention than its emphasis on the formal separation of powers, and the consequences this may have for executive-legislative relations. Much has been written about the conflict between the White House and Capitol Hill, and about the different groups of interests to which the Presidency and the Congress often appeal and respond.[1] The frequent occasions when an American President comes into conflict with members of his own party, as well as with the official opposition on Capitol Hill, underscore the real and persistent differences that may exist even between the congressional and presidential wings of the same party.

Yet, if there are elements of conflict embedded in the American constitutional system, there are also numerous devices that facilitate collaboration between the Congress and President of the day. And despite the differences of emphasis between each party's presidential and congressional wing, a major source of that collaboration is the presence in Congress of members of the President's own party. Democratic Representatives do not always support a Democratic Chief Executive, and a G.O.P. Congressman will not invariably heed a Republican President's appeal. But the occupant of the White House can reasonably expect to obtain more support for his legislative program from his party's side of the aisle than from opposition Congressmen.[2] And in an occasional session of Congress, when the President has firm majorities of House and Senate members of his own party who are committed to most of his legislative objectives, the amount of executive-legislative collaboration can be truly startling, as Lyndon Johnson and the heavily Democratic 89th Congress made clear in 1965.

This tie of party, of course, reflects a more fundamental bond that underlies the relationship between the White House and Capitol Hill. Between President and Congress there exists a common link—

1. Writing in the 1950's and early 1960's, James McGregor Burns, for example, perceived a "four-party system" in the United States. Both major parties, he contended, were split between a presidential wing, which supported "urban liberalism," and a congressional wing, which represented rural and semi-rural opposition to the demands of urban interest groups. James M. Burns, "America's 'Four-Party' System," *The New York Times Magazine*, August 5, 1956, p. 10. See also Burns, *The Deadlock of Democracy* (Englewood Cliffs, N.J.: Prentice-Hall, 1963).

2. For a demonstration of this tendency during 1953–1954, when G.O.P. Representatives, faced with a President of their own party for the first time in 20 years, gave his program substantially more support than did their Democratic colleagues, see V. O. Key, Jr., "The Eisenhower Program and the Congressional Elections," *The Christian Science Monitor*, October 5 and 7, 1954.

the electorate to which both are ultimately responsible. The President's constituency and the particular constituencies of individual Congressmen are, to be sure, radically different. The President, along with his vice-presidential running mate, is the only elected official in the United States for whom the entire electorate may vote. Individual Congressmen, on the other hand, are elected in local districts whose residents make up but a small fraction of the total national electorate. It is even possible for a President to win the election in his own national constituency while losing a majority of the House districts, as John F. Kennedy demonstrated in 1960 when he carried only 206 of the constituencies from which the country's 437 House members were elected in that year. Under the present electoral system, many Congressmen from safe districts are also insulated from shifts of sentiment that can have a decisive effect on the outcome of the presidential contest.

Nevertheless, the members of the House as a whole, like the President, are elected by voters scattered throughout the country; and the consequences this can have for executive-legislative relations are far-reaching. The voters in most districts can, if they choose, vote for Congressmen who will tend to support the nation's Chief Executive. They can thus mitigate the cleavage between the coordinate branches of government. Or the voters can send Congressmen to Washington who will oppose the President on a good many issues of the day. After elections of this sort, the net effect of party sentiment may actually be to hinder executive-legislative cooperation.

Yet even when control of the Congress and the Presidency is divided, the presence in the legislature of members of the President's own party serves to bring the policies of the two branches of government more closely into line. The process by which this takes place may be a complex mixture of conflict and collaboration. But a disciplined legislative minority, backed by the threat of presidential vetoes, can go a long way toward tempering the demands of a legislative majority, as President Eisenhower and the Republican minority in the House demonstrated during the heavily Democratic 86th Congress in 1959 and 1960.

The relationship between the presidential election results and the outcome of the contests for the House thus has a powerful impact on the functioning of the nation's political system. To a considerable extent the general tenor of executive-legislative relations depends on the electorate's most recent expression of sentiment. And the changing character of successive electoral verdicts turns, fundamentally, on two broad sets of factors. First, of course, there is the variety of viewpoints—Hamilton's "diversity of disposition"—that always may be found among successful candidates for the Presidency and the Congress, even those nominated by the same party. The reelection of Virginia's Democratic Representative Howard W. Smith in 1960, for example, did not materially advance the prospects for President Kennedy's legislative program.

But the bonds of party are sufficiently important in America that there is a second set of factors that helps to indicate the significance of the electoral results in a presidential year. These factors are the differences and similarities between the sources of electoral support that each party's presidential and congressional wings are able to command. When the voters bestow their favors equally on presidential and congressional candidates of the same party, the victorious President is likely to have a legislative majority headed by his fellow partisans with which to work. But when the electorate discriminates between a party's presidential and congressional tickets, the relationship between the Congress and the Presidency may be altered. This unwillingness to vote a straight ticket at the national level may leave the President with a congressional wing of his party that is much weaker than he is, as happened to Eisenhower in 1956. Or it may leave a party with its congressional wing considerably stronger than its winning presidential nominee, as happened to Kennedy in 1960. In either event, the relationship between the presidential and congressional wings of the President's party is different from what it would have been if the electorate had voted a straight ticket at the national level.

This book explores the relationship between the vote for President and the outcome of House elections in presidential years. Subsequent chapters will focus on some of the differences between the vote for presidential and House candidates of the same party that lie embedded in the returns of past elections. Yet most Americans, if they vote at all, vote a straight ticket at the national level. One should begin, therefore, by emphasizing the substantial elements of similarity that exist between each major party's congressional and presidential electoral support.

Political Parties and the Presidential and Congressional Electoral Tides

THE OBJECTIVE OF the framers of the Constitution was to divide the presidential and congressional constituencies. It was a presupposition of Federalist theory that one part of the electorate would find its interests best represented by the Presidency while other groups would obtain their most effective political expression in the Congress.[3] By providing that House members should be elected directly by the people while the President was to be selected by a specially chosen electoral college, the electoral system itself was designed to give force to the separation of powers.

In practice, the consequences of three developments brought a measure of unity to the process by which the Chief Executive and the national legislature are selected. One was the modification of the role of the electoral college. Another was the concurrent election of the President and Congressmen in presidential years. But the most important development of all was the emergence of national political parties.

What Bagehot said of the British House of Commons—"party is inherent in it, is bone of its bone, and breath of its breath"[4]—can with equal truth be said of the public life of the United States almost from its inception in 1789. The new nation was a federal republic, but ties of party quickly spanned state boundary lines. Even during President Washington's first term, as a careful study of the Jeffersonian Republicans has demonstrated, much of the impetus and incentive for party organization at the state level came from a

---

3. Alexander Hamilton, among others, voiced this feeling clearly. He referred to the need for "energy in the Executive" in order to secure the "protection of property against those irregular and high-handed combinations which sometimes interrupt the ordinary course of justice . . . ." *The Federalist*, Number 70, (New York: The Modern Library, 1937), p. 454.
4. Walter Bagehot, *The English Constitution* (London: Oxford University Press, World's Classics Edition, 1952), p. 125.

party-minded Congress and from national figures like Jefferson and Madison.[5] In building a rival party to the Federalists, these men did not merely combine preexisting state and local party organizations. In some instances, they created the elements for their combinations. When Washington retired, the electorate was presented with an opportunity to choose between the presidential candidates of two great national parties.

In time the Federalist party dissolved, and it took the Federalists' descendants a few years to learn the lesson that the Republicans had given them in how to compete for support in a mass electorate. But with the exception of this brief period preceding 1824, and the turbulant years surrounding the Civil War, two national political parties have offered the voters a choice between rival candidates for the White House during every presidential election since 1796. At the same time, the electorate in most House districts could also vote for congressional candidates nominated by those same parties.

The consequences of this, both for executive-legislative relations and for the party system, were far-reaching. Hamilton had predicted that there was "little probability of a common interest" that would cement the different branches of government "in a predilection for any particular class of electors."[6] In part, however, he was wrong. Today a President and the Representatives of his party in the House rely to a great degree on the support of the same voters in the national electorate.

A rough indication of the extent to which the fortunes of each party's presidential and congressional nominees move in concert is provided by Figure 1.1. The data, which indicate the division of the two-party vote for President and Congressmen in the country as a whole, cover the 48 years between 1916 and 1964. During this period, there was usually a fairly close correspondence between the percentage of the popular vote polled by a major party's House ticket and that party's share of the presidential tally. Of the 13 elections analyzed, in only one did the difference between a major

5. Noble E. Cunningham, Jr., *The Jeffersonian Republicans: The Formation of Party Organization, 1789–1801* (Chapel Hill: North Carolina University Press, 1958).

6. *The Federalist*, Number 60, *op. cit.*, p. 390.

party's popular vote for President and Congressmen exceed 5 per cent.[7]

Individual elections vary, however, in the closeness of the correspondence between the total vote for President and the total vote for Congressmen. It is clear, for example, that third-party movements may widen the divergence between each major party's presi-

Figure 1.1—Popular votes for President and Congressman: A comparison of national tickets, 1916–1964

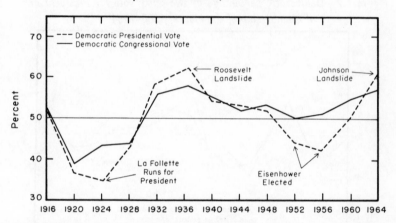

dential and congressional electoral support. Thus, in 1924, Senator Robert La Follette's minor-party presidential bid netted him nearly five million votes while third-party House nominees associated with his candidacy polled just over a million votes.[8] And in the four most recent presidential elections between 1952 and 1964, the discrepancy

7. Although the comparisons in Figure 1.1 are based on the division of the two-party vote, a presentation of each major party's percentage of the total vote for Congress and President would show roughly the same distinctions.

8. House candidates nominated by third-party groups who supported La Follette polled 1,029,014 votes—as against 4,831,289 votes for La Follette—in 1924. La Follette drew support both from former Republicans and former Democrats. But the House returns from districts where the Wisconsin Senator was strong suggest that most of the voters who supported him voted Democratic or Republican at the congressional level. For an examination of La Follette's 1924 electoral support, see V. O. Key, Jr., *Politics, Parties, and Pressure Groups*, Fourth Edition (New York: Thomas Y. Crowell Company, 1958), pp. 286–290.

between the presidential and congressional voting was also greater than in most previous elections. In 1952 and 1956, President Eisenhower was markedly more popular than his congressional running mates. In 1960 President Kennedy trailed the Democratic House ticket. And in 1964 the combination of Lyndon Johnson at the head of the Democratic ticket and Barry Goldwater as the Republican presidential nominee led to an election in which Johnson ran well ahead of many of his congressional running mates.

Figure 1.2—Democratic percentage of two-party vote for President and of Membership of the House, 1900–1964[a]

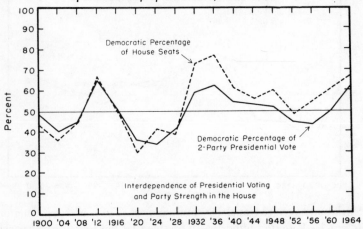

[a] Primary Source: V. O. Key, Jr., *Politics, Parties, and Pressure Groups*, Fifth Edition (New York: Thomas Y. Crowell Company, © 1964), p. 557. Used by permission of the publisher.

It also appears that the vote for President is more volatile than the vote for Congressmen—at least in elections when one of the presidential contenders makes a strong showing. Victorious Presidents who win by a healthy margin usually poll a higher percentage of the vote than their congressional running mates. Of the four elections (out of 13) when the winning President did not outpace his party's House ticket, two were in 1916 and 1948, both close elections, and another was in 1960—the closest presidential election of all.[9]

9. In 1948, President Truman probably lost a number of votes that were cast for the third-party candidacies of Wallace and Thurmond but which went to Democratic House nominees.

The other year when the winning President trailed his congressional running mates was 1940, when President Roosevelt was running for an unprecedented third term. Especially when there are great peaks of popular enthusiasm for a particular presidential candidate, as in the Roosevelt landslide of 1936 and the 1956 Eisenhower sweep, the division of the two-party congressional vote appears to be more resistant to the forces that propel the presidential electoral tide.

These variations draw attention to differences between the presidential and congressional vote—differences that can have a decisive impact on the outcome of particular elections. Yet the fact remains that over the years there has been a substantial similarity between the share of the popular vote polled by a party's presidential and congressional tickets. This similarity is in turn reflected by a tendency for the division of party strength in the House to parallel the movements of the presidential electoral tide (Figure 1.2). Again the correlation between the presidential voting and each party's strength in the House is by no means perfect. A given division of the popular presidential vote is not invariably associated with precisely the same division of House seats. Yet the relationship is close enough so that on only two widely separated occasions—in 1848 and in 1956, with a near miss in 1960—has the electorate sent a President to Washington without a House majority of the same party.[10]

Fate of the Party Ticket: Interdependence of the Vote for President and for Congressmen

FURTHER EVIDENCE OF THIS interdependence between the presidential and the congressional vote emerges if one probes behind the aggre-

10. There was an important difference between the 1848 and the 1956 results. When General Zachary Taylor defeated his Democratic opponent, Lewis Cass, by 1,360,101 votes to 1,220,544, his percentage of the two-party vote—52.7—and his plurality were rather small. General Eisenhower's share of the 1956 vote (57.8 per cent), by contrast, was enormous; and when Democratic candidates for the House outpolled their Republican opponents by more than 1,360,000 votes in 1956, they did so in the face of a G.O.P. presidential plurality that exceeded 9,500,000 votes. Figures cited for 1848 appear in *The World Almanac and Book of Facts for 1957* (New York: *The New York World-Telegram and The Sun,* 1957), p. 51.

gate relationships revealed in Figures 1.1 and 1.2 to examine the election returns in individual House districts. An analysis of this type appears in Table 1.1. The data, drawn from the 12 presidential years between 1920 and 1964, cover the returns for President and Congressman during that period in more than four fifths of the nation's House districts.

Table 1.1—Congressional Districts with Split Results: Districts Carried by a Presidential Nominee of One Party and by a House Candidate of Another Party, 1920–1964

Year	Number of Districts	Total Number of Districts With Split Results[a]	Per Cent	Number of Districts With Results Split Between Major-Party Candidates[b]	Per Cent
1920	345	11	3.2	11	3.2
1924	356	34	9.6	31	8.7
1928	358	68	19.0	67	18.7
1932	358	51	14.2	46	12.8
1936	361	51	14.1	41	11.4
1940	362	53	14.6	48	13.3
1944	366	40	10.9	39	10.7
1948	422	73	17.3	73	17.3
1952	435	82	18.9	81	18.6
1956	435	127	29.2	127	29.2
1960	437	111	25.4	111	25.4
1964	435	145	33.3	145	33.3
Total	4670	846	18.1	820	17.6

a The data in this column cover districts carried by a major-party presidential candidate and by a House candidate nominated either by the other major party or by a minor party.
b The data in this column cover districts carried by a House candidate of one major party and by a presidential candidate of the other major party.

Table 1.1 indicates just how closely the fortunes of a presidential candidate and his House running mate are tied together in individual districts. Between 1920 and 1964, the chances were better than four in five that the presidential and congressional nominees of the same party would win or lose a House district together. Individual elections, of course, vary widely in the number of districts that split their results. In 1920, a scant 3.2 per cent of the districts analyzed returned a mixed verdict. In 1964 a third of the nation's House districts split their results. Over 44 years, however, only 18.1 per cent of the districts supported a presidential candidate of one party while voting for an opposition House contestant.

Congressmen whose prospects of reelection are uncertain are well aware of the stake they have in the success of their party's national ticket. In the intraparty struggle that preceded the Republican National Convention in 1952, a heavy majority of the Republican

Table 1.2—Relationship between Presidential Vote in Congressional Districts and Results of House Elections, 1920–1964[a]

Winning President's District Percentage	Number of Districts	Number of Congressmen of Winning President's Party Elected	Per Cent of Districts Won by Congressmen of Winning President's Party
0–4.9	26	9[b]	34.6
5–29.9	194	8	4.1
30–34.9	83	3	3.6
35–39.9	244	15	6.1
40–44.9	327	37	11.3
45–47.4	218	38	17.4
47.5–49.9	278	80	28.8
50–52.4	311	138	44.4
52.5–54.9	301	191	63.4
55–59.9	714	510	71.4
60–64.9	628	534	85.0
65–69.9	434	390	89.9
70–94.9	849	815	96.0
95–100	63	63	100.0
Total	4670	2831	

[a] Districts for which no presidential figures are available for 1920, 1924, 1928, 1932, 1936, 1940, 1944, and 1948 are excluded from this table. The data for the period between 1920 and 1944 cover 82.3 per cent of the congressional contests held during those years. With the exception of 13 Cook County, Illinois results, all of the 1948 House races are included. For the four presidential years between 1952 and 1964, all House districts are covered by the data.

[b] The nine Congressmen in this unit were all Democrats elected in Alabama in 1948, when President Truman's name did not appear on that state's ballot.

Representatives from marginal districts, who expressed a preference, favored General Eisenhower over Robert A. Taft—a stance that, in some cases at least, was probably linked to a belief that Eisenhower would be a better vote-getter than the Ohio Senator.[11] For Congressmen who have had a close fight on their hands in the past, there can be a marked advantage in having a presidential

11. Malcolm Moos, *Politics, Presidents and Coattails* (Baltimore: The Johns Hopkins Press, 1952), pp. 83–84.

candidate heading their ticket who can win by a decisive margin.

The extent of this advantage becomes clear if the results of House elections are related to the size of the vote polled by a successful presidential nominee in individual districts. Since 1920, the larger a winning presidential candidate's lead in a particular constituency was, the brighter were the prospects that the district would also send a House nominee of the President's party to Washington. In Table 1.2, data drawn from the 12 presidential election years between 1920 and 1964 have been grouped together. In districts that a winning presidential candidate carried by a narrow margin (under 52.5 per cent), the chances that his congressional teammate would also win were not much better than four in ten. But as the President's strength in individual House districts went up, the outlook for his party's House ticket also improved. In districts where the winning presidential ticket polled between 60 and 65 per cent of the two-party vote, the President's congressional running mate also was destined for victory more than five times in every six.

The statistics in Table 1.2 are an average of the returns from 12 different elections. The results of individual elections may vary from the average. In any specific year, a given presidential percentage is not always paralleled by the same number of House victories. Thus, in 1960, Democratic congressional nominees, running well ahead of Kennedy, won many more districts that were lost by the successful presidential candidate than had been usual. Nevertheless, the general pattern revealed in Table 1.2 is to be found in every presidential election since 1920. Every four years, House candidates fare best in the districts where their party's presidential standard-bearer rolls up his biggest margins.

The average figures for the 1920-1964 period also conceal the fact that there has been an increase in split-ticket voting at the national level in recent elections. This discrimination between the parties' presidential and House tickets was particularly widespread during General Eisenhower's two campaigns, the 1960 Kennedy-Nixon contest, and the 1964 Johnson-Goldwater confrontation. But it has affected other elections as well. During the first five presidential contests following World War I (1920-1936), less than an eighth (12.1 per cent) of the nation's House districts were carried by presidential and congressional candidates of opposite parties. In the five most recent presidential years (1948-1964), the average number of districts with split election results jumped to nearly one in four (24.9 per cent). The proportion of districts with split results in 1956 alone was 29.2 per cent. In 1960 it was 33.3 per cent.

Yet even in the Eisenhower years, the congruence between each party's presidential and congressional support was substantial. The Survey Research Center at the University of Michigan has made available social survey data that indicate how individual voters cast their ballot in 1952 and 1956 (Table 1.3). Even in 1956—along with

Table 1.3—Straight-Ticket and Split-Ticket Voting for President and Congressman, 1952 and 1956

	1952		1956	
	Number of Voters[a]	Per Cent	Number of Voters[a]	Per Cent
Voters Supporting Presidential and Congressional Candidates of the Same Party	48,400,000	84.0	46,100,000	79.0
Voters Supporting Presidential and Congressional Candidates of Different Parties	9,200,000	16.0	12,300,000	21.0
Total	57,600,000		58,400,000	

[a] Estimates based on Survey Research Center data on the percentage of voters for presidential and congressional candidates who split their ticket at the national level. Source: Angus Campbell and Warren E. Miller, "The Motivational Basis of Straight and Split Ticket Voting," *American Political Science Review*, Vol. 51, No. 2, June, 1957, p. 295. The number of voters who actually split their ticket between presidential and House candidates of opposite parties is probably somewhat smaller than the figures in this table. The Survey Research Center's ticket-splitting data cover ballots that were split for Representative or for Senator; and some people may have split their ticket for Senator but not for the House. The estimates of the total number of split- and straight-ticket voters were almost certainly slightly inflated by another factor. To obtain them, the Survey Research Center percentages were related to the total number of people who voted for Congressmen, on the assumption that everyone who voted for Representative also voted for President. For a small fraction of the electorate, this assumption is probably incorrect.

1964 probably one of the peak years for ticket-splitting since World War I, nearly four voters in every five voted a straight ticket at the national level. In 1952, five voters in every six voted to give their presidential favorite a Representative of his own party.

It is unfortunate that comparable social survey data for many earlier presidential elections are not available. Nevertheless, the aggregate election statistics which can be examined provide clues to the amount of split-ticket voting that probably took place in other presidential years since 1920. Estimates of this type, of course, are vulnerable to error, because differing combinations of ticket-splitting among individual voters may cancel each other out and thus be concealed by the aggregate figures. But with the exception of 1924, when there was an important third-party presidential candidacy, the odds are that there was less ticket-splitting at the national level between 1920 and 1948 than occurred in 1956.[12] When it comes to the selection of national officers, voting the party ticket is the general custom in the American political system. It is split-ticket voting that is the exception.

Shifts in Party Strength for President and Congressman in Individual Districts

IN A GIVEN PRESIDENTIAL YEAR, both the presidential and congressional wings of the same party draw the bulk of their electoral support from the same voters. The tables that follow focus attention on this movement of opinion from one election to the next in the areas where the make-up of the next Congress is decided—in the individual House districts where congressional careers are extended or terminated. But first, a few remarks about the method of analysis are in order.

The increase or decrease between two presidential elections in a party's percentage of the vote for President in a given House district can, of course, be measured. A similar indication of the shift in support for the party's House candidate in that district can also

12. In recent elections, voters have split their ticket more frequently at the state and local levels of government than at the national level. The proportion of voters who split their ticket at the state or local levels in 1956 was 30 per cent; in 1952, it was 27 per cent. The proportion that split their ticket in at least one of the three levels of government were: 1956, 39 per cent; 1952, 34 per cent; and 1948, 25 per cent. See Angus Campbell and Warren E. Miller, "The Motivational Basis of Straight and Split Ticket Voting," *American Political Science Review*, Vol. 51, No. 2, June, 1957, p. 295; and Angus Campbell and Robert L. Kahn, *The People Elect a President* (Ann Arbor: Survey Research Center, University of Michigan, 1952), p. 13.

be computed. The congressional data, like the presidential figures, are thus based on the net shift of opinion—or swing—between two consecutive presidential years. If, for example, the Democratic party polled 50 per cent of the major-party vote in a district in one election and 55 per cent of the major-party vote at the next election, the district had a Democratic swing of 5 per cent. A drop by the Democratic party to 45 per cent of the two-party vote would indicate a Republican swing of 5 per cent.

Table 1.4—Relationship between the Swing for President and the Swing for Congressman in House Districts Outside the South, 1944–1948[a]

District's Presidential Swing: Range	Median Swing For Congressman	Number of Districts
Dem. 12.5–14.9%	Dem. 14.9%	3
Dem. 10.0–12.4	Dem. 11.0	4
Dem. 7.5–9.9	Dem. 8.5	13
Dem. 5.0–7.4	Dem. 6.6	22
Dem. 2.5–4.9	Dem. 4.7	37
Dem. 0.1–2.4	Dem. 2.6	31
Rep. 0.0–2.4	Dem. 1.2	24
Rep. 2.5–4.9	Rep. 1.2	20
Rep. 5.0–7.4	Rep. 4.1	12
Rep. 7.5–9.9	Rep. 3.8	3
Rep. 10.0–12.5	Rep. 10.3	1
Total		170

[a] The following nonsouthern districts are excluded from this table: districts where a major party failed to nominate a House candidate in 1944 or 1948; districts where the boundary lines were changed by redistricting between 1944 or 1948; districts where the minor-party presidential or congressional vote exceeded 3 per cent of the total vote in 1944 or 1948; and districts for which no presidential figures for 1944 or 1948 are available.

By comparing the swing for President and the swing for Congressman in individual House districts, a rough indication of the interrelationship between the presidential and congressional trends can be obtained.[13] An analysis of this type for the 1944-1948 period appears in Table 1.4, where the median swings for Congressmen in House districts with presidential swings of a given magnitude

13. The magnitude of the swing in a House district does not necessarily indicate how many individual voters within the district changed their vote between elections. If voters are switching in both directions, the effects of their changes may cancel each other out in the aggregate figures. Possible changes in the turnout and in the composition of the group actually voting are also not directly reflected in the swing.

are set forth. The data cover congressional districts outside the South where both major parties were likely to run a House candidate.

Nineteen-forty-four was the year Franklin D. Roosevelt made his last campaign for the Presidency. Four years later, after a midterm election in which the Democrats suffered extensive losses, Harry Truman was at the head of the national Democratic ticket. Moreover, although Thomas E. Dewey was the Republican presidential nominee in both 1944 and 1948, many House candidates nominated

Table 1.5—Relationship between the Swing for President and the Swing for Congressman in House Districts Outside the South, 1924–1928^a

District's Presidential Swing: Range	Median Swing For Congressman	Number of Districts
Rep. 15.0% plus	Rep. 10.4%	8
Rep. 12.5–14.9	Rep. 7.5	4
Rep. 10.0–12.4	Rep. 6.4	12
Rep. 7.5–9.9	Rep. 4.9	9
Rep. 5.0–7.4	Rep. 4.5	16
Rep. 2.5–4.9	Rep. 4.3	19
Rep. 0.1–2.4	Rep. 0.2	11
Dem. 0.0–2.4	Rep. 1.5	17
Dem. 2.5–4.9	Rep. 2.3	18
Dem. 5.0–7.4	Dem. 0.4	15
Dem. 7.5–9.9	Dem. 4.0	19
Dem. 10.0–12.4	Dem. 5.0	16
Dem. 12.5–14.9	Dem. 7.1	7
Dem. 15.0 plus	Dem. 9.4	43
Total		214

^a The following nonsouthern districts are excluded from this table: districts where a major party failed to nominate a House candidate in 1924 or 1928; districts where the boundary lines were changed by redistricting between 1924 and 1928; and districts for which no presidential figures for 1924 or 1928 are available. The remaining nonsouthern districts are included in this table regardless of the size of the minor-party vote for President or Congressman in the constituency. In many of these districts, the minor-party presidential vote cast for La Follette in 1924 was substantial. In all but seven of the districts analyzed, it exceeded 3 per cent of the total presidential vote.

by the two parties in 1948 had not stood for election in 1944. Yet despite these changes, the parallel between the swing for a party's presidential ticket and the four-year swing for its congressional ticket emerges clearly from the data in Table 1.4.

Individual districts can be found, of course, where the presidential and congressional electoral tides moved in opposite directions. Yet overall these constituencies were the exception rather than the rule. In general, the bigger the Democratic presidential swing in a particular district was, the larger the increase in the Democratic share of the House vote was likely to be. Similarly, in districts where Governor Dewey recorded his biggest gains over 1944, the largest swings to G.O.P. congressional hopefuls also occurred.

This relationship between the swing for President and the swing for Congressman is not unique to the period between 1944 and 1948. The same general pattern prevailed throughout both Roosevelt's and Eisenhower's terms in the White House. It also left its imprint on the returns from 1924 to 1928[14] (Table 1.5).

The way in which the swing for Congressman tends to parallel the swing for President, regardless of the direction the shift in presidential sentiment takes in individual House districts, is worthy of special note. In some presidential contests, a substantial number of House districts swing in both directions. At other times, however, the

Table 1.6—Relationship between the Swing for President and the Swing for Congressman in House Districts Outside the South, 1936–1940[a]

District's Presidential Swing: Range	Median Swing For Congressman	Number of Districts
Rep. 15.0% plus	Rep. 11.7%	19
Rep. 12.5–14.9	Rep. 7.5	19
Rep. 10.0–12.4	Rep. 8.5	28
Rep. 7.5–9.9	Rep. 6.5	43
Rep. 5.0–7.4	Rep. 5.2	46
Rep. 2.5–4.9	Rep. 3.6	37
Rep. 0.0–2.4	Rep. 0.1	23
Dem. 0.1–2.4	Dem. 1.1	9
Dem. 2.5–4.9	Rep. 0.3	2
Dem. 5.0–7.4	Rep. 5.5	3[b]
		———
Total		229

[a] The following nonsouthern districts are excluded from this table: districts where a major party failed to nominate a House candidate in 1936 or 1940; districts where the boundary lines were changed by redistricting between 1936 and 1940; districts where the minor-party presidential or House vote exceeded 3 per cent of the total vote in 1936 or 1940; and districts for which no presidential figures for 1936 or 1940 are available.

[b] These three districts where the presidential and congressional swings moved in opposite directions between 1936 and 1940 were all in Maine. In both years, the state's House delegation was elected in September while its presidential electors were chosen in November.

14. As a result of the extensive redistricting following each decennial census, there are fewer districts in which the swings can be analyzed between 1920–1924, 1928–1932, 1940–1944, 1948–1952, and 1960–1964. In the districts where the boundary lines were unchanged between those years, however, the swing for President and the swing for Congressman tended to move in concert.

shift of opinion for President is overwhelmingly in one direction. 1936-1940 was such a period, as the data in Table 1.6 indicate. In 1940, Mr. Wilkie improved upon Governor Landon's none-too-impressive 1936 showing in the great majority of districts. Nonetheless, in the few constituencies that did buck the national presidential trend, several Democratic House candidates also defied the Republican tide.[15]

Shifts in Party Strength for President and Congress: Three Types of Electoral Trends

A PARTY'S SLATE of congressional nominees and its national presidential ticket are swept along by the same general movement of opinion in the electorate. Individual elections vary, however, in the impact which the prevailing electoral trend may have upon the Presidency and the Congress. Sometimes a party's House nominees do relatively better compared with the preceding presidential year than even a winning presidential candidate of their party. In 1948, the swing to the Democratic House contestants in most districts exceeded the swing to President Truman (Table 1.4). In districts where Governor Dewey improved upon his 1944 showing by up to 2.4 percentage points, the median congressional swing to the Democratic House ticket was actually 1.2 per cent.

The number of districts that elected a Democratic Congressman even though the winning Democratic presidential nominee failed to carry them also increased sharply between 1944 and 1948. In 1944 these districts were a scant 1.4 per cent of the total. Four years later, they accounted for 8.3 per cent of the nation's House constituencies. In 1948, in short, there was a marked disparity in the shift of public sentiment as it affected the Democratic presidential and congressional tickets. The net effect of this discrepancy was

15. The chief exceptions were in Maine, where the presidential and congressional balloting were held on separate dates in 1936 and 1940. In 1940, Roosevelt's advocacy of aid to Britain resulted in an upsurge of support for the Democratic presidential ticket among the state's Yankee voters. See Samuel Lubell, *The Future of American Politics* (New York: Harper & Brothers, 1952), pp. 132–133. Although he lost the state by a narrow margin, Roosevelt actually carried two of Maine's three House districts in 1940. The percentage of the vote for Democratic House candidates in September before the November presidential election, however, was lower than it had been in 1936.

to leave President Truman relatively weaker in relation to the congressional wing of his party than President Roosevelt had been.

In other presidential election years there is a close articulation between the swing for President and the swing for Congressmen. Returns of this type indicate that the presidential and congressional wings of both parties have gained or lost public support in equal measure. The data in Table 1.7 suggest that 1936 was such an

Table 1.7—Relationship between the Swing for President and the Swing for Congressman in House Districts Outside the South, 1932–1936[a]

District's Presidential Swing: Range	Median Swing For Congressman	Number of Districts
Rep. 12.5–14.9%	Rep. 41.5%	1[b]
Rep. 10.0–12.4	—	—
Rep. 7.5–9.9	Rep. 6.1	6
Rep. 5.0–7.4	Rep. 5.7	11
Rep. 2.5–4.9	Rep. 4.9	20
Rep. 0.0–2.4	Rep. 1.7	14
Dem. 0.1–2.4	Rep. 0.8	20
Dem. 2.5–4.9	Dem. 2.0	20
Dem. 5.0–7.4	Dem. 4.1	18
Dem. 7.5–9.9	Dem. 5.5	8
Dem. 10.0–12.4	Dem. 10.6	12
Dem. 12.5–14.9	Dem. 12.2	6
Dem. 15% plus	Dem. 15.0	11
Total		147

[a] The following nonsouthern districts are excluded from this table: districts where a major party failed to nominate a House candidate in 1932 or 1936; districts where the boundary lines were changed by redistricting between 1932 and 1936; districts where the minor-party presidential or House vote exceeded 3 per cent of the total vote in 1932 or 1936; and districts for which no presidential figures for 1932 or 1936 are available.
[b] The district in this unit was the Nebraska 3rd.

election. In that year President Roosevelt's gains and losses were paralleled quite closely by increases and decreases in his House running mates' share of the vote. In the districts that swung Republican for President between 1932 and 1936, the swing to Republican House candidates corresponded remarkably closely to the swing from Hoover to Landon. In the constituencies where President Roosevelt picked up stength, the swing to Democratic congressional candidates lagged slightly behind the shift to the head of their ticket; but the correspondence was still fairly close.

This examination of the presidential and House results together underscores the full scope of the Democrats' electoral success in 1936. The returns were not only a great victory for President Roosevelt, who carried every state except Maine and Vermont; they were also a notable triumph for the Democratic party as a whole. Between 1932 and 1936, there was no increase at all in the number of House districts carried by President Roosevelt but lost by Democratic congressional aspirants.[16]

Table 1.8—Relationship between the Swing for President and the Swing for Congressman in House Districts, 1956–1960[a]

District's Presidential Swing: Range	Median Swing For Congressman	Number of Districts
Dem. 15% plus	Dem. 10.3	55
Dem. 12.5–14.9	Dem. 8.2	27
Dem. 10.0–12.4	Dem. 7.5	30
Dem. 7.5–9.9	Dem. 3.3	41
Dem. 5.0–7.4	Dem. 3.6	54
Dem. 2.5–4.9	Dem. 1.2	55
Dem. 0.0–2.4	Dem. 0.8	32
Rep. 0.1–2.4	Rep. 2.5	11
Rep. 2.5–4.9	Rep. 3.2	3
Rep. 5.0–7.4	Rep. 1.0	2
Rep. 7.5–9.9	Rep. 8.5	2
Total		312

[a] The following districts are excluded from this table: districts where a major party failed to nominate a House candidate in 1956 or 1960; districts where the boundary lines were changed by redistricting between 1956 and 1960; and districts where the minor-party presidential or House vote exceeded 3 per cent of the total vote in 1956 or 1960.

Still a third type of electoral verdict is rendered when the swing to the winning presidential candidate exceeds the swing to his House running mates. In 1960, President Kennedy raised the Democratic presidential tally higher proportionately than the Democratic House candidates increased their party's House vote compared with 1956 (Table 1.8). This relative increase in Democratic presidential strength occurred even though in absolute terms Kennedy still

16. This finding is based on the districts for which the presidential returns are available for 1932 and 1936—358 of the 435 districts in 1932 and 361 of the 435 districts in 1936. In both elections, 40 of the districts analyzed gave a majority to President Roosevelt while electing a Republican Congressman.

ran well behind the Democratic House ticket. As these 1960 results make clear, there can be a relative improvement in the strength of a party's presidential wing *vis-à-vis* its congressional wing between two presidential election years, even though in absolute terms the party's presidential ticket still remains weaker than its House ticket.[17] The first four Eisenhower years provide an even more extreme example of this kind of shift in the relative strength of the presidential and congressional wings of the two major parties. Even in 1952, President Eisenhower ran substantially better than his House teammates, carrying 82 districts where his party failed to elect a Congressman. Four years later, this gap widened still further. In 1956, President Eisenhower carried 127 districts that sent Democratic Representatives to Washington. Moreover, as the data in Table 1.9 indicate, in district after district the swing for Republican Congressmen lagged behind the swing for President.

This increase in the relative strength of the G.O.P.'s presidential wing in comparison with its congressional wing was, of course,

Table 1.9—Relationship between the Swing for President and the Swing for Congressman in House Districts, 1952–1956[a]

District's Presidential Swing: Range	Median Swing For Congressman	Number of Districts
Rep. 10.0–12.4%	Rep. 2.7%	5
Rep. 7.5–9.9	Rep. 2.1	30
Rep. 5.0–7.4	Rep. 1.1	56
Rep. 2.5–4.9	Dem. 0.5	62
Rep. 0.0–2.4	Dem. 1.8	68
Dem. 0.1–2.4	Dem. 2.3	48
Dem. 2.5–4.9	Dem. 5.6	25
Dem. 5.0–7.4	Dem. 11.4	13
Dem. 7.5–9.9	Dem. 15.8	5
Dem. 10.0–12.4	Dem. 20.9	1
Total		313

[a] The following districts are excluded from this table: districts where a major party failed to nominate a House candidate in 1952 or 1956; districts where the boundary lines were changed by redistricting between 1952 and 1956; and districts where the minor-party presidential or House vote exceeded 3 per cent of the total vote in 1952 or 1956. Five districts in which the Republican or Democratic presidential swings exceeded 12.4 per cent are also excluded.

17. Although he trailed most of his House running mates, Kennedy nevertheless made a better showing compared with the Democratic House ticket in 1960 than Adlai Stevenson had in 1956.

reflected by a shift in the opposite direction within the Democratic party. The Democrats who composed the party's House wing emerged from the election even stronger than before relative to the presidential wing of their party. Thus, the shift from the Presidency to the Congress as the more popular wing of the Democratic party, a trend that first appeared in 1948, continued through 1952 and 1956. Not until 1960 was the direction of this trend reversed; and not until 1964 did the Democratic presidential ticket again lead the party's slate of House nominees.

Comparisons of changes in the balloting for Congressman and for President over a period of time provide clues to the differing nature of particular electoral verdicts. They also afford insights into the functioning of the party system which analysis of the presidential returns alone may fail to provide. These variations in the prevailing electoral trends as they affect the Presidency and Congress suggest that over the years a continual process of change is taking place in the relative strength of the presidential and congressional wings of both major parties. The chances are that the scope and direction of these changes stem from the interaction of two broad sets of factors. First, there are the differences between the peculiar appeals of policy and personality that a presidential candidate and the House slate of the same party have for the electorate. And second, there are the differences in the special sources of organizational strength and weakness which the congressional and presidential wings of the same party may have in individual House districts.

The relationship between the swing for Congressman and the swing for President also may provide clues to the nature of the change going on within the electorate when there is a shift in party control of the White House. Sometimes a switch in control of the Presidency may herald a fundamental transformation of the electorate's party allegiance. The returns may signify the emergence of a new majority party. Basic changes of this sort may occur during a single election.[18] But it is perhaps more likely that they will take place over a period of several years.[19] And even a sharp change at

18. See V. O. Key, Jr., "A Theory of Critical Elections," *Journal of Politics*, Vol, 17, No. 1, February, 1955, pp. 3–18.
19. See Duncan MacRae, Jr., and James A. Meldrum, "Critical Elections in Illinois, 1888–1958," *American Political Science Review*, Vol. 54, No. 3, September, 1960, pp. 669–683.

one election must be ratified at a subsequent election before the full significance of the change becomes clear. 1932 and 1936 were two crucial election years during a period when the electorate was moving from a basically Republican to a basically Democratic majority, and it is significant that the movement of opinion to Franklin Roosevelt was paralleled closely by a swing to Democratic House candidates. In 1932 both Roosevelt and the Democratic congressional ticket were given control of the government by decisive margins. In 1936 the Democrats consolidated their position in both branches of the government as the nation's new majority party.

At other times when a change in party control of the White House takes place, the verdict may be less clear-cut. An election in which the swings for President and Congressmen are closely articulated probably provides a better indication of a basic change in the electorate's party allegiance than does an election when the winning presidential nominee far outdistances his House running mates. Thus, the extent to which Republican House candidates lagged behind Eisenhower in 1952 suggested that the electorate was not breaking with the Democratic party in 1952 in the clear-cut way they had broken with the Republicans in 1932. The 1956 returns made this message unmistakeably clear. As the Survey Research Center's data indicate, the proportion of the electorate who considered themselves Republicans was no larger at the end of Eisenhower's eight years in office than at the beginning.[20]

House Elections and National Electoral Tides

THE OBVIOUS VARIATIONS in the effect that shifts in party strength have had on the Presidency and the Congress in the past inevitably raise questions about why a party's presidential and congressional vote might diverge. Perhaps the great differences that may exist between a party's presidential and congressional ticket in different House districts point to some possible reasons. Consider the range and variety that can be found throughout the nation in the House

20. Angus Campbell, Philip E. Converse, Warren E. Miller, and Donald E. Stokes, *The American Voter* (New York: John Wiley & Sons, 1960), p. 124; and Philip E. Converse, Angus Campbell, Warren E. Miller, and Donald E. Stokes, "Stability and Change in 1960: A Reinstating Election," *American Political Science Review*, Vol. 55, No. 2, June, 1961, p. 274.

nominees who appear under the same party label. These candidates may benefit from relatively strong organizations in some districts and have weak organizations in other districts. To the extent that they are visible to the electorate, they may appear as strong liberals in some contests and as arch-conservatives in other contests. And they may be exceptionally attractive candidates in some areas and be very unappealing indeed in other districts.

Their party's presidential nominee, by contrast, is but one man. His utterances and activities are reported extensively by the national media of communication. And, although the amount of local organizational effort that goes into a presidential campaign can vary widely, the national nominee is more likely to be identified with the same policy views and must present the same personality in each of the nation's House districts. Presidential nominees have been known to try to adjust their image to reflect nuances of sentiment in individual areas. But it is far more difficult for a party's presidential nominee than for its congressional nominees to espouse differing policy proposals in different districts and regions in order to attract votes in particular House districts.

Perhaps in part because of differences of this kind, there are individual House candidates whose standing with the electorate is relatively unaffected by the tides of presidential voting in their district. Thus, in three different presidential years between 1924 and 1960, one of the most powerful men of his era in the House, Missouri's Democratic Representative Clarence Cannon, was reelected while his presidential running mate was going down to defeat in his constituency. Numerous other districts are so overwhelmingly dominated by one party that even when the presidential and the House vote move in concert it has little practical effect. Even a considerable increase in the opposition presidential vote fails to convert the district from safely Republican or safely Democratic at either the presidential or the congressional level.

Nonetheless, the general tendency revealed in Tables 1.4 through 1.9 for the House vote to parallel the presidential vote points to the operation of broader trends affecting most contests for Representative in presidential years. The direction taken by the national electoral tide leaves an unmistakable imprint not only on the presidential returns but on the outcome of congressional elections as well. Whether in these fluctuations in partisan strength it is the presidential candidate who carries the House candidates into office or the congressional candidates who give the presidential candidate a boost poses an interesting question, though one that need not be answered for the purposes of the argument here.[21] Whatever the relation of mutual reinforcement or hindrance between the presidential and congressional tickets, the House contests clearly do not operate independently of the broad sweeps of public sentiment that determine the outcome of the national presidential race. In the great majority of districts, candidates of the same party for the House and the Presidency win or lose together.

The difference between the way House candidates of the party that wins the Presidency do in the districts their presidential running mate carries and their showing in the districts where he is defeated underscores this interdependence between the vote for President and the vote for Congressmen. The following figures show this relationship during the 12 elections between 1920 and 1964:

Type of District	Percentage of Districts where a House Nominee of Winning President's Party was Elected
Districts Carried by Winning Presidential Nominee	80.0%
Districts Lost by Winning Presidential Nominee	13.9

In districts the winning presidential nominee carried, the chances that his congressional running mate would also win were eight in ten. In districts the President lost, the chances of his party winning the local House seat were not much better than one in eight.

21. For two analyses of the effect the presidential voting may have on congressional contests, and *vice versa*, see Warren E. Miller, "Presidential Coattails: A Study in Political Myth and Methodology," *Public Opinion Quarterly*, Vol. 19, No. 4, Winter 1955–1956, pp. 353–368; and Angus Campbell, "Surge and Decline: A Study of Electoral Change," *Public Opinion Quarterly*, Vol. 24, No. 3, Fall, 1960, pp. 397–418. See also John W. Meyer, "A Reformulation of the 'Coattails' Problem," Chapter 2 in William N. McPhee and William A. Glaser, Editors, *Public Opinion and Congressional Elections* (New York: The Free Press of Glencoe, 1962), pp. 52–64.

Even when the presidential balloting shifts in opposite directions in different types of districts, the returns for Congressmen tend to move in concert with the presidential vote. In constituencies where the presidential nominee picks up support, the prospects for his party's House candidates also improve. But in districts where the head of the national ticket is losing strength, some Congressmen of his party are likely to be in serious trouble.

This is not to say that special issues, personalities, and other factors unique to individual House contests do not affect the returns for Congressman. There is abundant evidence that they do, and in subsequent chapters considerable attention will be devoted to examining the special features of individual House results. Local issues and individual candidates can make all the difference in determining who wins a district's congressional seat. In a few constitutencies, they may render the House contest virtually autonomous of the presidential electoral tide. But the efforts of these individual House candidates are made harder or easier by the direction taken by the presidential electoral tides, which condition if they do not determine the outcome of the contests in individual House districts.[22] National party trends, which affect both presidential and congressional candidates, have a powerful influence on the races for Congressman in presidential years.

The consequences of this for relations between the President and the House of Representatives during the next two years are substantial. Party majorities for the Presidency and the Congress are usually forged and broken together; and winning control of the White House is commonly a party's best insurance against finding itself in a minority in the House of Representatives. The tendency of the great majority of the nation's House districts to support

22. In some presidential election years, as in 1952, there is a dominant trend to one party's presidential ticket in virtually every area of the country. In election years of this type, nearly all of the gains in House seats are recorded by the winning presidential candidate's party. In other election years, however, there may be more than one broad trend in the presidential voting. Thus, in 1956, Eisenhower generally gained strength outside the South in areas east of the Mississippi River, while losing strength west of the Mississippi. The gains and losses of House seats by each party tended to parallel the direction taken by these contradictory presidential trends. West of the Mississippi it was the Democratic party that gained House seats. East of the Mississippi most of the House gains were registered by the Republicans.

presidential and congressional nominees of the same party reflects the fact that most individual voters mark a straight ticket at the national level. Moreover, in district after district, most of the voters who switch their party preference for President also change their vote for Congressman. Thus is a measure of collaboration injected into American executive-legislative relations by the functioning of the electoral system.

CHAPTER 2

Split-Ticket Voting and the
Presidency and Congress

In October, 1956, as the national election campaign entered its final weeks, Colorado's Governor Edward Johnson took stock of public sentiment and predicted: "The voters are going to scratch their ballot in this election just like an old hen scratching for corn."[1] The returns confirmed the veteran politician's prognostication, and with the possible exception of 1964, it is likely that more voters split their ticket at the national level in 1956 than in any other presidential year since World War I. According to one estimate, some 12 million people supported the presidential nominee of one party while voting for an opposition House candidate.[2] In any event, the 1956 returns were an emphatic reminder that, although the great majority of voters do not split their ballot at the national level, a

1. Quoted in Curtis Martin, "The 1956 Election in Colorado," *Western Political Quarterly*, Vol. 10, No. 1, March, 1957, p. 117.
2. Estimate based on the percentage of the electorate that split its ticket at the national level as reported by the Survey Research Center at The University of Michigan. The estimate may be somewhat high, because some voters who reported having split their ticket at the national level may have split their ticket for Senator and not for Representative. See Angus Campbell and Warren E. Miller, "The Motivational Basis of Straight and Split Ticket Voting," *American Political Science Review*, Vol. 51, No. 2, June, 1957, p. 295.

sizable minority of the electorate often does discriminate between the parties' congressional and presidential tickets.

The influence that this minority of voters can have on the workings of the party system can be profoundly important. Republican Congressmen who were unable to organize the House and to serve as chairmen of its committees after the 1956 election could blame their fate on the perversity of an electorate that had voted for a Republican President and a Democratic Congress. If every 1956 Eisenhower voter had also supported a G.O.P. congressional nominee, the Republicans would have had a top-heavy 328-107 majority in the House in the 85th Congress. Instead, House Republicans found themselves in a minority by 29.

In 1956, all of the House seats that were denied to the Republicans were filled by Democrats. One result of this extraordinary amount of ticket-splitting was to weaken the power of the President vis-à-vis the Congress. But the voters also can reduce the President's party supporters in the House by splitting their ballot to elect third-party or independent Representatives. In the 1930's, several minor-party congressional candidates were elected in districts that were carried by Franklin Roosevelt but not by his House running mates. And in 1952 the electorate in Ohio's 9th District gave General Eisenhower a comfortable majority while bypassing the regular Republican House nominee to reelect an independent Representative. During the next two years Eisenhower probably received less support in the House from Congressman Frazier Reams than he would have obtained from his congressional running mate.

The discrimination that part of the electorate exercises between each party's congressional and presidential wings can have other effects on the national legislature. While at times ticket-splitting increases the number of minor-party House members, at other times it may reduce the size and importance of third-party blocs in Congress. This is particularly likely to happen when a minor-party presidential nominee polls a sizable vote. If every district carried by Robert La Follette in 1924 had also elected a Progressive Representative, at least 13 minor-party Congressmen, instead of only three, would have taken seats in the House in 1925.

The impact of ticket-splitting on the Dixiecrats' third-party rebellion in 1948 is more difficult to evaluate, because in all but one of the districts that voted for Thurmond, the South Carolinian appeared on the ballot as the Democratic presidential nominee. Nevertheless, the absence of Dixiecrat House nominees in most southern districts points up the differential impact that American third-party movements may have on the presidential and congressional wings of the major parties. If every Thurmond voter had also supported a House nominee who ran as a Dixiecrat, 31 minor-party Congressmen would have appeared in the House in 1949.[3]

The consequences of split-ticket voting are thus extraordinarily complex. At times ticket-splitting has played a role in preserving the two-party character of the House by reducing the number of minor-party candidates who are elected to Congress. In 1960 it increased the number of President Kennedy's Democratic party supporters on Capitol Hill.[4] These 1960 consequences of split-ticket voting were unusual, however. Far more often, it has strengthened the President's opponents in the House. Ticket-splitting can thus both mitigate and exacerbate the executive-legislative struggle. But the most frequent consequence has probably been to strengthen the checks on the power of the President that are built into the American system of government.

The existence of districts that return majorities for presidential

3. Thirty of the 31 districts carried by Thurmond were in Mississippi, Alabama, South Carolina, and Lousiana, where Dixiecrat supporters succeeded in having the electors chosen through the regular Democratic party machinery instructed to vote for Thurmond and Wright. The Tenth District in Tennessee (Memphis) was the only district where Thurmond outpolled Truman when Truman headed the Democratic party ticket. The chances are, however, that Thurmond would have carried some districts in Mississippi, Alabama, South Carolina, and Louisiana, even if Truman had appeared as the regular Democratic nominee in those states. Alexander Heard, *A Two-Party South?* (Chapel Hill: University of North Carolina Press, 1952), p. 22. For fuller discussions of the Dixiecrat movement, see *ibid.*, Chapter 2, and V. O. Key, Jr., *Southern Politics in State and Nation* (New York: Alfred A. Knopf, 1949), Chapter 15.

4. Kennedy won the extraordinary 1960 election while carrying only a minority (206) of the nation's 437 House constituencies. Yet 263 Democratic House candidates won in the 1960 election. The new Democratic President had difficulty enough getting the more controversial domestic measures in his legislative program passed by Congress with a nominal Democratic House majority of 89. Had there not been extensive ticket-splitting in 1960 in favor of the Democratic congressional ticket his difficulties would have been even greater.

and House candidates of opposite parties poses intriguing questions for the analyst of American politics. But before one can speculate about their significance in the political system, a look at the facts is in order. What types of House districts return a mixed verdict at the national level? How many such districts are there? What are the circumstances in which voters are likely to vote for a presidential candidate of one party while supporting another party's congressional nominee? Has the electorate's willingness to vote a straight ticket been declining steadily over the past four decades? Or does the balance between straight-ticket and split-ticket voting shift erratically from election to election? By probing behind the district-by-district returns for President and Congressmen it should be possible to obtain tentative answers to questions of this kind.

Split-Ticket Voting: Extent and Incidence since 1920

IN EVERY PRESIDENTIAL YEAR since World War I, some unfortunate House candidates have gone down to defeat in districts that their presidential running mate carried. The impact of split-ticket voting on the fortunes of individual House nominees—as well as on their presidential teammates—is thus a persistent characteristic of American elections. Its effect on the membership of the House, however, has varied widely from election to election. Since World War I, the number of House candidates who survived in opposition presidential territory has ranged from just over three in every hundred in 1920 to one in every three in 1964[5] (Table 2.1).

The incidence of House districts with split results involving major-party candidates for national office between 1920 and 1964 appears in graphic form in Figure 2.1. As one would expect, the trend line suggests that ticket-splitting was especially widespread in the Eisenhower-Stevenson races of 1952 and 1956, the Kennedy-

5. The total number of House districts with split results from 1920 to 1964, including those carried by minor-party or independent candidates as well as those where the results were split between candidates of opposite major parties, are listed in Table 2.1. In this and subsequent tables, data from districts for which the presidential returns were not available (between 1920 and 1948) are omitted.

Table 2.1—Congressional Districts with Split Election Results: Districts Carried by a Presidential Nominee of One Party and by a House Nominee of Another Party, 1920–1964[a]

Year and Party of the Winning Presidential Candidate	Number of Districts	Number of Districts With Split Results	Per Cent
1920 R	344	11	3.2
1924 R	356	42	11.8
1928 R	359	68	18.9
1932 D	355	50	14.1
1936 D	361	51	14.1
1940 D	362	53	14.6
1944 D	367	41	11.2
1948 D	422	90	21.3
1952 R	435	84	19.3
1956 R	435	130	29.9
1960 D	437	114	26.1
1964 D	435	145	33.3
Total	4668	879	18.8

[a] Districts listed in this table as having split results include every district analyzed where a presidential candidate of one party and a House nominee of another party obtained a plurality. Of the 879 districts with split results, 806 were carried by presidential and House candidates of opposite major parties. In 26 districts a major-party presidential nominee and a third-party House candidate won. Another 47 districts were carried by a third-party or independent presidential electors ticket while a major-party candidate won the House seat. Of these, 11 were affected by La Follette's candidacy in 1924; two were the result of T. Coleman Andrews' race in 1956; three were carried by the Unpledged Democratic Electors' ticket in Mississippi in 1960; and 31 were affected by the Thurmond candidacy of 1948. All but one of the Thurmond results, however, came from districts where Thurmond was listed as the regular Democratic presidential nominee, and it is a moot point whether all of them should be counted as split results. Nevertheless, these 30 districts were in South Carolina, Alabama, Mississippi, and Louisiana, where anti-Truman sentiment was particularly strong, and some of them would undoubtedly have had split results even if Thurmond had run on an independent Dixiecrat ticket.

Nixon contest in 1960, and th Goldwater-Johnson race in 1964. (More House districts split their results in the four most recent elections than in the eight presidential elections between 1920 and 1948.) Yet whatever trend there has been toward increased split-ticket voting has been anything but steady. There was also a marked jump in districts with split results in 1928 when Al Smith ran against Herbert Hoover for President. And during the four succeeding election victories by Franklin Roosevelt, the number of districts with split results dropped substantially and remained fairly constant. It should be noted, too, that congressional districts with split election results were relatively rare in most of the presidential election years covered by our analysis. Since 1920 there have been only three elections—1956, 1960, and 1964—when much more than a fifth of the nation's House districts returned a mixed verdict for President and Congressman.

Figure 2.1 indicates some of the variations in ticket-splitting since 1920 in the country as a whole. An idea of the regional pattern of split-ticket voting emerges if the returns from nonsouthern districts are compared with the results from the districts in the 11 states of the former Confederacy. This analysis, to be found in Figure 2.2, underscores some of the marked differences in the impact that ballot-splitting has had in the North and in the South.

Figure 2.1—Congressional districts with split election results: Percentage of house districts carried by a congressional candidate of one major party and by a presidential candidate of the other major party, 1920–1964

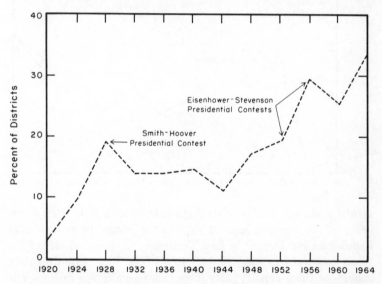

Between 1920 and 1932, the number of districts with split results in the North increased substantially. Since 1932, however, the variation in the number of split results outside the South has been much less extensive. In the three most recent elections (1956-1964) there were substantially more such districts than in 1932. But in four other elections that followed Franklin Roosevelt's first campaign for the

Presidency, the number of northern districts which returned a mixed verdict was about the same as in 1932.

In the South, by contrast, the appearance of districts with split results has fluctuated violently. In all four elections during the Roosevelt Era, every southern district that returned a Democratic Congressman to Washington also supported the Democratic presi-

Figure 2.2—Congressional districts with split election results in the north and the south: Percentage of southern and nonsouthern house districts carried by a congressional candidate of one major party and by a presidential candidate of the other major party, 1920–1964

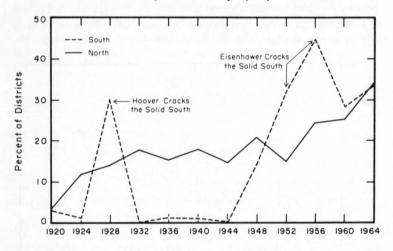

dential nominee. The only southern district with a partisan divergence at the national level in 1936 and 1940 was the traditionally Republican 2nd District in East Tennessee. There a majority of the voters continued to support their Republican Representative while enough of them crossed party lines to give majorities to Roosevelt over Landon and Wilkie. In 1920 and in 1924, the southern electorate was almost equally steadfast in its loyalty to the entire Democratic national ticket.

The response of southern voters to the Smith-Hoover contest in 1928, however, was of a different order. Nearly a third of the South's districts deserted the Democratic presidential nominee to give

Hoover a majority while continuing to send a Democratic Representative to Washington. And in the presidential elections that followed World War II, when questions of civil rights and (in 1960) religion, and the candidacies of Truman, Eisenhower, Kennedy, Goldwater, and Johnson were important political factors, ticket-splitting was also widespread in the South. In 1956, the number of southern districts with split results rose to nearly 45 per cent of the total.[6]

The number of districts in which the electorate supports candidates for the Presidency and the House of opposite parties, of course, does not give a complete picture of ticket-splitting in American congressional elections. Often widespread ballot-splitting may take place in districts that do not actually divide their partisan allegiance for President and Representative. Some House districts may turn in pluralities for both the presidential and the congressional candidate of the same party, yet the winning presidential nominee may still run behind or ahead of his congressional teammate by as much as 10 per cent, or even more, of the district's total vote.

This discrepancy, or spread, between the percentage of the vote polled by presidential and House candidates of the same party can be measured. The size of the spread can then be used to provide a more precise indication of the incidence of ticket-splitting in individual districts since 1920.[7] In election years when the spread

6. The remarkable increase in 1956 in southern House districts with split results could be the end rather than the beginning of a trend. A southern third-party movement that drew more votes for President than for Congressmen, or a Republican presidential nominee who outpolled even General Eisenhower, could bring forth still more ticket-splitting in the South. Yet either an improved showing by southern Republican House candidates, or a drop in the number of southern votes for G.O.P. presidential aspirants, or some combination of the two, could reduce the number of southern House districts with split results in future years.

7. The spread, like any analytical tool based upon aggregate election statistics, is an imperfect measure of the amount of straight-ticket and split-ticket voting during a given election year. Both the presidential and the House candidate of the same party could receive 55 per cent of the vote in a district, and the spread would be zero. Yet this coincidence could conceal widespread ticket-splitting by voters who supported a Republican presidential nominee and a Democratic House candidate if they were counter-balanced by an equally large number of voters who split their ticket in the opposite direction. It should also be noted that the spread is based upon the major-party candidates'

in most districts is relatively small, the chances are that the balloting has been characterized by extensive straight-ticket voting.[8] In elections in which the average spread is large, substantial split-ticket voting has taken place.

An examination of the spread between the presidential and House returns in individual districts appears in Table 2.2. In general, the data reveal some of the same variations in split-ticket voting that were reflected in our figures for the number of House districts with split results. There are, however, some differences. It is clear that there was widespread ticket-splitting in 1924, much of it probably caused by La Follette's third-party presidential candidacy, that was not reflected in split election results in particular House districts. Inspection of the spreads in individual constituencies also suggests that there was some split-ticket voting in the South before 1948 that also did not show up in split election results. In some southern districts where the Democratic presidential nominee received 60 to 65 per cent of the vote, for example, his House running mate garnered 75 per cent or more of the congressional poll. Nevertheless, the dominant themes of our earlier data are also reflected in Table 2.2.

Again it is clear that there are wide variations from election to election in the amount of ticket-splitting that takes place. In 1932, Democratic House nominees ran within 2.5 per cent of Franklin

share of the two-party vote. It is a measure of the discrepancy between the percentage of the two-party presidential vote and the percentage of the two-party House vote polled in a district by candidates of the same major party. Both third-party congressional votes and third-party presidential votes are excluded from the computation. In practice, however, this turns out to be a less serious problem than it first might appear to be. When minor-party candidacies divert votes from the presidential and House nominees of the same major party unequally, as they usually do, this discrepancy shows up in a widening of the spread. Inferences about ticket-splitting drawn from analysis of the spreads in individual districts from 1948 to 1964 can be checked against the relevant findings of social survey studies of those election years. The findings that emerge from the two types of data concerning split-ticket voting correspond closely.

8. Unless, of course, the coincidence of the aggregate figures masks extensive ticket-splitting in opposite directions by individual voters whose effects on the total figures thus cancel each other out. See preceding footnote.

Roosevelt's percentage in nearly half of the nation's congressional districts. The large proportion of voters who scratched a straight ticket at the national level indicates that the electorate's shift to the Democratic party in the depression year of 1932 was unequivocal and decisive.

Table 2.2—The Spread Between the Percentage of the Two-Party Vote Polled by Victorious Major-Party Presidential Candidates and the Percentage of the Two-Party Vote Polled by House Nominees of their Party, 1920–1964[a]

YEAR, PARTY OF WINNING PRESIDENT, AND NUMBER OF DISTRICTS ANALYZED		NUMBER OF DISTRICTS IN WHICH SPREAD WAS:			PERCENTAGE OF DISTRICTS IN WHICH SPREAD WAS:		
		Under 2.5%	Under 5.0%	Over 10.0%	Under 2.5%	Under 5.0%	Over 10.0%
1920 R	332	157	206	79	47.3	62.0	23.8
1924 R	356	71	139	128	19.9	39.0	36.0
1928 R	359	87	142	143	24.2	39.6	39.8
1932 D	355	169	235	57	47.6	66.2	16.1
1936 D	361	149	236	60	41.3	65.4	16.6
1940 D	362	139	211	97	38.4	58.3	26.8
1944 D	367	131	209	92	35.7	56.9	25.1
1948 D	422	144	207	135	34.1	49.1	32.0
1952 R	435	139	226	142	32.0	52.0	32.6
1956 R	435	72	142	184	16.6	32.6	42.3
1960 D	437	96	178	162	22.0	40.7	37.1
1964 D	435	81	157	189	18.6	36.1	43.4
Total	4656	1435	2288	1468	30.8	49.1	31.5

[a] The spread is the difference between the percentage of the vote polled by a presidential candidate and the percentage polled by a congressional candidate of the same major party, e.g., if in a district the Democratic presidential candidate received 59.0 per cent of the presidential vote and the Democratic House nominee received 55.0 per cent of the House vote, the spread was 4.0 per cent, with the presidential candidate leading. All computations in this and subsequent tables dealing with the spread are based upon the major-party candidates' share of the major-party vote. Votes cast for third-party candidates are excluded from consideration. The data also include every district for which figures on the presidential vote are available. They therefore include a substantial number of districts for each year in which one of the major parties failed to run a House candidate and where the spread was often large.

At the other extreme was 1956, when the electorate's response to the appeals of the parties' presidential and congressional wings was noteworthy for its ambivalence. Then, only one Republican House candidate in eight ran within 2.5 per cent of the G.O.P. standard-bearer's share of the vote. In more than four districts out of every ten, the spread between the Republican congressional and presidential tickets exceeded 10 per cent.

Other elections also reflect a bewilderingly sharp variation in the proportion of the electorate who may decide to split their ticket in a presidential year. In 1920, the voters not only turned to Harding and "normalcy"; they also registered a ringing endorsement of the Republican congressional ticket. The magnitude of the difference between the 1920 electoral verdict and that of 1956 is indicated in Figure 2.3, which compares the spreads in individual districts out-

Figure 2.3—The spread between the Republican presidential and congressional candidates' percentage of the major two-party vote in northern house districts, 1920 and 1956

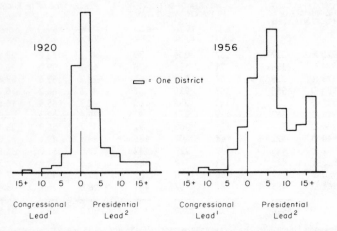

[1] Percentage lead of Republican congressional candidate over Republican presidential candidate.
[2] Percentage lead of Republican presidential candidate over Republican congressional candidate.

side the South in those years. In 1920, G.O.P. congressional candidates ran within 2.5 per cent of Senator Harding's vote in half of the northern House districts. The most common situation was for the victorious Republican presidential nominee to run slightly ahead of his congressional running mate. In some districts, Harding ran substantially ahead of his congressional candidate; in only a few districts did he run very far behind the congressional ticket. In the great bulk of the constituencies, the fortunes of the G.O.P. presidential and congressional candidate were closely linked.

The results of the 1956 balloting were of a different nature. Only in a small minority of districts were the results of the presidential and congressional contest closely articulated. The most common result was for President Eisenhower to run between 5 per cent and 7.5 per cent ahead of the Republican congressional nominee. In nearly a third of the districts his lead was even greater.

Split-Ticket Voting and the Nature of the Electoral Verdict

FEW TASKS ARE MORE difficult than that of reading meaning into the election returns of a nation as vast and as diverse as the United States. As an impressive number of voting behavior studies indicate, the motivations individual citizens may have when they vote are both highly varied and extraordinarily complex.[9] Yet perhaps in the amount of ballot-splitting that takes place at the national level lies one clue to the dominant nature of the verdict given by the electorate in a presidential year. In some elections, when the successful presidential candidate wins by a decisive margin and large numbers of voters cast a straight ticket thus giving the President big majorities of his fellow partisans in the House, the public seems to give a solid mandate to one of the parties to get on with the business of governing. Such situations allow maximum scope for the ties of party to overcome the obstacles to action inherent in the separation of powers.

But if in some elections the voters seem to speak with one voice, at other times they clearly speak with two. The results of elections in which there is widespread ticket-splitting to the disadvantage

9. Among the major studies of voting behavior are: Bernard Berelson, Paul F. Lazarsfeld, and William M. McPhee, *Voting* (Chicago: University of Chicago Press, 1954); Eugene Burdick and Arthur J. Brodbeck, *American Voting Behavior* (Glencoe, Illinois: The Free Press, 1959); Angus Campbell and Robert L. Kahn, *The People Elect a President* (Ann Arbor: Survey Research Center, 1952); Angus Campbell, Gerald Gurin, and Warren E. Miller, *The Voter Decides* (Evanston: Row, Peterson, 1954); Angus Campbell and Homer C. Cooper, *Group Differences in Attitudes and Votes* (Ann Arbor: Survey Research Center, 1956); Angus Campbell, Philip E. Converse, Warren E. Miller, and Donald E. Stokes, *The American Voter* (New York: Wiley, 1960); Louis Harris, *Is There a Republican Majority?* (New York: Harper, 1954); V. O. Key, Jr., *The Responsible Electorate: Rationality in Presidential Voting, 1936–1960* (Cambridge: Harvard University Press, 1966); and Paul F. Lazarsfeld, Bernard Berelson, and Hazel Gaudet, *The People's Choice* (New York: Duell, Sloan and Pearce, 1944).

of the winning presidential candidate's party are both more ambiguous and more difficult to fathom. Sometimes the special qualities of one of the presidential nominees may wrench many voters loose from their traditional party moorings and account for much of the ticket-splitting that ensues. The odds are, for example, that the Goldwater presidential candidacy accounted for a sizable part of the exceptionally heavy ticket-splitting in 1964. Yet in other such election years, perhaps the checks and balances limiting vigorous governmental action which were implanted in the American political system are more deeply reflected in the electorate itself.

Table 2.3—Split-Ticket Voting for President and for Representative: Elections Grouped According to the Size of the Spread Between the Percentage of the Two-Party Vote Polled by Major-Party Presidential Candidates in Individual House Districts and the Percentage of the Two-Party Vote Polled by House Nominees of their Party, 1920–1964[a]

ELECTION YEAR AND PERCENTAGE OF DISTRICTS IN WHICH THE SPREAD WAS:

Under 2.5%		Under 5.0%		Over 10.0%	
1932	47.6	1932	66.2	1932	16.1
1920	47.3	1936	65.4	1936	16.6
1936	41.3	1920	62.0	1920	23.8
1940	38.4	1940	58.3	1944	25.1
1944	35.7	1944	56.9	1940	26.8
1948	34.1	1952	52.0	1948	32.0
1952	32.0	1948	49.1	1952	32.6
1928	24.2	1960	40.7	1924	36.0
1960	22.0	1928	39.6	1960	37.1
1924	19.9	1924	39.0	1928	39.8
1964	18.6	1964	36.1	1956	42.3
1956	16.6	1956	32.6	1964	43.4

[a] The number of districts analyzed is identical to that in Table 2.2. Districts in which one of the major parties failed to run a House nominee are included in the table.

In Table 2.3 the data of Table 2.2 are rearranged so that one can view the returns from presidential election years in terms of the amount of split-ticket voting that accompanied them. In classifying the results of elections, the danger of emphasizing the differences among elections at the expense of the similarities is always present.

Nevertheless, broadly speaking, the verdicts of the 12 elections for President and a House of Representatives between 1920 and 1964 were of three types. In three of those years—1920, 1932, and 1936— the dominant characteristic of the election returns was a straight-line party vote. Both major parties' presidential and congressional wings received support from the electorate in almost equal measure. In 1932, the congressional and presidential candidates of both parties ran within 5 per cent of each other in nearly two thirds of the nation's House districts. In only about a sixth of the constituencies did the spread exceed 10 per cent, and some of those results came from districts where one of the major parties failed to run a congressional candidate. In 1920 and in 1936, the vote for President and for Congress was almost equally closely articulated.

At other elections during this period, the electorate discriminated more sharply between the presidential and congressional tickets which the parties placed before it. President Roosevelt's last two elections, Mr. Truman's victory in 1948, and General Eisenhower's first election in 1952 were all accompanied by a moderate, though fairly substantial, amount of ticket-splitting. In those elections, the fortunes of the presidential and congressional slates of each party were closely linked in about a third of the country's districts. At the same time, the number of constituencies where the spread exceeded 10 per cent varied from a quarter to just under a third of the total.

Even by comparison with this amount of split-ticket voting, however, the electoral verdicts of 1924, 1928, 1956, 1960, and 1964 were of a different order. In 1924, Robert M. La Follette polled some 4,822,856 votes as a third-party presidential nominee. Congressional candidates who ran on a third-party ticket with the Wisconsin Senator, by contrast, drew only about a fifth as many votes.[10] This discrepancy alone would have showed up in a widening of the spread between the major-party presidential and House candidates. But it was accentuated still further because La Follette drew most of his support from Republican ranks in some states, while

10. In a few cases, it is difficult to determine whether a third-party congressional nominee was associated with the La Follette candidacy. Even if the marginal cases are interpreted generously, however, the third-party congressional vote of candidates who supported the La Follette presidential ticket was only 1,029,014.

siphoning off predominantly Democratic presidential votes in other areas. As a result, there was widespread ticket-splitting for President and Congressman in nearly every part of the country.

Al Smith's campaign for the Presidency in 1928 also placed severe strains on the traditional party allegiance of many voters. In a sizable bloc of normally Democratic districts, large numbers of people shifted their support to Hoover while continuing to vote for the Democratic party's congressional ticket. Simultaneously, however, the issues and emotions surrounding the New York Democrat's candidacy raised the Democratic presidential vote in some erstwhile Republican strongholds that still remained steadfast in their support for G.O.P. House candidates.

The reelection of President Eisenhower in 1956 also took place in a year when it was difficult for party managers to persuade the electorate to support their ticket from top to bottom. Although the General's tenure in the White House was extended by a sweeping plurality exceeding nine and a half million votes, Democratic House nominees secured a majority of the votes cast for Representatives. In 1960 the nomination of another Roman Catholic by the Democrats and in 1964 the nomination of Barry Goldwater by the Republicans were also followed by elections in which split-ticket voting was especially heavy. In all five elections—1924, 1928, 1956, 1960, and 1964, congressional and presidential nominees of the same party ran within 2.5 per cent of each other in less than a quarter of the districts. In 1924, 1956, and 1964, the spread between the two parts of the national ticket exceeded 10 per cent in about four in every ten House constituencies.

The marked variation in the nature of the electoral verdict which occurs from year to year invites speculation about the role of ticket-splitting in the American political system. Who are the ticket-splitters, and why do they mark their ballot for one party's presidential nominee while voting for an opposition Congressman? Perhaps one clue to the answer emerges from a study based on social survey data of ticket-splitting in 1956.[11] Both the straight-

11. Angus Campbell and Warren E. Miller, "The Motivational Basis of Straight and Split Ticket Voting," *American Political Science Review*, Vol. 51, No. 2, June, 1957, p. 312. At the conclusion of their article, Campbell and Miller remark: "As a final note it may be appropriate to remind the reader that the

ticket voters and the ticket-splitters, Angus Campbell and Warren Miller suggest, fall into one of two broad categories: the politically motivated voters and those who are relatively indifferent to activities of a political nature.

Members of the electorate who are politically motivated are likely to express a lively interest in either the issues, the candidates, or the parties that play a role in the campaign. Some may even have strong convictions about all three. They are also likely to feel that both the outcome of the election and their getting to the voting booth to help to determine that outcome are matters of importance.

Their fellow citizens who are less politically involved, by contrast, are relatively indifferent to the electoral battle that swirls around them, even though they may make it to the polls to vote. Yet on occasion, both the voters whose interest in politics is keen and their neighbors who are indifferent to the political struggle may either split their ticket or cast a straight-party vote. One can thus identify four broad types of people in the electorate: the motivated straight-ticket voter, the motivated split-ticket voter, the indifferent straight-ticket voter, and the indifferent split-ticket voter.

This 1956 study suggests that different types of voters may vote the same way for different reasons. It also indicates that the reasons which impel both the politically involved and the politically indifferent to vote as they do are as varied as they are bewildering in their complexity. A feeling of "right or wrong—my party," gratitude to the Congressman who endorsed a son's application for admission to West Point, or even a response to a reasoned, sustained argument by a politician—all these, and many more elements may enter into the voter's decision. Moreover, between the most and the least politically motivated voters there probably lies a series of minute gradations in the amount of political involvement that individual voters feel.

Despite the complexities of voter motivation, examples spring to

---

data we have been considering refer specifically to the 1956 election. The concepts with which we have been concerned, however, are not peculiar to any particular election situation. We would expect them to apply with equal validity in any presidential election in this country and we are confident that subsequent research will demonstrate this to be the case." *Ibid., loc. cit.*

mind that suggest the usefulness of the categories which Campbell and Miller propose. The citizen who voted for a Republican Congressman in 1956 because he felt that a G.O.P. Representative would best support the Republican President whose policies he favored was a motivated straight-ticket voter. But the conservative Virginia Democrat who split his ticket to vote for President Eisenhower while continuing to support a Democratic House nominee of Senator Byrd's political coloration may have been an equally motivated voter. Both voters had clear policy preferences, and the votes of both were probably best calculated to give effect to those preferences.[12]

Quite different are the votes of the less politically motivated members of the electorate. They care relatively little about the issues, the candidates, or the parties that are involved in the campaign. Nevertheless, a vague sense of civic duty, the admonition of a relative, or even the request of a party worker may get them to the polling booth. There they participate in the solemn ritual by which the governors of the land for the years immediately ahead are selected. If they can do the job with one motion, many of these voters are likely to simplify the whole business by voting a straight ticket.

Although some indifferent voters may support all of the candidates of one party, others may swell the ranks of the ticket-splitters. Some superficial interest in a particular candidate, the request of a friend or a campaign worker, or some last-minute influence may lead them to bypass the straight-party vote to pick out some particular candidate. In states where it is impossible to vote a straight ticket easily by marking a party circle or pulling a party lever, relatively more of the indifferent voters are likely to split their ticket. Voters who have a clearer idea of what they wish to accomplish in the political realm, by contrast, are less likely to be

12. Both of these voters, one should add, would probably be more informed about public policy questions and the instrumental use of their vote than many members of the American electorate. For a discussion of some of the limitations on the extent to which policy preferences serve as a guide to the way people vote, see Angus Campbell, Philip E. Converse, Warren E. Miller, and Donald E. Stokes, *The American Voter*, (New York: Wiley, 1960), Chapters 8–10.

influenced by the form of the ballot or the arrangement of the voting machine.[13]

The foregoing remarks suggest something of the broad types of motivation that underlie straight- and split-ticket voting in a presidential election year. Yet both the number of voters who are indifferent to the outcome of the campaign and the ratio between ticket-splitters and straight-ticket voters among the politically involved probably vary from year to year. The chances are that the ranks of the unmotivated expand or contract as the political seas become alternately placid and stormy; and some campaigns probably induce more of the politically involved voters to split their tickets than others. Issues change, and no election is ever exactly like the preceding one.

In addition, the specific voters who are the ticket-splitters may change enormously from year to year (even leaving aside, for the moment, differences caused by the changes that occur over time in the composition of the electorate). The type of voters who bolted the party ticket in 1928 were quite different from the ticket-splitters of 1940. And most voters who discriminated between the parties' presidential and congressional slates in 1948 were not the same as the voters who split their ballot in 1932. As the general political situation, the leading issues, and the particular candidates who are nominated change from election to election, so too does the relative appeal of the presidential and congressional slates that each party places before the voters. Nevertheless, although the extent and kind of split-ticket voting may vary, the chances are that in every presidential year it will have at least some practical effect on the working of the political system.

13. In their study of ticket-splitting in 1956, Campbell and Miller divided their sample of voters from the North into two categories: those who came from states where it was possible to vote a straight ticket by marking a party circle or pulling a party level (single-choice states); and those who came from states where it was necessary to vote for a candidate for each office separately (multiple-choice states). In 1956, 77 per cent of the northern voters who felt a strong sense of identification with one of the parties voted a straight ticket in both the single-choice states and the multiple-choice states. Of the weak party identifiers, however, 70 per cent voted a straight ticket in single-choice states, compared with only 55 per cent in multiple-choice states. Angus Campbell and Warren E. Miller, "The Motivational Basis of Straight and Split Ticket Voting, "*American Political Science Review,* Vol. 51, No. 2, June, 1957, pp. 305–308.

This practical impact reaches its maximum in districts where the voters give a majority to a presidential candidate of one party while electing an opposition Congressman to swell the ranks of his opponents in the House. But before examining those districts, it might be well to survey the drift of the argument thus far. Although more voters split their ticket in 1956 and in 1964 than in any other election since World War I, there has been no regular, steady increase in ticket-splitting since 1920. The data suggest rather that the amount of split-ticket voting varies markedly from election to election in response to the special characteristics of each individual campaign. As has been noted, on the average there has been more ticket-splitting since World War II than before; and it is possible, of course, that repeated experience of split-ticket voting and long-term changes in the nature of American politics and society are accustoming a larger proportion of the electorate to splitting their ticket. If this is the case, then a similar political siuation might bring forth more split-ticket voting today than it would have elicited in an earlier election. Even so, variations from year to year in the general political situation are still likely to be reflected in variations in the amount and kind of ticket-splitting. The three most recent presidential years of 1956, 1960, and 1964 were years when ticket-splitting was unusually widespread. But so also were 1924 and 1928.

The electorate's willingness to cross party lines in a presidential year also varies sharply from region to region. Since World War I, southern voters have been much more volatile about ticket-splitting than the electorates in northern districts where there has been greater two-party competition. Despite these variations in the electorate's behavior from year to year and from region to region, however, most general election verdicts fall into three broad categories. Sometimes an overwhelming majority of the voters cast a straight-line party vote. In other years, a moderate amount of ticket-splitting takes place. Occasionally, however, the minority of voters who split their ticket at the national level becomes so large that the effect on the distribution of party strength in the Presidency and the Congress becomes substantial.

That it is only a minority who fail to heed the pleas for party loyalty, even in elections when ticket-splitting is widespread, should be emphasized. Even in the extraordinary election of 1956, only about 21 per cent of the voters failed to mark a straight ticket at the national level. But even in elections when there is far less crossing of party lines, the voters' selectivity can be profoundly important to the individual candidate for the House when he meets his moment of truth.

Congressmen and the Presidential Tide

AT FIRST GLANCE the variety of districts with split election results seems bewildering in the extreme. Yet something of what the electorate may be up to emerges if the results of individual House contests are viewed in relation to the impact of the dominant presidential tide that sweeps the country in most presidential election years. When the House returns are looked at from this standpoint, two conclusions become clear: (1) in most presidential years, it is mainly House candidates of the party that lost the Presidency who survive an opposition presidential tide in their district; and (2) most split results occur in districts where the presidential race is close.

A substantial number of the House candidates of the party that loses the presidential election may survive in districts carried by the victorious opposition presidential candidate. Unless the presidential contest itself is extremely close, however, the chances are slim that a congressional candidate of the winning party will be sent to Washington from a district that his party's standard-bearer does not also carry (Table 2.4).

In years of big presidential landslides, the chances that a congressional nominee of the victorious party will win in a district the President failed to carry frequently drop to nearly zero. In 1964 Democratic Congressmen were elected in a number of southern districts where President Johnson lost to Barry Goldwater.[14] But in the Eisenhower landslide of 1956, John F. Baldwin, an incumbent Representative with a liberal voting record from the 6th District in

14. Johnson's 1964 landslide was in fact sectional in character. In the 11 states of the former Confederacy he had only a modest lead in the popular vote over Barry Goldwater. The irregular relationship between the presidential and House results in the South in 1964 resembled the relationship between the presidential and congressional voting in the country as a whole in election years when the presidential contest is close.

California, was the only Republican to carry a district where Eisenhower lost to Stevenson.[15] In the Republican presidential sweep of 1920, again there was just a solitary Republican Representative who managed to win in a district which Harding did not also carry. And in 1936, not one Democratic congressional aspirant made it to Washington from a district that Franklin Roosevelt lost.

Table 2.4—Congressional Districts with Split Election Results and the Presidential Tide: Districts Carried by a Presidential Nominee of One Major Party and by a House Nominee of the Other Major Party; and the Result of the Presidential Contest in those Districts, 1920–1964[a]

YEAR, PARTY OF WINNING PRESIDENTIAL CANDIDATE, AND NUMBER OF DISTRICTS ANALYZED	NUMBER OF DISTRICTS WITH SPLIT RESULTS IN WHICH:			
	Victorious President Lost While House Candidates of His Party Won	Per Cent	Victorious President Won While House Candidates of His Party Lost	Per Cent
1920 R 344	1	0.3	10	2.9
1924 R 356	2	0.6	28	7.9
1928 R 359	8	2.2	59	16.4
1932 D 355	10	2.8	34	9.6
1936 D 361	0	0.0	41	11.4
1940 D 362	9	2.5	39	10.8
1944 D 367	6	1.6	34	9.3
1948 D 422	20	4.7	38	9.0
1952 R 435	3	0.7	80	18.4
1956 R 435	1	0.2	127	29.2
1960 D 437	83	19.0	28	6.4
1964 D 435	32	7.4	113	26.0
Total 4668	175	3.7	631	13.5

[a] In this Table, only districts carried by presidential and congressional candidates of opposite major parties are recorded as having split election results.

In years when the presidential contest is more evenly fought, by contrast, more of the winning party's House candidates may carry districts that are lost by the head of the ticket. Nearly half of the would-be Congressmen who pulled off this feat between 1920 and 1964 did so during the 1960 Kennedy-Nixon contest—the closest presidential election in this century. Aside from 1964, the other jump in House results of this kind occurred during the 1948

15. In 1956 the California 6th, a district to the north and east of Oakland and Berkeley in the San Francisco Bay area, included Contra Costa and Solano Counties.

Truman-Dewey contest, another unusually close presidential election.[16]

Despite these exceptions, in most presidential years few of the winning party's congressional candidates can hope to be elected from districts that are not swept along by the dominant presidential tide. The prospects for the losing party's House nominees, however, are better, and a sizable number of them may succeed in withstanding the presidential tide in their district. During the 1920-1964 period analyzed in Table 2.4, more than one district in every eight elected a Congressman from the losing party while being carried by the opposition's winning presidential ticket.

If most districts with split election results are constituencies that are carried by the winning presidential nominee, most are also districts in which the presidential contest was closely fought. On occasion, some of the most notable Congressmen to serve in the House have had to withstand a mild opposition presidential tide in their district. In 1924, for example, the national Republican sweep brought the Coolidge vote in the 9th District in east-central Missouri up to 51.7 per cent of the two-party total.[17] At the same time, however, Representative Clarence Cannon, a Democrat who had first been sent to Washington in his party's upsurge in 1922, was reelected by nearly 9,000 votes. The voters in the Missouri 9th thus enabled Mr. Cannon to continue what was to become a career of more than four decades of uninterrupted service in Congress.

In 1944, the voters in the 10th District of Massachusetts, a constituency embracing Brookline, Newton, and part of Boston, reelected their incumbent Republican Congressman, Christian A. Herter. Simultaneously, Franklin Roosevelt edged to a 2,700-vote victory in the district. Both Cannon, a rural Democrat, and Herter, an urban Republican, had one thing in common: the opposition presidential tide in their district was not very strong. A relatively few tickets

16. Third-party or unpledged presidential tickets that divert votes from the winning presidential nominee also may create a situation in which more House candidates of his party than usual win, despite a poor showing by their party's presidential ticket in their district. Thus in 1948, in several districts where third-party discontent hurt the Truman candidacy, Democratic House nominees won with ease.

17. Only 3,382 votes (4.9 per cent of the total) went to La Follette or to other third-party presidential candidates in the Missouri 9th in 1924.

split in their favor were sufficient to save their seats in the House. Nor was their success unusual—a point underpinned by the data in Table 2.5. Between 1920 and 1964, opposition congressional candidates survived in more than half of the districts which a winning presidential nominee carried with less than 52.5 per cent of the vote.

Table 2.5—Congressional Districts Carried by House Candidates of the Major Party which Lost the Presidency and the Size of the Winning Opposition President's Vote in the District, 1920–1964

Winning President's District Percentage	Number of Districts	Number of House Candidates of Party Which Lost the Presidency Who Won[a]	Per Cent
0–4.9	26	17[b]	65.4
5–29.9	194	186	95.9
30–34.9	83	80	96.4
35–39.9	244	229	93.8
40–44.9	327	288	88.1
45–47.4	218	180	82.6
47.5–49.9	279	199	71.3
50–52.4	311	171	55.0
52.5–54.9	301	110	36.5
55–59.9	714	199	27.9
60–64.9	628	87	13.8
65–69.9	433	38	8.8
70–94.9	849	29	3.4
95–100	63	0	0.0
Total	4670	1813	

[a] 26 successful minor-party House nominees who also were not of the winning President's party are excluded from this column.
[b] In nine districts in Alabama in 1948 where Truman, the winning presidential nominee, was not on the ballot, no opposition G.O.P. House candidates were elected.

The number of the winning party's House candidates who receive the electorate's blessing in districts lost by their presidential running mate, of course, is far smaller. Nevertheless, the redoubtable Congressman Cannon pulled that feat as well, and thus became one of only six Democrats to win in a district Franklin Roosevelt lost in 1944. While Governor Dewey was squeaking to a tenuous 56-vote margin in the Missouri 9th, the veteran Democratic Congressman polled 53.2 per cent of the district's vote for Representative. Once again, relatively few split tickets were sufficient to save

Mr. Cannon's seat. In fact, throughout the country between 1920 and 1964 about half of the winning party's House candidates who won in districts the President lost came from districts where their party's presidential nominee did manage to poll at least 47.5 per cent of the vote.

This general relationship between districts with split election results and districts with close presidential contests emerges clearly from the following summary of the results from 1920 to 1964:

Winning President's District Percentage	Number of Split Election Results	Per Cent of Total Split Results
47.5–52.4%	239	29.6%
45.0–54.9	380	47.1
40.0–59.9	609	75.6
Over 59.9 or Under 40.0	197	24.4

Between 1920 and 1964, close to a third of the split results occurred in districts where the margin between victory or defeat in the presidential race was less than 2.5 per cent. Nearly half took place in constituencies where a shift of 5 per cent of the presidential vote would have swung the district to the other party. Many split election results, in short, do not reflect widespread ticket-splitting— even though the selectivity exercised by a few voters in the district can be of crucial importance for the individual House candidates concerned.

Occasionally, however, a Congressman will win deep in opposition presidential territory. In 1936, Charles A. Wolverton, the G.O.P. Representative from a district which included Camden, New Jersey, and two adjacent counties was reelected at the same time that the New Jersey 1st District gave two thirds of its presidential vote to Franklin D. Roosevelt.[18] In the same election, William Lemke and Usher Burdick, both North Dakota Republicans, won two At-Large seats while the Democratic standard-bearer was drawing 69.2 per cent of their state's two-party presidential vote.

18. In addition to Camden County, the New Jersey 1st contained Gloucester and Salem Counties in 1936. Roosevelt's share of the two-party presidential vote was 66.6 per cent.

These men won in the face of a nationwide opposition presidential tide. Extraordinary as their achievement was, the success of House candidates of the party that wins the Presidency in districts where the President is soundly beaten is even more remarkable. In 1940, Harry B. Coffee, a three-term Democratic incumbent, stood for reelection in the 5th District in Nebraska. Representative Coffee had first been sent to Washington in the midterm Democratic congressional landslide of 1934, when his district was in the throes of

Table 2.6—Congressional Districts with Split Election Results and the Winning President's Share of the Two-Party Presidential Vote in those Districts, 1920–1964[a]

Winning President's District Percentage	Number of Districts With Split Results	Per Cent of Total Number of Split Results
0–4.9	9[b]	1.1
5–29.9	8	1.0
30–34.9	3	0.4
35–39.9	15	1.9
40–44.9	36	4.5
45–47.4	37	4.6
47.5–49.9	77	9.6
50–52.4	162	20.1
52.5–54.9	104	12.9
55–59.9	193	23.9
60–64.9	89	11.0
65–69.9	41	5.1
70–94.9	32	4.0
95–100	0	—
Total	806	

[a] Split election results involving minor-party candidates for President or Congressman are excluded from this table.
[b] The nine districts in this unit were in Alabama in 1948, where President Truman's name did not appear on the ballot.

an acute agricultural depression. In 1932 and 1936, Franklin Roosevelt also won the Nebraska 5th with votes to spare, but in 1940 his share of the district's vote plummeted to 39.7 per cent.[19] At the same time, however, Representative Coffee was reelected comfortably with an even 58 per cent of the congressional vote.

19. In 1932 Roosevelt polled 62.2 per cent of the two-party presidential vote in the Nebraska 5th. Four years later he received 57.2 per cent.

Two years later, the Nebraska 5th had been redistricted, and Representative Coffee, who was the last Democrat to represent a rural district in Nebraska until 1958, was out of office. The magnitude of his achievement in 1940, however, is underscored by the data in Table 2.6. From 1920 to 1964, only 34 other Representatives of the party which won the Presidency succeeded in carrying districts where the head of their ticket polled less than 40 per cent of the vote.[20]

Relatively more of the losing party's House candidates succeed in bucking even a strong opposition presidential tide. Since 1920 about one in eight of those running in districts where the victorious presidential nominee received between 60 and 65 per cent of the vote have been elected. As the winning President's margin goes even higher, however, the prospects for opposition Congressmen dim perceptibly. Eventually, in districts where the President polled over 95 per cent of the vote, the point is reached where no opposition House candidate has been successful between 1920 and 1964. Yet like their counterparts in the winning party, most House candidates of the party that loses the Presidency who buck an opposition presidential tide in their own district do so in constituencies where the presidential contest is close.

Split-Ticket Voting and the Political System

THE IMPACT ON THE functioning of the political system of these Congressmen who withstand an opposition presidential tide invites reflection. Most of them are candidates for the House who win despite a dominant national trend that is carrying the opposition's presidential ticket to victory. When the presidential race is close, as in 1960, the winning presidential nominee may not always lead his congressional teammates. But a presidential nominee who wins by a decisive margin almost invariably carries more districts than his party's House slate.

20. Most of these other 34 successful House candidates were southern Democrats elected in 1960 and 1964 in districts that went for Richard Nixon or Barry Goldwater. Another nine were southern Democrats elected in 1948 in Alabama, where Truman's name did not appear on the ballot and Dixiecrat J. Strom Thurmond was listed as the regular Democratic nominee.

The tendency since World War I for the popular vote for President to fluctuate more widely than the popular vote for Congressmen has already been noted. In its impact on the partisan makeup of the House, however, this difference is accentuated. If the congressional vote had exactly paralleled the presidential vote in 1952, President Eisenhower would have gone into office with 297 Republican House members instead of 221. If the same voters who suppor-

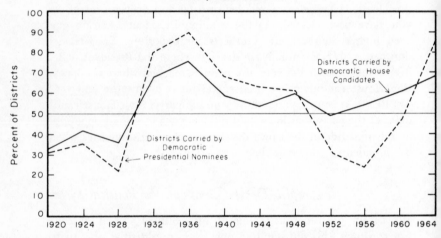

Figure 2.4—*Congressional districts carried by Democratic presidential nominees and congressional districts carried by Democratic house candidates, 1920–1964*

ted Hoover in 1928 had also backed a Republican House candidate, Hoover would have had about 320 Republican Representatives to work with in 1929 instead of 267. Particularly in years when there is a presidential landslide, when an additional few percentage points in the popular vote enable one of the major parties to carry numerous districts for President where normally that party is not strong, opponents of the winning presidential nominee may manage to retain House seats in a substantial number of districts that their presidential teammate is unable to carry.

This tendency is depicted graphically in Figure 2.4. The trend lines indicate clearly that the electorate in individual House districts changes its party allegiance for President more readily than it shifts its choice for Representative. In the years of Republican presidential victories between 1920 and 1964, the G.O.P. carried more districts for President than for the House. In elections when the Republican party lost the Presidency decisively, by contrast, it was the Democratic presidential nominee who won more districts than his party's congressional slate. Only in the extraordinarily close presidential contest of 1960 did a successful Democratic presidential candidate trail his party's congressional ticket in the number of House districts carried.

Throughout the period from 1920 to 1964 covered by the data, the percentage of districts that the Democrats carried for President fluctuated violently—from just over 22 per cent to nearly 90 per cent. The variation in the number of districts carried by Democratic House candidates, which ranged from a third to slightly over three quarters of the total, also was large. But it involved substantially fewer districts than the number that shifted for President. Public sentiment for a Chief Executive, it would seem, is more volatile than the shifts in popularity suffered by the candidates who comprise each party's congressional wing.

The consequences of this ticket-splitting for the partisan composition of the national legislature are clear. Shifts in party strength within the House are less mercurial than they would be if every voter cast a straight ticket for President and Congressman. As a result, elements of continuity, stability, and perhaps even resistance to change are strengthened in the House. In its impact on executive-legislative relations, too, the voters' selectivity conditions as well as it reflects the nature of American politics. The survival of these opposition Congressmen in the House represents a check on the incoming President that is built into the functioning of the nation's electoral system.

Incumbent Congressmen and
the Electoral Verdict

Since World War I, about an eighth of the nation's House districts have supported presidential and congressional candidates of opposing parties. Most of these split results occur in districts where the presidential race is hotly contested. Most also occur in districts where the winning presidential nominee makes a stronger showing than his less-successful House running mate. Yet every four years, in some districts where the victorious presidential candidate ekes out a narrow margin, the congressional nominee of his party also wins. Meanwhile, in other districts with split results, even a successful presidential nominee may falter despite a victory by his congressional running mate in the district. Results such as these suggest that individual House candidates sometimes conduct campaigns that enjoy at least a measure of autonomy from the national presidential tide. The pertinent question here, however, is why.

Most politicians would probably have a ready answer. The overwhelming majority of the House candidates in question, they would point out, are incumbents. The special ties that most Congressmen are able to develop in their local constituency, once they are in the

House, are a potent source of support on election day. The proposition that the incumbent candidate generally enjoys a marked advantage in an electoral contest is, in fact, one of the cardinal tenets of the nation's political folklore. If true, it could also be one of the principal factors influencing the outcome of congressional contests in presidential years. On the average, more than four of every five candidates for Representative who win are already House members.[1] But first, it might be well to test this widely accepted assumption against the facts of American congressional politics.

Incumbent Congressmen, the Presidential Tide, and Congressional Survival

IN 1944, WILLIAM A. PITTENGER, the G.O.P. candidate for Representative in Minnesota's 8th District, edged to victory over his Democratic-Farmer-Labor opponent with 51.9 per cent of the vote. At the same time his constituency, which embraced northeastern Minnesota's iron range country and included the city of Duluth, gave nearly 70 per cent of its presidential vote to the Democrats' Franklin D. Roosevelt. In New Jersey's 1st District in 1936, Charles A. Wolverton won a House victory for the Republican party while Roosevelt was winning an even two thirds of the district's presidential vote. And in 1964, Frances P. Bolton won the House election in the Ohio 22nd District while in the presidential race her district was going for Lyndon Johnson by 70.1 per cent.

Although these three House nominees who withstood an opposition presidential landslide came from widely differing types of districts, they had one thing in common: all of them were already duly accredited members of the House. When Representative Wolverton withstood the Roosevelt tide in his district in 1936, he had had 10 consecutive years of service in the House. When Congressman Pittenger bucked the Democratic presidential sweep in his district in 1944, he had, with but two exceptions, been chosen to

1. During the 11 presidential years between 1924 and 1964, 86.0 per cent of the successful House candidates of the party that lost the Presidency were incumbents. For the winning party, 77.4 per cent of its successful House nominees were incumbents during the comparable period.

represent the constituency in every election since 1928.[2] And when Mrs. Bolton was elected despite the Johnson landslide in her district in 1964, she was in her 25th year of continuous service in the House.

The extraordinary victories of Pittenger and Wolverton in 1936 and 1944 were not isolated cases. Throughout the years when Roosevelt and Truman occupied the White House, the G.O.P. House candidates who withstood a heavy Democratic presidential vote in their districts were all incumbents. This finding is underpinned by the data in Table 3.1. Between 1932 and 1948, the larger

Table 3.1—Incumbency, the Presidential Tide, and Congressional Survival: Number of Winning House Candidates of the Party that Lost the Presidency Who Were Incumbents and the Victorious Presidential Candidate's Vote in their Districts, 1932–1948[a]

Winning Presidential Candidate's District Percentage	Number of Districts	Number of House Candidates of Party That Lost the Presidency Who Won[b]	Number Who Were Incumbents	Per Cent Who Were Incumbents
0–39.9	111	101	95	94.1
40–44.9	127	122	111	91.0
45–47.4	99	88	77	87.5
47.5–49.9	114	84	65	77.4
50–52.4	119	62	51	82.3
52.5–54.9	136	35	31	88.6
55–59.9	230	36	31	86.1
60–64.9	166	15	15	100.0
65–69.9	93	6	6	100.0
70–94.9	347	4	4	100.0
95–100	48	0	0	—
Total	1590	553	486	

[a] Congressional districts for which no presidential figures are available are excluded from this table.
[b] Only House nominees of the major party that lost the Presidency are included in this column. Successful minor-party House nominees are excluded.

the Democratic presidential candidate's margin was in a district, the greater were the chances that an opposition House candidate who managed to survive would be an incumbent. In districts where

2. Representative Pittenger's only two defeats between 1928 and 1944 came in 1932 and 1936. In 1932, the entire Minnesota congressional delegation had to run for At-Large House seats whose occupants were elected on a state-wide basis.

Roosevelt and Truman polled more than 60 per cent of the vote, not a single would-be Republican Congressman who was not already in the House was able to win.

Limitations to the Electoral Advantage Usually Enjoyed by Incumbent Congressmen

THE RESULTS FOR House and President do not always fit this pattern, however. In the 1920's and the 1950's, and again in 1960 and 1964, House nominees who bucked a strong opposition tide for the winning presidential candidate in their district were about as likely not to be incumbents as to be incumbents. Quite clearly, in certain circumstances incumbents are not the only House nominees who can survive in districts where the opposition presidential ticket is strong. An examination of individual results reveals what some of these special circumstances are.

Regional Revolts Against the Dominant Party in a Region. Sometimes major regional revolts against the heretofore dominant party in a region may widen the divergence between a party's presidential and congressional vote and create a situation in which new candidates for the House can win despite a poor showing by their presidential running mate in their district. During the years of the Roosevelt coalition, both the Democratic presidential and congressional tickets did well not only in the party's traditional southern stronghold but also throughout much of the North. From 1932 to 1948, virtually every district in the North that gave the Democratic presidential ticket a large margin was also captured by a Democratic congressional aspirant. Incumbent Republican Representatives managed to stay in office in only a few constituencies where the Democratic presidential nominee was strong. Meanwhile, in the South, Roosevelt and even Truman ran ahead of their Republican presidential adversaries in nearly every district in the region. In all of these constituencies, Democratic Congressmen were elected.

The elections in the 1920's, the 1950's, and in 1960 and 1964 were of a different order. Several nonincumbent House candidates of the party that lost the presidential contest won decisive victories in districts where the winning presidential nominee ran exceptionally well. These elections of 1924, 1928, and 1952-1964 are covered by the data in Table 3.2. During those years, 15 nonincumbent opposition House candidates carried districts where the winning presidential candidate polled over 60 per cent of the vote.

Table 3.2—*Incumbency, the Presidential Tide, and Congressional Survival: Number of Winning House Candidates of the Major Party that Lost the Presidency Who Were Incumbents and the Victorious Presidential Candidate's Vote in their Districts, 1924, 1928, 1952, 1956, 1960, and 1964*[a]

Winning Presidential Candidate's District Percentage	Number of Districts	Number of House Candidates of Party That Lost the Presidency Who Won	Number Who Were Incumbents	Per Cent Who Were Incumbents
0–4.9	11	11	10	90.9
5–29.9	136	128	110	85.9
30–34.9	40	37	32	86.5
35–39.9	115	105	81	77.1
40–44.9	158	125	98	78.4
45–47.4	87	62	53	85.5
47.5–49.9	124	77	65	84.4
50–52.4	132	81	70	86.4
52.5–54.9	129	62	54	87.1
55–59.9	370	141	128	90.8
60–64.9	355	63	54	85.7
65–69.9	252	26[b]	22	84.6
70–94.9	353	19	17	89.5
95–100	1	0	0	—
Total	2263	937	794	

[a] Congressional districts for which no presidential figures are available are excluded from this table.
[b] The Maine 2nd, a district which gave President Eisenhower 68.7 per cent of its vote but also elected Frank M. Coffin, a nonincumbent Democratic House candidate, in 1956, is not included in this unit. The 1956 balloting for President and for Congressman took place on different days in Maine.

Two of these nonincumbents who bucked a strong opposition presidential tide in their constituency were southern Democrats. In 1928, the voters in the 4th District of Florida elected Ruth Bryan Owen, a Democrat then making her first race for the House, by nearly two to one. Mrs. Owen's district extended along most of Florida's eastern coast and included the cities of Miami, West Palm Beach, and Jacksonville. On the same day the voters there gave

Herbert Hoover a decisive margin over Al Smith.[3] In 1956, the voters in the Texas 3rd, a district in east-central Texas, discriminated equally sharply between the G.O.P. presidential nominee and the party's local House candidate. In this 1956 contest, Lindley G. Beckworth, a nonincumbent Democratic House nominee (through one who had previously served in the House) defeated his Republican opponent by nearly five to one. In the same constituency President Eisenhower received an even 60 per cent of the vote.[4]

In both 1928 and 1956, as well as in 1952, a widespread regional revolt took place in the previously Democratic South against the Democratic presidential ticket. Yet, though the number of votes cast by southerners for a Republican President increased sharply during those elections, the Democratic House candidates in most of the region's districts could still look forward to election by a comfortable margin—whether they were incumbents or not. In some instances, the more conservative political orientation of the new Democratic House nominee was probably more in keeping with the dominant sentiments in the constituency than was the national Democratic presidential ticket. But whatever the reasons, most nonincumbent Democratic House aspirants were not swept to defeat in the Republican presidential tide. In all three elections, nonincumbent Democrats also carried southern districts where the G.O.P. presidential nominee polled between 55 and 59.9 per cent of the vote.[5]

The 1956 returns bore the imprint of yet another regional revolt—this time against the congressional ticket of the party that won the Presidency. This peculiarity of the voting in certain sections of the country also resulted in House victories for nonincumbent Democrats in the face of heavy Republican presidential margins in

3. The two-party vote: Ruth Bryan Owen, Democrat, 64.9 per cent; Herbert Hoover, Republican, 62.4 per cent. No minor-party votes for Representative were reported. The minor-party presidential total was 1.7 per cent.
4. The 1956 House vote in the Texas 3rd: Beckworth, 83.5 per cent. No minor-party congressional votes were reported. The minor-party presidential total was 0.7 per cent.
5. In 1928, 1952, and 1956, the Republican presidential candidate received between 55 and 59.9 per cent of the two-party vote in a total of 40 southern districts. In three of them, Democrats making their first House race were elected. Several constituencies that were redistricted shortly before the 1952 election are excluded from this calculation.

their districts. In the wheat-raising counties of southwestern Kansas, the voters in the Kansas 5th District elected a Democrat making his first try for Congress, J. Floyd Breeding, even though they voted for President Eisenhower by more than two to one.[6]

In the 7th District in southwestern Missouri, another area hard hit by sagging agricultural prices and drought, not even a 61.1 per cent margin for the Republican presidential ticket could save Mr. Dewey Short, the district's veteran G.O.P. Representative. His opponent, Charles H. Brown, like Mr. Breeding, was making his first race for the House.[7]

The 1956 returns from the 29th District in southeastern California were also particularly noteworthy. This rural and small-town constituency included the renowned Imperial Valley, perhaps the lushest site for irrigated truck farming in the country. In 1956 the local Democrats nominated D. S. Saund, a former judge who had been born in India; and in November he won the local House seat despite an Eisenhower margin of 61.5 per cent in his district.[8] The personalities of both major-party House contestants made for a contest of unusual interest—Judge Saund's Republican opponent was the well-known aviatrix, Mrs. Jacqueline C. Odlum. The chances are, however, that the Democrat's narrow victory also reflected a general regional revolt against the Republican House ticket which was noticeable in nearly all of the rural and small-town districts west of the Mississippi in 1956.

These extraordinary victories by new House candidates in districts where the opposition's share of the presidential vote exceeded 60 per cent of the total were unusually dramatic. But they were paralleled by the election of nonincumbent Democrats in several other districts where President Eisenhower won by comfortable, if somewhat smaller, margins. In four districts where the

6. Mr. Breeding defeated his Republican opponent by a narrow margin, with 50.5 per cent of the total congressional vote. No minor-party House votes were recorded. In the presidential race, Eisenhower received 67.9 per cent of the two-party vote. The minor-party presidential vote was 0.4 per cent.

7. Brown received 50.3 per cent of the House vote in the Missouri 7th in 1956. No minor-party votes for President or for Congressman were recorded.

8. Saund polled 51.5 per cent of the California 29th's two-party congressional vote. The minor-party percentages were: for Congressman, 0.05 per cent; for President, 0.5 per cent.

Eisenhower vote ranged between 55 and 57.5 per cent of the total, nonincumbent Democratic congressional nominees won in the same regional revolt which benefitted Messrs. Brown, Breeding, and Saund.

Even the President himself was not immune from the discontent reflected by these unusual election results. In all the rural and small-town districts cited above, Eisenhower's share of the presidential vote was smaller than it had been in 1952; and the Democratic presidential swings in the districts ranged from 3.2 per cent up to 11.5 per cent. The shift of sentiment against the G.O.P. congressional standard-bearers in the same districts, however, was generally even more pronounced. The Republicans' loss of support in parts of the farm belt and the West in 1956 thus constituted a general regional revolt which affected the party's congressional slate more severely than its presidential ticket.

Hard Times and the Officeholder. These returns from rural constituencies in 1956 demonstrate that sometimes nonincumbent House nominees can win despite an opposition presidential landslide in their district. They do not preclude the possibility, however, that an incumbent congressional candidate of the same party might have done even better in the districts in question. Nevertheless, the results suggest that sometimes, if events take a markedly unfavorable turn, it may be a positive disadvantage to be an officeholder. The 1956 campaign came at a time when drought and sliding agricultural prices were causing many farmers to experience a painful decline in their revenue, and it was no secret that Secretary of Agriculture Benson's popularity was less than the Republican National Chairman might have hoped. A number of G.O.P. Congressmen from districts in the prairie states where the cash-crop farming population was particularly large had actually voted against the Republican Administration's farm program. Even so, they experienced a marked loss of support on election day.

President Eisenhower, as has been noted, also lost ground in these districts, even though in most other parts of the country he ran more strongly than he had run in 1952. The episode suggests the possibility that, when things go wrong, some voters reckon that those who took credit for the good times should be made to pay for the bad.[9] In any event, regional revolts that have a differential impact on a party's presidential and congressional tickets may create circumstances in which even nonincumbent House nominees can ride to victory over a strong opposition presidential tide in their district.

Third-party Candidacies. Occasionally another broad election trend may make it easier for nonincumbent House nominees to win in districts where an opposition presidential candidate has a long lead over his nearest competitor. In 1924, Brooks Fletcher, the new Democratic hopeful in Ohio's 8th District, was elected to Congress. In the same general election, President Coolidge decisively defeated the Democrats' John W. Davis in the constituency by 39,099 votes to 25,902. This margin gave Coolidge 60.2 per cent of the two-party presidential vote. But if the district's sizable third-party vote polled by Robert La Follette for President—13.4 per cent of the total—is taken into consideration, it is clear that the regular Republican presidential tide which Mr. Fletcher had to buck was less formidable than the two-party figures alone would suggest.[10] Opponents of Mr. Coolidge polled 47 per cent of the district's total presidential vote.

In elections marked by a large minor-party presidential vote, it is obvious that the interrelationship between the presidential and congressional contests in individual districts takes on a new and often more complex form. Even a nonincumbent House nominee may win in districts that are carried with ease by an opposition presidential hopeful, if the rest of the presidential votes are divided

9. The election of 1932, held in the midst of the Great Depression, followed a campaign in which the time-honored cry of "Throw the Rascals Out" could be used to good effect. And the returns indicate that incumbent Republican Congressmen were less successful that year than incumbents normally are in withstanding an opposition presidential tide in their district. In 1932, in districts for which the presidential returns are available, only 22.5 per cent (9 of 40) of the G.O.P. Representatives who were up for reelection in districts the Democratic presidential nominee carried survived the Roosevelt tide in their constituency. In the other 10 presidential elections between 1924 and 1964, 69.4 per cent (474 of 683) of the incumbent House candidates of the party that lost the Presidency survived an opposition presidential tide in their district.

10. Mr. Fletcher polled 53.6 per cent of the Ohio 8th's two-party congressional vote in a race in which minor-party candidates drew 0.8 per cent of the total vote. The third-party presidential vote in the district totaled 10,083.

among two or more additional candidates for the White House. Moreover, an important third-party presidential movement, like a regional revolt against a major-party presidential or congressional ticket, has general consequences that may affect the fate of nonincumbent House candidates in a sizable number of districts.

Special Local Factors. A quite different situation prevails when some local factor peculiar to the congressional contest in an individual district enables a nonincumbent House candidate to win despite strong sentiment for the opposition's presidential ticket in the constituency. The 1924 and the 1952 returns provide notable examples of House contests whose outcome was probably determined in large part by local issues or personalities. Shortly before the 1952 campaign began, the G.O.P. Representative from the normally Republican 1st District in Kansas, Albert M. Cole, voted to authorize construction of a flood-control dam in his constituency. Congressman Cole's district included several cities, perched along the Kansas River, which had suffered severe flood damage during the summer of 1951; and his vote for a Tuttle Creek dam was applauded warmly by his constituents in river-bottom towns like Manhattan and North Topeka who had had several feet of water in their living rooms. His stand was opposed equally emphatically, however, by people living on some of the best cropland in the state who would have seen their farms inundated by the planned reservoir.

Amid cries of "large reservoir dams" versus "small dams for upstream watershed development" and a sharpening political cleavage between the townspeople in the river valley and the farmers in the uplands, a Democratic congressional nominee, himself a farmer, entered the fray. Howard Miller, the Democratic hopeful, was a practicing soil conservationist of many years' standing, and his numerous contacts with conservationist groups throughout the district probably strengthened his candidacy. But the principal plank on which he ran was straightforward: "End Big Dam Foolishness."

A hot congressional campaign ensued. The wives of farmers whose land would have been flooded by the dam, many of them normally Republicans, drove through the district in automobile caravans urging their fellow citizens to vote Democratic—for

Congressman. When the returns were in, Representative Cole had been bested by the Democrats' Howard Miller by nearly 4,000 votes, despite an overwhelming Eisenhower vote in the district of 71.3 per cent.[11] Veteran political observers could not recall another occasion, even in the New Deal's heyday, when the 1st District of Kansas had sent a Democrat to Washington.[12]

In 1924, Kansas was the scene of another remarkable congressional contest. In that year, the voters in the state's 2nd District elected Chauncy B. Little, a Democrat making his first race for the House, while giving President Coolidge 71.7 per cent of the two-party vote; but here, also, there hangs a tale. Late in June, 1924, the district's incumbent Republican Representative with a long record of service in the House, Edward C. Little, died. In the general election campaign that followed, the G.O.P. entered Mr. Russell Dyer as its new congressional nominee. The Democrats, however, ran Chauncy B. Little, a man whose name closely resembled that of the district's former Representative. In November, after a contest in which minor-party candidates also demonstrated some strength, Mr. Little won.[13]

These unusual Kansas election results are intrinsically interesting; but they also illustrate a more general, if obvious, point. Incumbent Congressmen who ill-advisedly vote wrong on an issue of burning concern to large numbers of their constituents may be vulnerable on election day even though their party's presidential ticket is strong in the district. And nonincumbent congressional

11. Miller received 51.5 per cent of the Kansas 1st House vote in defeating Representative Cole by 68,909 votes to 64,963. No minor-party presidential or congressional votes were reported for the district.

12. Two years later, in 1954, after a Republican primary contest that again reflected a sharp cleavage between city voters in the Kansas River valley and farmers in the area directly affected by the proposed dam, State Representative William Avery was chosen as the G.O.P. House nominee. Avery came from Clay County, where many farms, including his own, were doomed by the planned reservoir, and he campaigned as a staunch opponent of the dam. In November he defeated Congressman Miller, despite Democratic gains elswhere in the country.

13. Little drew 52.3 per cent of the two-party congressional vote in the Kansas 2nd in 1924, The minor-party totals were: for Congressman, 6.6 per cent; for President, 12.8 per cent. The G.O.P. percentage of the total presidential vote, although substantially smaller than its 71.7 per cent of the two-party poll, was still sizable at 62.2 per cent.

aspirants whose personal qualities make them especially attractive to the electorate can, on rare occasions, win deep in opposition presidential territory.

Other circumstances, as well, may limit an incumbent's drawing power at the polls. Congressmen who find themselves on the shady side of the law are likely targets for irate constituents. And a host of other personal disabilities can have a similar effect upon an incumbent's popular appeal if they obtain sufficient publicity to become known to a significant portion of the voters. Marital problems, misbehavior by members of the candidate's family, other domestic difficulties, questions concerning the Congressman's loyalty, an ill-advised offhand remark—all these and other problems may bedevil an incumbent's bid for reelection. When they do, they also affect the interrelationship between the presidential and the congressional vote in the incumbent's constituency. Usually, however, the electoral impact of such considerations is limited to individual congressional districts.[14]

Incumbency and the General Political Situation. Congressional contests whose outcome is determined chiefly by local issues or by local candidates can crop up in any presidential year. The remarkable showing made by a few nonincumbents in elections marked by party revolts of regional or national scope, on the other hand, may merit a more general explanation. The point to be made is conjectural, but the data presented earlier in Table 3.2 should be pondered with some care.

The statistics cover six elections when the traditional party allegiance of large sections of the electorate was subjected to severe

14. A general policy stand taken by a presidential candidate can, of course, also have a particular impact on the presidential balloting in individual House districts, if the general issue is of special local concern to the voters in a particular constituency. In 1956, Wallowa County, Oregon, was one of the few counties in eastern Oregon which had a predominantly Republican registration. But the county also lay next to the site of a possible multipurpose federal dam on the Columbia River at Hell's Canyon. Opposition to the Republican Administration's "partnership" approach to the development of electric power was strong in the area; and in the November general election, Wallowa was one of only three counties in the state which the Democrats' Adlai Stevenson carried for President. Four years earlier, President Eisenhower had won the county by nearly three to two. See John M. Swarthout, "The 1956 Election in Oregon," *Western Political Quarterly,* Vol. 10, No. 1, March, 1957, p. 146.

strain. In 1928, 1952, and in 1956, 1960, and 1964, close to half of the voters in the normally Democratic South felt constrained to desert the Democratic presidential standard-bearer. In 1964, also, there was a heavy desertion of the G.O.P.'s presidential ticket by many normally Republican voters. And in 1924, when La Follette's third-party candidacy drew one of every eight votes cast for President, the preexisting ties of party also were put to a severe test. It is in elections like these, Table 3.2 suggests, that an occasional nonincumbent House candidate may win in a district where sentiment for the opposition presidential candidate is strong. New House nominees, however, were not able to pull this feat between 1932 and 1948, when party ties held more strongly and when, in general, there was less ticket-splitting. Then only incumbents won House seats in districts where their presidential running mate was weak.

General Appraisal of the Electoral Advantage Usually Enjoyed by Incumbent Congressmen

THE THEME OF THE foregoing discussion is that certain circumstances may limit the advantage that incumbent House candidates supposedly enjoy over other congressional nominees. Yet if a major assumption on which politicians operate is correct, incumbent Congressmen generally should do better at the polls than other House contestants. Moreover, if their advantage is real, it should show up particularly clearly in districts where their presidential running mate finds himself in trouble. It is here that the electoral tide is running against the incumbent Representatives' party. The fact is, most incumbent Congressmen do enjoy a marked advantage in such constituencies. How substantial this advantage is may be demonstrated by a comparison of the showing made by incumbents and nonincumbents of the same party in districts with a similar division of the presidential vote.

In Table 3.3 the success of Congressmen of the party that lost the presidential election who sought reelection is contrasted with the fate of nonincumbent House aspirants of the same party. The data cover the elections between 1924 and 1964. All these House nominees entrusted their fate to the outcome at the polls on a day when the opposition's presidential ticket was winning a nationwide victory. Many ran in districts where sentiment for the opposition's presidential nominee was strong. Except in districts where their party had a long lead in the presidential balloting anyway, Congressmen who were up for reelection did much better than nonincumbent House candidates of the same party.

Table 3.3—*Incumbent and Nonincumbent House Nominees and the Winning Presidential Tide: The Fate of Congressional Candidates of the Party that Lost the Presidency, 1924–1964*

WINNING PRESIDENTIAL CANDIDATE'S DISTRICT PERCENTAGE	NUMBER OF DISTRICTS[a]	HOUSE CANDIDATES OF THE PARTY THAT LOST THE PRESIDENCY				PERCENTAGE OF INCUMBENTS AND NONINCUMBENTS WHO WON:	
		NUMBER OF INCUMBENTS WHO:		NUMBER OF NONINCUMBENTS WHO:			
		Ran	Won	Ran	Won	Incs.	Nonincs.
0–4.9	20	10	10	5[b]	1[b]	100.0	20.0
5–29.9	139	113	113	19[c]	18[c]	100.0	94.7
30–34.9	61	52	52	7	6	100.0	85.7
35–39.9	193	153	153	33	29	100.0	87.9
40–44.9	285	213	209	59	38	98.1	64.4
45–47.4	186	132	130	48	20	98.5	41.7
47.5–49.9	238	144	132	87	29	91.7	33.3
50–52.4	251	146	120	99	21	82.2	21.2
52.5–54.9	265	129	85	122	12	65.9	9.8
55–59.9	600	247	160	316	18	64.8	5.7
60–64.9	521	122	69	360	9	56.6	2.5
65–69.9	345	52	28	267	5	53.8	1.9
70–94.9	700	27	21	460	2	77.8	0.4
95–100	49	—	—	28	0	—	0.0
Total	3853	1540	1282	1910	208		

[a] Districts for which no presidential figures are available are excluded from this table. Since some House seats are uncontested, the number of districts analyzed may exceed the total number of ncumbent House nominees run by the party losing a presidential election.

[b] Four of the five districts covered in these units were in Alabama in 1948, where President Truman, the regular Democratic party presidential nominee, was excluded from the ballot but where no Republican House candidates were elected.

[c] In 1964, Robert B. French, a nonincumbent Republican House candidate, lost to Democratic Representative Armistead I. Selden, Jr., in Alabama's 5th District.

Nonincumbents of the party that lost the Presidency faced an uninviting prospect in their attempt to buck the winning presidential tide. Only in districts where the winning President was held to less than 40 per cent of the vote were more than two thirds of the opposition's House candidates certain to win. In districts were the victorious presidential nominee polled between 45 and 49.9 per cent of the vote, only a little more than a third of the nonincumbents on the losing party's House ticket made it to Washington.

The outlook for nonincumbent opposition House candidates was even bleaker in the districts that the winning President carried. In constituencies where the President-elect won by a whisker—with less than 52.5 per cent of the vote—only about one in five managed to win. In the remaining districts, where the winning President's margin swelled to increasingly larger proportions, the chances that a nonincumbent House candidate could be elected dropped steadily until they were virtually nil.

The showing made by incumbent Congressmen faced with an opposition presidential sweep is far more impressive. Between 1924 and 1964, only four Representatives were defeated in a district where an opposition President-elect was held to less than 45 per cent of the vote. Moreover, at practically every level of opposition presidential strength, incumbent House nominees of the party that lost the Presidency did better than their nonincumbent fellow partisans. In districts where the winning President received between 55 and 59.9 per cent of the vote, the odds were little better than one in twenty that a nonincumbent House candidate of the losing party would win. In districts with a comparable division of the presidential vote, nearly two thirds of their party conferees who were already House members were elected.

This same general relationship between the presidential tide and the fate of incumbent and nonincumbent House nominees is examined from a slightly different angle in Table 3.4. The data in this table also cover the years 1924 to 1964. In it the showing of House nominees of the party that won the Presidency is related to the size of their presidential standard-bearer's margin in individual districts. Once again the weakness of nonincumbent House nominees in comparison with incumbent candidates of the same party emerges with striking clarity.

Only a handful of the nonincumbents of the party that won the Presidency were elected in districts that their presidential running mate failed to carry. While this result will occasion no amazement, nonincumbent House nominees of the winning President's party also ran surprisingly poorly in the districts that their President carried by small or even by comfortable margins. Less than half of them won in districts where the head of their ticket polled between 50 and 60 per cent of the vote. Even in districts that the winning President carried decisively, with 60 to 70 per cent of the vote, less than two thirds of his congressional running mates were likely to win if they were not already members of the House.

Table 3.4—Incumbent and Nonincumbent House Nominees and the Winning Presidential Tide: The Fate of Congressional Candidates of the Party that Won the Presidency, 1924–1964

WINNING PRESIDENTIAL CANDIDATE'S DISTRICT PERCENTAGE	NUMBER OF DISTRICTS[a]	HOUSE CANDIDATES OF THE PARTY THAT WON THE PRESIDENCY				PERCENTAGE OF INCUMBENTS AND NONINCUMBENTS WHO WON:	
		NUMBER OF INCUMBENTS WHO:		NUMBER OF NON-INCUMBENTS WHO:			
		Ran	Won	Ran	Won	Incs.	Nonincs.
0–4.9	20	6[b]	6[b]	3[b]	3[b]	100.0[b]	100.0[b]
5–29.9	139	11	7	49[c]	1	63.6	2.0
30–34.9	61	4	3	46	0	75.0	0.0
35–39.9	193	18	12	132	1	66.7	0.8
40–44.9	285	41	28	205	8	68.3	3.9
45–47.4	186	35	28	140	7	80.0	5.0
47.5–49.9	238	64	52	142	24	81.2	16.9
50–52.4	251	74	70	159	38	94.6	23.9
52.5–54.9	265	106	102	146	65	96.2	44.5
55–59.9	600	295	290	271	127	98.3	46.9
60–64.9	521	343	340	166	101	99.1	60.8
65–69.9	345	255	255	87	51	100.0	58.6
70–94.9	700	577[d]	575	117	97	99.7	82.9
95–100	49	43	43	6	6	100.0	100.0
Total	3853	1872	1811	1669	529		

[a] Districts for which no presidential figures are available are excluded from this table. Since some House seats are uncontested, the number of districts analyzed may exceed the total number of incumbent and nonincumbent House nominees run by the party winning a presidential election.
[b] The districts in these units were all in Alabama in 1948. President Truman, the regular Democratic party nominee, was excluded from the ballot; but the Democratic House candidates, incumbents and nonincumbents alike, were all elected.
[c] The one nonincumbent House candidate in this unit who won was Maston O'Neal, a Democrat. elected in the Georgia 2nd District in 1964.
[d] The two incumbent House nominees in this unit who failed in their bids for reelection were Albert M. Cole, from the 1st District in Kansas in 1952, and Joseph W. Byrns, Jr., from the 5th District in Tennessee in 1940. Byrns, a Democrat, was defeated by an Independent.

Quite different was the showing made by incumbent Congressmen of the President-elect's party. The data bring into sharp focus the stake that House members from potentially marginal constituencies have in the nomination of a presidential candidate of their party who can win. Even in districts where the winning President lost, well over half of his congressional running mates who were incumbents were able to retain their seats in the House. In districts carried by the winning President, even those where he won by a narrow margin, the House candidates of his party who were already in Congress were nearly invincible. Between 1924 and 1964, only 18 incumbents from the party that won the Presidency were defeated in districts carried by their presidential standard-bearer. In constituencies with a comparable division of the presidential vote, some 1,675 Congressmen of the winning President's party were returned for another term.[15]

Nonincumbent House Nominees in Two Situations: Opposing an Incumbent or Opposing a Nonincumbent

NONINCUMBENT HOUSE NOMINEES, of course, may run in a variety of situations. The majority take on the unenviable job of attempting to oust an opponent who is already in the House. Others, however, face an adversary who, like themselves, is not already a House member. In Table 3.5, the fate of incumbent and nonincumbent House nominees of the party that lost the Presidency between 1924 and 1964 is again compared. These new data, however, also bring out a contrast between the showing made by nonincumbents who were opposed by a House member and nonincumbents who ran against a nonincumbent.

Few politicians are likely to covet the job of the nonincumbent House nominee who must run against a Congressman of the party that wins the Presidency. Even those few nonincumbents who attempted to unseat an opposition House member in districts carried by their own presidential candidate had less than a 50-50 chance of winning. In constituencies that the winning President carried—even those where he barely squeaked to victory—their chances of success were negligible.

Nonincumbents of the party that lost the Presidency who did not have to face a sitting Congressman, on the other hand, did a bit better. Most survived in the districts carried by their party's presidential nominee, and a fair proportion of them were able to with-

15. Both figures would probably be somewhat larger if the presidential returns were available for every district back to 1924.

stand a moderate opposition presidential tide in their constituency. In districts where the winning President's proportion of the vote exceeded 55 per cent, however, the chances of victory of nonincumbents who were opposed by a nonincumbent were also slim. Only their party colleagues who were already in the House enjoyed

Table 3.5—Nonincumbent House Nominees Opposed by Incumbent and by Nonincumbent Opponents; Incumbents; and the Winning Presidential Tide: The Fate of Congressional Candidates of the Party that Lost the Presidency, 1924–1964

WINNING PRESIDENTIAL CANDIDATE'S DISTRICT PERCENTAGE[a]	HOUSE CANDIDATES OF THE PARTY THAT LOST THE PRESIDENCY								
	NONINCUMBENTS OPPOSED BY AN INCUMBENT WHO:			NONINCUMBENTS OPPOSED BY NON-INCUMBENTS WHO:			NUMBER OF INCUMBENTS WHO:		
	Ran	Won	%Won	Ran	Won	%Won	Ran	Won	%Won
0–4.9	2[b]	0[b]	0.0	3[c]	1[c]	33.3	10	10	100.0
5–29.9	5	4	80.0	14	14	100.0	113	113	100.0
30–34.9	2	1	50.0	4	4	100.0	52	52	100.0
35–39.9	11	6	54.5	22	21	95.4	153	153	100.0
40–44.9	29	12	41.4	30	26	86.7	213	209	98.1
45–47.4	30	7	23.3	19	14	73.7	132	130	98.5
47.5–49.9	58	12	20.7	29	17	58.6	144	132	91.7
50–52.4	68	5	7.4	31	16	51.6	146	120	82.2
52.5–54.9	92	4	4.3	30	8	26.7	129	85	65.9
55–59.9	266	5	1.9	52	12	23.1	247	160	64.8
60–64.9	310	3	1.0	50	6	12.0	122	69	56.6
65–69.9	238	0	0.0	29	5	17.2	52	28	53.8
70–94.9	395	1[d]	0.2	66	1	1.5	27	21	77.8
95–100	24	0	0.0	5	0	0.0	0	0	—
Total	1530	60		384	145		1540	1282	

[a] The number of districts analyzed is identical with that in Table 3.4.
[b] The two districts covered in these units were in Alabama in 1948. President Truman's name did not appear on the state's ballot that year.
[c] The two districts covered in these units that were lost by House candidates of the party that lost the Presidency were in Alabama in 1948. President Truman's name did not appear on the state's ballot in that year.
[d] Howard Miller, a Democrat, beat Republican Representative Albert M. Cole in the 1st District in Kansas in 1952.

any substantial degree of success in these constituencies where sentiment for the winning presidential candidate was strong. In short, the prospects of nonincumbents who run against a nonincumbent are rosier than the outlook for candidates who try to take the measure of a sitting Congressman. But incumbents running for reelection do markedly better than both groups of nonincumbent

House nominees, especially in districts where a winning opposition presidential candidate polls a heavy vote.

This advantage enjoyed by incumbents also emerges from Table 3.6, in which the relationship between the presidential balloting and the fate of various types of House candidates of the party that won the Presidency is set forth. The general pattern of the data is by now familiar: in districts that the winning President carries,

Table 3.6—Nonincumbent House Nominees Opposed by Incumbent and by Nonincumbent Opponents; Incumbents; and the Winning Presidential Tide: The Fate of Congressional Candidates of the Party that Won the Presidency, 1924–1964

HOUSE CANDIDATES OF THE PARTY THAT WON THE PRESIDENCY

WINNING PRESIDENTIAL CANDIDATE'S DISTRICT PERCENTAGE[a]	NONINCUMBENTS OPPOSED BY AN INCUMBENT WHO:			NONINCUMBENTS OPPOSED BY NON-INCUMBENTS WHO:			NUMBER OF INCUMBENTS WHO:		
	Ran	Won	%Won	Ran	Won	%Won	Ran	Won	%Won
0–4.9	0	0	—	3[b]	3[b]	100.0	6[b]	6[b]	100.0
5–29.9	42	0	0.0	6	0	0.0	11	7	63.6
30–34.9	43	0	0.0	3	0	0.0	4	3	75.0
35–39.9	137	0	0.0	19	1	5.3	18	12	66.7
40–44.9	179	4	2.2	26	4	15.4	41	28	68.3
45–47.4	121	2	1.6	18	5	27.8	35	28	80.0
47.5–49.9	130	15	11.5	27	10	37.0	64	52	81.2
50–52.4	129	25	19.4	30	13	43.3	74	70	94.6
52.5–54.9	117	44	37.6	29	22	75.9	106	102	96.2
55–59.9	221	87	39.4	49	39	79.6	295	290	98.3
60–64.9	114	54	47.4	52	47	90.4	343	340	99.1
65–69.9	54	23	42.6	32	27	84.4	255	255	100.0
70–94.9	22	5	22.7	94	91	96.8	577	575	99.6
95–100	0	0	—	6	6	100.0	43	43	100.0
Total	1309	259		394	268		1872	1811	

[a] The number of districts analyzed is identical with that in Table 3.4.
[b] The districts in these units all were in Alabama in 1948. President Truman's name did not appear on the state's ballot that year.

less than half of the opposition Congressmen who seek reelection are dislodged. By contrast, nearly all of the President's incumbent running mates from such districts are reelected.

But note the showing made by the nonincumbents of the party that wins the Presidency when they oppose a nonincumbent. Such candidates do not fare so well as the incumbents from their party, but in the districts that the President carries, most of them also ride to victory. Save for districts where the victorious President wins by a very narrow margin, the outcome of House contests where neither party ran an incumbent tends to resemble the results in constituencies where the President had an incumbent running mate. At least it parallels those results more closely than it resembles the outcome in districts where the President's party had an opposition Congressman to dislodge.

The Importance of Previous Party Control of a House Seat

THE PRECEDING DISCUSSION might seem to indicate that in districts where the opposition's presidential ticket is strong, an incumbent House member is well-nigh indispensable to his party on election day. In districts the winning President carries, almost all of the incumbent House nominees of his party are returned to office. In similar districts where an opposition Congressman is up for reelection, the winning President's House running mates have less than a 50-50 chance of being elected. The outcome of House contests in which no incumbent candidates are involved, on the other hand, appears to follow fairly closely the drift of the district's presidential tide.

This line of reasoning, of course, attaches tremendous importance to the individual Congressman's decision to run or not to run again. It is possible, however, that our analysis of the elements of which an incumbent's electoral advantage may be composed has still not probed deeply enough. The data presented in Table 3.7 deal once again with the fate of nonincumbent House nominees of the party that lost the Presidency. (For purposes of comparison, data indicating how the Congressmen of the losing party who were running for reelection fared are also presented.) The analysis is focused, however, on the showing made by would-be Congressmen who were opposed by a nonincumbent candidate.

Some of these nonincumbents ran in districts formerly represented by a Congressman of the opposite party. Others ran in constituencies where a Congressman from their own party had previously occupied the local House seat. What is noteworthy is how much better nonincumbents who were bucking an opposition presidential tide did in these latter districts than they did in districts where their opponent's party had previously controlled the congressional seat.

Table 3.7—The Winning Presidential Tide and Nonincumbent House Nominees in Three Situations: Opposing an Incumbent; Opposing a Nonincumbent for a Seat Formerly Held by the Opposing Party; and Opposing a Nonincumbent for a Seat Formerly Held by their Own Party. A Comparison of the Fate of Congressional Candidates of the Party that Lost the Presidency, 1924–1964

	HOUSE CANDIDATES OF THE PARTY THAT LOST THE PRESIDENCY								
WINNING PRESIDENTIAL CANDIDATE'S DISTRICT PERCENTAGE[a]	NONINCUMBENTS OPPOSED BY AN INCUMBENT			NONINCUMBENTS WITH NONINCUMBENT OPPONENT, OPPONENT'S PARTY HAD HELD SEAT			NONINCUMBENTS WITH NONINCUMBENT OPPONENT, OWN PARTY HAD HELD SEAT		
	No. Ran	No. Won	%Who Won	No. Ran	No. Won	%Who Won	No. Ran	No. Won	%Who Won
0–4.9	2[b]	0[b]	0.0	2[b]	0[b]	0.0	1	1	100.0
5–29.9	5	4	80.0	1[c]	1[c]	100.0	13	13	100.0
30–34.9	2	1	50.0	0	0	—	4	4	100.0
35–39.9	11	6	54.5	3	2	66.7	19	19	100.0
40–44.9	29	12	41.4	10	7	70.0	20	19	95.0
45–47.4	30	7	23.3	6	3	50.0	13	11	84.6
47.5–49.9	58	12	20.7	10	2	20.0	19	15	78.9
50–52.4	68	5	7.4	16	7	43.7	15	9	60.0
52.5–54.9	92	4	4.3	11	1	9.1	19	7	36.8
55–59.9	266	5	1.9	35	4	11.4	17	9	52.9
60–64.9	310	3	1.0	40	1	2.5	9	5	55.6
65–69.9	238	0	0.0	24	2	8.3	5	3	60.0
70–94.9	395	1	0.2	63	1	1.6	2	0	0.0
95–100	24	0	0.0	4	0	0.0	0	0	—
Total	1530	60		225	31		156	115	

[a] The number of districts analyzed is identical with that in Table 3.4.
[b] The districts in these units were all in Alabama in 1948. President Truman's name did not appear on the state's ballot that year.
[c] In 1964, W. Jack Edwards, a nonincumbent Republican, was elected in Alabama's 1st District.

A word of caution is in order. The number of cases to be examined, even during a 40-year period embracing 11 presidential elections, is small. Nevertheless, the discrepancy between the results in the two groups of districts where the former partisan control of the House seat differed is both clearcut and persistent. In districts where the party winning the Presidency formerly controlled the

House seat, nonincumbent congressional candidates of the losing party did somewhat better against a new opponent for the House than did their fellow partisans who took on an incumbent Congressman. The prospects for nonincumbents who defended a seat that their own party had formerly controlled, however, were consider-

Table 3.8—The Winning Presidential Tide and Nonincumbent House Nominees in Three Situations: Opposing an Incumbent; Opposing a Nonincumbent for a Seat formerly Held by the Opposition Party; and Opposing a Nonincumbent for a Seat formerly Held by their Own Party. A Comparison of the Fate of Congressional Candidates of the Party that Won the Presidency, 1924–1964

	HOUSE CANDIDATES OF THE PARTY THAT WON THE PRESIDENCY								
WINNING PRESIDENTIAL CANDIDATE'S DISTRICT PERCENTAGE[a]	NONINCUMBENTS OPPOSED BY AN INCUMBENT			NONINCUMBENTS WITH NONINCUMBENT OPPONENT, OPPONENT'S PARTY HAD HELD SEAT			NONINCUMBENTS WITH NONINCUMBENT OPPONENT, OWN PARTY HAD HELD SEAT		
	No. Ran	No. Won	%Who Won	No. Ran	No. Won	%Who Won	No. Ran	No. Won	%Who Won
0–4.9	0	0	—	0	0	—	3[b]	3[b]	100.0
5–29.9	42	0	0.0	5	0	0.0	1	0	0.0
30–34.9	43	0	0.0	3	0	0.0	0	0	—
35–39.9	137	0	0.0	16	0	0.0	3	1	33.3
40–44.9	179	4	2.2	17	1	5.9	9	3	33.3
45–47.4	121	2	1.6	12	2	16.7	6	3	50.0
47.5–49.9	130	15	11.5	20	4	20.0	10	8	80.0
50–52.4	129	25	19.4	14	4	28.6	17	10	58.8
52.5–54.9	117	44	37.6	18	12	66.7	11	10	90.9
55–59.9	221	87	39.4	16	8	50.0	34	31	91.2
60–64.9	114	54	47.4	9	5	55.6	42	41	97.6
65–69.9	54	23	42.6	5	2	40.0	27	22	81.5
70–94.9	22	5	22.7	2	1	50.0	92	90	97.8
95–100	0	0	—	0	0	—	6	6	100.0
Total	1309	259		137	39		261	228	

a The number of districts analyzed is identical with that in Table 3.4.
b The districts in these units were in Alabama in 1948. President Truman's name did not appear on the state's ballot that year.

ably better. Fully half of them survived even in districts where the winning opposition President polled over 55 per cent of the vote.

This same general relationship between former party control of a House seat and greater success for the same party in winning the seat again is brought out in Table 3.8. Here the analysis focuses

on nonincumbent House nominees of the party that won the
Presidency, but the import of the data when viewed from this new
angle is still fundamentally the same. Would-be Congressmen who
faced a nonincumbent in districts where their opponent's party
formerly occupied the House seat did a little better than members
of their party who had to oppose a Representative seeking reelection.
Even so, only half of them managed to win in districts carried by the
winning President. On the other hand, nonincumbents of their party
who sought to win a seat that their own party had formerly controlled did much better. In districts where their presidential standard-bearer polled more than 52.4 per cent of the vote,
about nine in every ten were sent to Washington.

A more general picture of the relationship between the national
presidential tide and the results of House races involving different
types of contestants emerges from the figures that appear below.
The figures cover incumbents seeking reelection and nonincumbents in three different campaign situations: opposing an incumbent Congressman; opposing a nonincumbent when the opposition
previously controlled the House seat; and opposing a nonincumbent
where their own party previously controlled the House seat. Here,
for the party that lost the Presidency, are the House results in
districts carried by the winning presidential nominee during the 11
elections between 1924 and 1964.

House Nominees of Party that Lost the Presidency Running in Districts Carried by Winning Opposition President	No. Who Ran	No. Who Won	Per Cent Who Won
Nonincumbents Opposing an Incumbent Congressman	1393	18	1.3
Nonincumbents Opposing a Nonincumbent, Opponent's Party Had Held Seat	193	16	8.3
Nonincumbents Opposing a Nonincumbent, Own Party Had Held Seat	67	33	49.2
Incumbent Congressmen Running for Reelection	723	483	66.8

The fate of the House nominees who sought to ride with the winning presidential tide also reveals much the same relationship. In the districts the winning presidential candidate carried, here is how various types of House nominees of the party that won the Presidency fared between 1924 and 1964:

House Nominees of Party that Won the Presidency Running in Districts Carried by Their Own Presidential Nominee	No. Who Ran	No. Who Won	Per Cent Who Won
Nonincumbents Opposing an Incumbent Congressman	657	238	36.2
Nonincumbents Opposing a Nonincumbent, Opponent's Party Had Held Seat	64	32	50.0
Nonincumbents Opposing a Nonincumbent, Own Party Had Held Seat	229	210	91.7
Incumbent Congressmen Running for Reelection	1693	1675	98.9

These data invite speculation about the impact that former party control of a House seat appears to have on a subsequent congressional contest in a district when no incumbents are involved. For the returns suggest that the advantage that an incumbent House nominee usually takes into a campaign is often composed of far more than his own personal strengths as a candidate. Unquestionably incumbent House members usually do add a measure of personal strength to their party's congressional ticket. Some of them become sufficiently well known and popular that the presence of their name on the ballot can mean the difference between victory and defeat for their party in a House contest. In districts where their presidential running mate was defeated, nearly 67 per cent of the incumbent House candidates of the party that lost the Presidency were able to survive, compared with about 49 per cent of their nonincumbent party colleagues who ran in districts where the name of a previous incumbent of their party did not appear on the ballot.

Nevertheless, in districts the winning President carried, nonincumbents of the party that lost the Presidency did almost as well as incumbents in defending a House seat previously controlled by their party. By contrast, only 8 per cent of their fellow partisans opposing a nonincumbent for a House seat that their opponent's party had previously controlled could win.

Thus, the very fact that a Congressman of a particular party has occupied a seat in the House may be of greater importance than his own decision to run or not to run again. The odds are that an incumbent's prior election to the House both reflects and fosters persistent sources of strength for his party at the congressional level. In some cases, this strength may stem from traditional voting support for the party at the local level, or the identification of the party locally with some issue of particular concern to the area. Moreover, the odds are that once he is elected, a Congressman and his fellow partisans do what they can to foster continued support for their party in the district. Much of this may be done by an incumbent bent on creating a personal organization. Nevertheless, even support cultivated for reasons such as these may benefit another candidate of the same political persuasion at a later election.

Perhaps one reason for this is that the domination of a district by a Representative of one party is usually paralleled by the relative weakness of the other party in his constituency. If the party's domination of the district's House elections has been of long standing, a gradual gravitation of the more promising political leaders in the community into the ranks of the locally prominant party may have taken place. Parties deprived of officeholders seldom flourish. When they do have a better than usual prospect for victory, they may be unable to put forward a good enough candidate, backed by adequate organizational strength, to take full advantage of an upsurge of sentiment for their presidential nominee in their constituency.

The advantage enjoyed by a new House nominee in a district formerly represented by a Congressman of his party is thus probably conditioned by two broad sets of factors: the elements of strength at the congressional level of the formerly dominant party and the opposition's relative weakness in the district. Both factors probably play a role in the advantage incumbent Congressmen usually enjoy at the polls. To be sure, incumbents who stand for reelection to the House are often formidable candidates. Many of them enjoy at least a measure of autonomy from the vagaries of the presidential electoral tide in their district; and a few, such as the Republicans' Jacob Javits, who was regularly elected in a heavily Democratic district in New York City between 1946 and 1952, are undoubtedly indispensable to their party's continued success in their district. But many incumbents are strong candidates as much because their tenure of a House seat reflects and stimulates strength for their party at the congressional level, as because of the personal strength which the presence of their names on the ballot brings to the party ticket.

Incumbent Congressmen, the Presidency, and the Party System

DISCUSSIONS THAT EMPHASIZE THE success of some incumbent Congressmen in resisting an opposition presidential tide in their district have their dangers. They may give an exaggerated impression of the divergence between the presidential and congressional balloting that is associated with incumbency. Yet two factors serve to limit the number of districts with split election results in which incumbent Congressmen are involved. The outcome of all House contests, those involving incumbents and nonincumbents alike, tend to parallel the contours of the presidential vote. And most incumbent Congressmen who stand for reelection do so in districts that are carried by the presidential nominee of their own party[16] (Table 3.9).

These findings, of course, reflect the fact that many congressional districts in the United States maintain the same partisan allegiance —both for President and for Congressman—over fairly long periods of time. A major consequence of this is to reduce the number of incumbent House members who find themselves in opposition presidential territory when they seek reelection. The partisan convergence that exists in many districts through a series of elections

16. Between 1924 and 1964, 70.1 per cent of the incumbents who ran in districts carried by the victorious President were House members of the President's own party. In districts carried by the losing presidential nominee, 84.3 per cent of the incumbents who stood for reelection were of the same party as the presidential candidate who carried their constituency (Table 3.9).

augments the congruence between the presidential and congressional balloting that prevails in individual presidential election years.

Table 3.9—Incumbent House Nominees Tend to Belong to the Same Party as the Presidential Candidate Who Carries their District: The Winning Presidential Tide and the Party Affiliation of Incumbent House Nominees in Individual Congressional Districts, 1924–1964

| | | INCUMBENT CONGRESSMEN | | | |
| WINNING PRESIDENTIAL CANDIDATE'S DISTRICT PERCENTAGE[a] | TOTAL NUMBER WHO RAN | INCUMBENT HOUSE NOMINEES OF PARTY THAT LOST THE PRESIDENCY: | | INCUMBENT HOUSE NOMINEES OF THE PARTY THAT WON THE PRESIDENCY: | |
		No. Who Ran	% of Total	No. Who Ran	% of Total
0–4.9	16	10	62.5	6[b]	37.5
5–29.9	124	113	91.1	11[c]	8.9
30–34.9	56	52	92.9	4[d]	7.1
35–39.9	171	153	89.5	18	10.5
40–44.9	254	213	83.9	41	16.1
45–47.4	167	132	79.0	35	21.0
47.5–49.9	208	144	69.2	64	30.8
50–52.4	220	146	66.4	74	33.6
52.5–54.9	235	129	54.9	106	45.1
55–59.9	542	247	45.6	295	54.4
60–64.9	465	122	26.2	343	73.8
65–69.9	307	52	16.9	255	83.1
70–94.9	604	27	4.5	577	95.5
95–100	43	0	0.0	43	100.0
Total	3412	1540		1872	

[a] The number of districts analyzed is identical with that in Table 3.4.
[b] The districts in this unit were in Alabama in 1948. President Truman's name did not appear on the ballot that year.
[c] The 11 incumbents in this unit ran in southern districts carried by Senator Barry Goldwater in 1964.
[d] The four incumbents in this unit ran in southern or Border-State House districts where Kennedy or Johnson ran poorly in 1960 or 1964.

Even so, every four years some incumbent Congressmen buck an opposition presidential tide in their district. The consequences of these defensive victories by incumbent House candidates become relevant to the operation of the political system by their effect on the number of likely opponents and supporters of the President's program they cause to be sent to Capitol Hill. These effects on the balance of party strength between the White House and Capitol Hill, however, have not always been the same.

One type of consequence occurred in 1960. That election, as V. O. Key observed, manifested an unusual combination of oddities.[17] The presidential race was exceptionally close, religious loyalties and antagonisms left a deep imprint on the pattern of the voting, and the final returns gave the United States its first Roman Catholic President in history. In addition, 1960 was the first election since World War I in which the successful presidential nominee carried far fewer House districts than his congressional running mates. In all, more than 60 incumbent Democratic House candidates who were reelected had to buck a Republican presidential tide in their district.

Democratic strength in the House was reduced by the 1960 election results. But there undoubtedly would have been still fewer Democrats in the new 87th Congress if the Democrats had not had so many incumbent candidates defending House seats in districts carried by Richard M. Nixon, the G.O.P. presidential nominee. The net effect of incumbency in 1960 was to increase the number of Democratic Congressmen President John F. Kennedy had to work with when he entered the White House.

Yet in this respect, too, the 1960 results were highly unusual. Since 1920 most presidential contests have not been close, and the victorious presidential candidate has nearly always carried more House districts than his party's congressional slate managed to win. In House districts the losing presidential nominee carries, there are usually relatively few incumbents of the winning presidential candidates party who buck an opposition presidential tide.[18] But in districts the winning presidential nominee carries, the number of opposition party Congressmen who run for reelection is often surprisingly large.

During the 11 presidential elections between 1924 and 1964, more than four in every ten of the losing party's Congressmen who were

---

17. V. O. Key, Jr., "Interpreting the Election Results," in Paul T. David, ed., *The Presidential Election and Transition 1960–1961* (Washington: The Brookings Institution, 1961), p. 150.

18. Over half of the 179 instances reported in Table 3.9 when incumbent House nominees of the party that won the Presidency had to run in districts lost by their presidential running mate occurred in 1960. That year 94 Democratic House members had to run for reelection in districts that John Kennedy was unable to carry.

up for reelection found themselves in opposition presidential territory. Over a third of the party's incumbents who were reelected
had to withstand an opposition presidential tide in their district.
The data on which these findings are based appear in Table 3.10.

*Table 3.10—Partisan Affiliation of Incumbent House Candidates Who
Ran for Reelection and Who Won, and the Winning Presidential Candidate's Share of the Vote in their District, 1924–1964*

WINNING PRESIDENTIAL CANDIDATE'S DISTRICT PERCENTAGE—	INCUMBENT HOUSE NOMINEES OF THE PARTY THAT WON THE PRESIDENCY				INCUMBENT HOUSE NOMINEES OF THE PARTY THAT LOST THE PRESIDENCY			
	No. Who Ran	% of Total No. Who Ran	No. Who Won	% of Total No. Who Won	No. Who Ran	% of Total No. Who Ran	No. Who Won	% of Total No. Who Won
0–4.9	6[b]	0.3	6[b]	0.3	10	0.6	10	0.8
5–29.9	11[c]	0.6	7[c]	0.4	113	7.4	113	8.8
30–34.9	4[d]	0.2	3[d]	0.2	52	3.7	52	4.1
35–39.9	18	1.0	12	0.7	153	9.8	153	11.9
40–44.9	41	2.2	28	1.5	213	13.7	209	16.3
45–47.4	35	1.9	28	1.5	132	8.5	130	10.1
47.5–49.9	64	3.4	52	2.9	144	9.3	132	10.3
50–52.4	74	3.9	70	3.9	146	9.4	120	9.4
52.5–54.9	106	5.7	102	5.6	129	8.3	85	6.6
55–59.9	295	15.8	290	16.0	247	16.0	160	12.5
60–64.9	343	18.3	340	18.8	122	7.8	69	5.4
65–69.9	255	13.6	255	14.1	52	3.8	28	2.2
70–94.9	577	30.8	575	31.7	27	1.7	21	1.6
95–100	43	2.3	43	2.4	0	—	0	—
Total	1872	100.0	1811	100.0	1540	100.0	1282	100.0

ᵃ The number of districts analyzed is identical with that in Table 3.4.
ᵇ The districts in these units were in Alabama in 1948. President Truman's name did not appear
on the state's ballot that year.
ᶜ The 11 incumbents covered in these units, including four who lost, ran in southern districts
carried by Senator Barry Goldwater in 1964.
ᵈ The four incumbents covered in these units ran in southern or Border-State House districts
where Kennedy or Johnson ran poorly in 1960 or 1964.

Here, for the years between 1924 and 1964, is a summary of the
figures:

In Districts the Losing Presidential Nominee Carried:

9.6% of the Opposition's Incumbent House Nominees Ran
7.5% of the Opposition's Winning Incumbent House Nominees Ran

In Districts the Winning Presidential Nominee Carried:

46.9% of the Opposition's Incumbent House Nominees Ran
37.7% of the Opposition's Winning Incumbent House Nominees Ran

Between 1924 and 1964, the House returns involving incumbents from districts with split election results which had the greatest impact on the distribution of party strength in the House took place in constituencies where the winning President's party was unable to translate a victory for its presidential nominee into success for its House candidate.

A little reflection on the figures in Table 3.10 will underscore the import for executive-legislative relations of these defensive victories by incumbent opposition Congressmen. Between 1924 and 1964 there were 483 split election results of this type. If the preceding analysis of the importance of previous party control of a House seat has validity, most of these districts would have sent an opposition Congressman to Washington even if the incumbent dropped out of the race. A few more House members of the winning President's party would probably have been elected in such circumstances, but hardly enough to cause a substantial alteration of the prevailing relationship between the White House and Capitol Hill.

On the other hand, if the winning President's party had controlled those 483 districts at the congressional level, nearly all of them would have elected a Congressman of the winning President's party. (In districts the winning President's party previously controlled, as already noted, 91.7 per cent of the party's nonincumbent and 98.9 per cent of its incumbent candidates were elected.) House victories for the winning President's party in 90 per cent of the 483 districts would have sent about 435 more Congressmen of the winning President's party to Washington over the 11 election years between 1924 and 1964.

On the average, this would have meant nearly 40 more of the President's fellow partisans in the House after each presidential election. It also would have meant about 40 fewer opposition Congressmen—an increase of 80 in the winning party's majority in the House of Representatives.[19] The decision of incumbents to run or not to run again in a particular election may not have a major effect on the balance of power between the White House and Capitol Hill. But the fact that in most presidential years the opposition party controls a sizable bloc of House seats in districts the winning President carries clearly does.[20]

19. The odds are that the magnitude of the effect these defensive victories by incumbent Congressmen have on the party balance in the House varies from election to election. In some years many more incumbent Congressmen of the party that loses the Presidency encounter an opposition presidential tide than in others. Thus, in 1964, 143 Republican Representatives had to run in districts carried by President Johnson. Of these 104 were reelected. If every district that went for Johnson had also elected a Democratic Congressman, the Republican party would have been all but wiped out in the House in 1964.

20. The exact size of this bloc of House seats is affected by the midterm election results preceding a presidential election. The preceding midterm electoral verdict can both increase or decrease the number of House seats in districts carried by the winning President which are controlled by the party that loses the presidential election. In midterm elections where there is a significant change in party strength in the House, the results can thus both increase or decrease the number of House seats the winning President's party is likely to win in the next presidential year. (This relationship probably prevails, even though it is likely that partisan control of a House seat for one term does not have as strong an effect on the House vote in the next presidential year as does control of the House seat for more than one congressional term.) Between 1922 and 1962, nine of the 11 midterm elections resulted in House seat losses of varying but substantial magnitudes for the party then in control of the Presidency. Of these midterm results, those which preceded a turnover in party control of the White House (1930, 1950, and 1958) reduced the number of House seats controlled by opponents of the presidential nominee who won the subsequent presidential election. As a result of these midterm electoral verdicts, therefore, President Roosevelt, President Eisenhower, and President Kennedy probably had more Congressmen of their own party elected in the subsequent presidential election year than would have been elected if there had been no midterm congressional elections. On the other hand, the midterm elections which were followed by another victory for the party controlling the White House (1922, 1926, 1934, 1938, 1942, 1946, and 1954) increased the number of House seats controlled by the President's opponents in districts that the winning President carried. These midterm electoral verdicts, therefore, probably weakened the showing in the House that the winning President's party made in the subsequent presidential election year. In the 1934 and the 1962 midterm contests, there was little net change in the distribution of party strength in the House. Nevertheless these two verdicts also probably had an important effect on the House results in the next presidential year. Both left the Democratic party with more House seats than the party that controls the White House usually has after a midterm election. As a consequence the Democrats were in a stronger position when they entered the House contests in the next presidential year.

The foregoing remarks underscore the importance of incumbent Congressmen to the party that finds itself on the defensive in a presidential year. Always an influence on the distribution of party strength in the national legislature, incumbent Representatives may sometimes determine whether the Democrats or the Republicans win control of the House. There are other reasons for stressing the impact that former party control of a House seat can have on the functioning of the nation's electoral system. Some causes of divergence between the presidential and congressional vote assume importance in some elections but are a negligible factor in other presidential election years. But members of the House usually run for election again, and a winning President almost always carries districts where his party's congressional slate must attempt to dislodge sitting Representatives of the opposition party. The impact of incumbent House nominees on split-ticket voting for President and for Congressmen is thus a persistent one.

It is also of considerable practical effect on the working of the political system. With but one exception between 1920 and 1964, the net effect of the incumbent nominees who run on each party's House ticket has been to reduce the strength of the President's party in the legislature. On occasion, incumbency works counter to the advocates of party government: those who would like to see the electorate place a President and a solid House majority of the same party in office together, and then hold them collectively responsible for both their deeds and their misdeeds. Incumbent opposition Congressmen thus make the nation's political system more complicated and intricate. But they also constitute one of the primary checks in the political system on the power of the American Presidency.

CHAPTER 4

Policy and Personality Differences between the Presidential and House Tickets

A s our probings of the congressional returns in presidential years proceed, something of the extraordinary complexity of the elements determining the concurrent selection of a House of Representatives and a Chief Executive gradually begins to emerge. The great majority of American voters support a President and a Congressman of the same party. And many voters who split their ticket at the national level support a presidential candidate of one party while voting for an incumbent opposition House nominee. Nevertheless, some incumbent Congressmen are much more successful than others in insulating themselves from the effects of an opposition presidential tide. And sometimes there is extensive split-ticket voting in districts where neither party places an incumbent Congressman before the electorate. Evidently other special circumstances, too, may contribute to a divergence between the vote polled by the presidential and congressional candidates of the same party.

A cherished tenet of the American political tradition is summed up in an adage: "It's not the party that matters—it's the man." Even a cursory examination of the interrelationship between the presidential and congressional returns in individual districts makes it clear that a candidate's party affiliation often has a powerful influence on his chances of election. In fact, on more than one occasion the electorate's party regularity has elevated candidates of dubious merit to high public office. Yet the slogan—"it's the man who counts"—is of importance; for, although the amount of information the electorate has about such matters is often limited, voters sometimes do discriminate among candidates of the same party whose personal characteristics vary or whose policy pronouncements differ. And part of the ticket-splitting for President and Congressman may stem from this fact.

Few items in an election campaign receive more publicity and attention than the personal characteristics and background of a major-party candidate for the presidency. The nominee's childhood romances, his early career, his family life, his religion—all these items, and many more, become the subject of conversation and comment from Eastport, Maine to San Diego, California. So pervasive is the publicity attracted by a candidate's personal qualities that the puzzled onlooker may even wonder whether the nominee's political views matter at all. The fact is, however, that a presidential aspirant's stands on the major issues of the day also may receive widespread public scrutiny.

A priori, one might suppose that both the special personal qualities of a presidential nominee and his positions on public issues would have a greater appeal to some voters than to others. In fact, even among the normal adherents of the candidate's own party, there is likely to be considerable variation in the enthusiasm with which the choice of their party's national nominating convention is viewed. In some parts of the country, the nominee may bring new strength to the party ticket; in other areas, the appearance of his name on the ballot may threaten to depress the party's presidential tally well below the level attained by its House candidates in recent years. The special characteristics of a party's presidential ticket, in short, may create divergence between the party's presidential and congressional vote.

Although would-be Presidents who try to talk out of both sides of their mouth are not unknown, fundamentally the policy stands of a national presidential candidate, like the nominee's personality, must be the same in all parts of the country. But the personal and policy appeals made by his party's congressional ticket, composed as it is of several hundred individual House nominees, may vary greatly from district to district and region to region. And in this very diversity may lie a second potent source of partisan divergence at the national level.

Again, *a priori,* one might expect that in a few districts an unusually attractive congressional nominee would induce a substantial number of voters to split their ticket in order to give him their support. The success of a House nominee of this type might stem either from personal appeals or from policy appeals, or from a combination of the two; yet whatever the reasons, the result would be the same. The party's congressional candidate would run well ahead of the party's presidential ticket in the constituency. Conversely, in districts where the local House nominee's personal qualities or stands on issues failed to inspire public confidence, the party's vote for Representative might fall well below its presidential tally.

If these lines of speculation are correct, part of the divergence between the vote for President and the vote for Congressmen may stem from the special personal and policy characteristics of a major-party presidential ticket. The net effect of these unique elements in a presidential candidate is to make the presidential ticket more attractive than the party's congressional slate in some parts of the country, while causing it to be less appealing than the party's House ticket in other sections of the nation. At the same time, another portion of the divergence stems from the special qualities of particular congressional nominees. These make their impact on the nation's political system by raising or depressing the party's congressional poll above or below its presidential strength in individual House districts.

Actually, to provide an adequate explanation of the split-ticket voting associated with the differing personal and policy appeals of candidates of the same party for national office, a further expansion and modification of the argument would be in order. For the odds are that the relative electoral strength of a party's presidential and congressional ticket is not only a function of the appeals that the party's own nominees for President and for Representatives have for the voter: it may also be influenced by the relative attractiveness of the opposition's candidates for these offices. Even a mediocre candidate for Representative may make a better showing than a formidable presidential vote-getter on the same party ticket—if the opposition's House candidate has been indicted for income-tax evasion.

The relative appeal of one party's presidential and congressional ticket in a constituency depends in part on the relative appeal of the other party's candidates for Congressman and President. Nevertheless, the basic notion to be explored is that differences in the personalities and policy stands of congressional and presidential candidates of the same party do in fact underlie part of the split-ticket voting at the national level. It would require an appalling amount of work to demonstrate all the conditions under which this factor operates, and probably the amount of ticket-splitting that is caused by such differences varies from election to election. Nevertheless, in the pages that follow some initial test borings of the available electoral data are presented, and these test borings suggest that, in some instances at least, our general notion fits the facts.

Differential Appeal of the National Presidential Ticket: Al Smith Runs for President

FEW EVENTS IN AMERICAN political history have been more widely debated than why Al Smith lost the Presidency in 1928. As he listened to the returns, the New York Governor himself gave the most common explanation of his defeat. "Well," he is reported to have said, "the time just hasn't come yet when a man can say his beads in the White House."[1] This religious interpretation of the 1928 Democratic debacle may have been oversimplified; yet the fact is that Smith's defeat meant that for a generation it was an axiom of American politics that no Roman Catholic could be elected President of the United States.

Other observers, however, pointed to different reasons for the defeat of the man with the brown derby who came from the sidewalks of New York. Smith actually made a much stronger showing than the Democratic presidential nominee had made in 1920 and

---

1. Quoted in James MacGregor Burns, *Roosevelt: The Lion and the Fox* (New York: Harcourt, Brace and Company, 1956), p. 104.

1924.[2] Nevertheless, he was nominated during a period when the Republicans, not the Democrats, were the normal majority party of the United States. In the era of the "Noble Experiment," Smith also was on record as an opponent of Prohibition. While in some parts of the nation, this policy stand met with approval, in others the Prohibition issue undoubtedly cost Smith some greatly needed votes.[3] Moreover, as the candidate who seemed to typify the city, Smith had definite personal characteristics that weakened his appeal for many voters. As James M. Burns notes, "His Bowery mien, his harsh resonance over what he called the 'raddio', his natty dress with the bright pocket handkerchief—all these clashed with their idea of the man who should occupy the White House."[4]

Above all else, there was the extraordinary prosperity that prevailed in the industrial sector of the American economy in 1928. Herbert Hoover summoned his fellow countrymen to a New Era: "given a chance to go forward with the policies of the past eight years, we shall soon with the help of God be in sight of the day when poverty will be banished from this nation."[5] Perhaps any candidate who had been put up by the opposition Democrats would have been foredoomed to failure.

The interrelationship among the elements of personality and policy that influenced Smith's electoral appeal undoubtedly was extremely complex, and a good deal of time and effort can be

2. Smith raised the Democratic share of the total presidential vote from 34.1 per cent in 1920 and 28.8 per cent in 1924 to 40.8 per cent in 1928. Ruth C. Silva, *Rum, Religion, and Votes: 1928 Re-examined* (University Park: Pennsylvania State University Press, 1962), p. 4.

3. After an analysis by partial correlation of the 1928 vote in 173 counties chosen largely at random in Massachusetts, New York, Ohio, Illinois, Wisconsin, Colorado, Montana, and California, Ogburn and Talbot concluded that the vote for Smith was more closely associated with anti-Prohibition sentiment than with Catholicism. See W. F. Ogburn and N. S. Talbot, "A Measurement of the Factors in the Presidential Election of 1928." *Social Forces*, Vol. 8, No. 2, December, 1929, pp. 175–183. The Ogburn-Talbot study was limited to the eight states where the electorate had voted on some form of the wet-dry issue during 1926, 1927, or 1928, a procedure which meant that their measures of wet sentiment and of Smith's electoral strength were close together in time. For additional comments on the Ogburn-Talbot study, see Silva, *op. cit.*, pp. 41–42.

4. Burns, *op. cit., loc. cit.*

5. Quoted in Arthur M. Schlesinger, Jr., *The Crisis of the Old Order, 1919–1933* (Boston: Houghton Mifflin Company, 1957), p. 128.

expended on an attempt to determine the precise effect of each of those elements on the outcome of the 1928 presidential voting.[6] But the 1928 returns can also be analyzed for another purpose. For they illustrate, perhaps in extreme form, the differential impact which the selection of a particular presidential nominee can have on his party's vote for President, and, as a result, on the relationship between the party's presidential and congressional strength.

The chances are that every presidential nominee attracts the support of a coalition of voters which, to some extent, at least, is unique. The selection of Al Smith by the Democratic party in 1928, however, was particularly well designed to evoke strong emotions for and against his party's presidential ticket. In some parts of the country, including areas where the Democrats had long been strong, his nomination aroused powerful antagonisms among many of his party's traditional supporters. To George Fort Milton of Tennessee, it was obvious that the Smith candidacy was designed to appeal "to the aliens, who feel that the older America, the America of the Anglo-Saxon stock, is a hateful thing which must be overturned and humiliated; to the northern negroes, who lust for social equality and racial dominance; to the Catholics who have been made to believe that they are entitled to the White House; and to the Jews who likewise are to be instilled with the feeling that this is the time for God's chosen people to chastise America yesteryear." "If the dominance of such groups represents the new America which Smith is seeking to arouse," Milton wrote to California Democrat William Gibbs McAdoo, "the old America, the America of Jackson, and of Lincoln and Wilson, should rise up in wrath and defeat it."[7]

Lifelong Democrats of Milton's generation had been called on to support at least five different presidential nominees—William Jennings Bryan, Alton B. Parker, Woodrow Wilson, James Cox, and John W. Davis. Yet no Democrat had ever before seen his party

---

6. From an extensive series of statistical tests, using states as the units of analysis, Ruth C. Silva has concluded that nation-wide Smith's 1928 strength (and weakness) had a far closer relation to variations in the population proportions of foreign white stock (persons born abroad or with at least one parent born abroad) than to variations in the Catholic percentage of the population or sentiment on the liquor question. Silva, *op. cit.*, pp. vii and 47.

7. Letter of July 31, 1928, from George Fort Milton to William Gibbs McAdoo. Quoted in Edmund A. Moore, *A Catholic Runs for President* (New York: Ronald Press, 1956), p. 114.

run a candidate like Al Smith. In scores of districts across the country it is evident that the New York Governor was rejected by many of his own party's normal supporters; for he ran well behind the rest of the party ticket. Yet while in some areas thousands of people crossed party lines to vote against Smith, in other constituencies his name brought an unprecedented outpouring of votes in support of the Democratic presidential ticket. In many of these districts, Smith ran well ahead of the rest of the candidates for public office who were put up by his party.

Figure 4.1—Al Smith and the Democratic congressional ticket: Relationship between the Democratic presidential candidate's share of the two-party presidential vote and the Democratic party's share of the two-party congressional vote in individual House districts in 1928

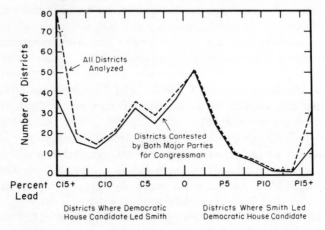

An idea of the relationship between the vote for Al Smith and that for Democratic House nominees in individual congressional districts is indicated by the trend lines in Figure 4.1. The data measure the discrepancy between Smith's share of the presidential vote and the Democratic House nominee's portion of the congressional vote in each of the districts analyzed. In some constituencies, those grouped near the center of the graph, Smith and his party's House candidate ran nearly neck and neck. But in more than a hundred districts, Smith lagged 10 and 15 percentage points, or even more, behind his congressional running mate. In 47 of these latter districts, the divergence between the Democratic presidential and congressional tickets was undoubtedly widened by the G.O.P.'s failure to run a House candidate. Nevertheless, most of these constituencies were in the South. In many of them, Smith probably would have fared considerably worse than the Democratic House nominee even if the Republicans had run a congressional candidate.

Although in these districts, Smith ran far behind his party's House ticket, in a smaller number of constituencies he decisively outdistanced his congressional running mates. In some 39 of the districts analyzed, his lead over the Democratic House nominee exceeded 7.5 per cent. The data in Figure 4.1 suggest that Smith alienated many Democratic voters in some areas while attracting new supporters to the party in other sections of the nation. A more rounded picture of the 1928 voting pattern emerges if some of the individual districts where Smith made a relatively poor showing are contrasted with constituencies where he led his party's House nominee.

Consider, for example, the 1928 returns for President and Congressman in the eight House districts of Oklahoma. When the campaign began, all but one of the Congressmen from the normally Democratic Sooner State were Democrats. Many Democratic voters in the state, however, were unhappy with their party's choice for President. When the Smith campaign train approached Oklahoma City, the New York Governor could see the fiery crosses of the Ku Klux Klan burning on the countryside. In his speech delivered that evening, Smith once again denounced the Klan.[8]

His forthright stand may have won him votes elsewhere, but in Oklahoma Smith's presence on the Democratic ticket was almost catastrophic. In the general election, he trailed his congressional running mate by more than 10 percentage points in all eight of the state's House districts. In four Oklahoma districts, the gap exceeded 15 per cent; yet even that discrepancy was not enough to save two incumbent Democratic Congressmen from defeat.

Nor was Oklahoma the only state in which Smith made a poor showing relative to his House running mates. In the South, he

8. Arthur M. Schlesinger, Jr., *op. cit., loc. cit.*

trailed his party's congressional ticket by more than 10 percentage points in some 81 districts. He lagged behind the Democratic House nominees by sizable, though somewhat smaller, margins in the great majority of constituencies in the Border States. And in the North Smith ran 10 percentage points or more behind his congressional teammate in a score of rural and small-town districts scattered from Pennsylvania to the Pacific Northwest.[9]

But what of the constituencies where Smith led his congressional ticket by a wide margin? Broadly speaking, these districts were of two types. In the upper reaches of the Mississippi basin—an area where the Democratic party long had been notoriously weak at the congressional level—Smith led nearly all of his party's congressional candidates by a wide margin. In Wisconsin, for example, he ran ahead of his party's House ticket by more than 10 percentage points in every district in the state; he also rolled up similar margins both in Minnesota and in North Dakota.[10] In 1924, close to five of every ten voters in these districts had supported Robert M. La Follette for President, leaving John W. Davis, the Democratic nominee, a poor third behind Calvin Coolidge. Four years later, the swings to the Democratic presidential ticket in the districts in this area were enormous—ranging as high as 36.8 per cent.[11] Even so, in most cases Smith still fell somewhat short of a majority.[12]

9. The districts outside the South and the Border States where Smith ran 10 percentage points behind his House running mate included: Pennsylvania 22 and 30; Ohio 6, 8, 11, 16, and 17; Indiana 7; Illinois 20; Kansas 3 and 8; Nebraska 1, 3, 4, and 5; Colorado 4; Wyoming At Large; Montana 1; Arizona At Large; and Washington 5.

10. In many of these districts, Smith's lead over the Democratic House ticket was larger than 10 per cent. It exceeded 15 per cent in the following districts in Wisconsin, Minnesota, and North Dakota: Wisconsin 1, 2, 3, 6, 8, 10, and 11; Minnesota 3 and 8; and North Dakota 1 and 2. Two Milwaukee districts for which no presidential figures are available are excluded from this analysis.

11. In the 14 districts in Wisconsin, Minnesota, and North Dakota where Smith's lead over the Democratic House ticket exceeded 10 per cent, the median presidential vote for La Follette in 1924 was 53.2 per cent. The median Democratic presidential swing in these districts in 1928 was 25.6 per cent. The swings cited for these districts are the difference between the Democratic presidential nominees' share of the major-party vote in 1924 and 1928. If the swings were based on the Democrats' share of the total presidential vote in 1924 and 1928, they would be even larger.

12. The median vote for Smith in this group of districts was 42.7 per cent. In 5 of the 14 districts analyzed, Smith received between 45 and 49.9 per cent of the vote; in one, he obtained a clear majority.

Taken together, this cluster of districts in the northcentral part of the country had several factors in common: heavy previous support for the La Follette Progressive movement; a longstanding weakness of the Democratic party at the congressional and local level; and the general economic distress that afflicted large parts of the farm belt in 1928. In some of these constituencies, where there were relatively few voters of Smith's religious faith, his Catholicism was probably a liability. Yet in other districts in the area it may have been an asset.

The 9th District in northeastern Wisconsin, where more than four residents in every ten were Roman Catholics, is a case in point. Many of the district's voters were of German or Irish extraction, and one town in the area, Appleton, was the birthplace of a future Republican Senator from Wisconsin who was destined for considerable notoriety on the national scene—Joseph R. McCarthy. In 1924, La Follette carried the district, which gave the Democratic presidential ticket less than 9 per cent of its vote. Four years later, with Smith on the ballot, the Democratic presidential vote in the Wisconsin 9th increased more than sevenfold, jumping from 6,726 in 1924 to 50,712 in 1928.[13] This was more than enough to enable Smith to carry the district—he led Herbert Hoover by nearly 6,000 votes. But it was a victory that the local Democrats could not match at the congressional level. When all returns were in, the district's Democratic candidate for the House had been badly beaten, after a race in which he ran more than 14 percentage points behind the head of the ticket.[14]

All the districts discussed so far where Smith was in the lead were concentrated in a single area, broadly speaking, the region between the center of North Dakota and the northern reaches of Lake Michigan. By contrast, the other group of constituencies

13. The 1924 presidential vote in the Wisconsin 9th was: Democratic 6,726; Republican 28,693; La Follette 39,177; and others 659. Votes for third-party presidential nominees accounted for 52.9 per cent of the total. The 1928 presidential returns in the district were: Democratic 50,712; Republican 44,744; and others 673. Smith received 53.1 per cent of the major-party presidential vote.

14. Smith's congressional running mate in the Wisconsin 9th polled 38.9 per cent of the district's two-party vote for Congressman. He ran 14.2 percentage points behind Smith.

where Smith's appeal exceeded the electoral strength of local Democratic House nominees was more dispersed—including districts scattered here and there over a sizable portion of the country, from St. Louis, Missouri, to Baltimore, Maryland, and from Pittsburgh, Pennsylvania, to the north of Maine. In many of these districts, Smith's strong showing was accompanied by extraordinary increases both in the Democratic presidential vote and in the total turnout for President. In the Pennsylvania 1st, a Philadelphia

Figure 4.2—The relative electoral appeal of Al Smith and the Democratic congressional ticket—A regional contrast between the South and New England: The relationship between Smith's share of the two-party Presidential vote and the Democratic party's share of the two-party congressional vote in contested house districts in the South and in New England in 1928

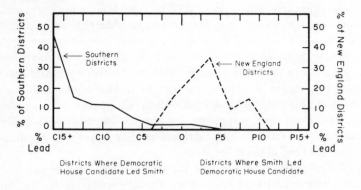

district once represented by William S. Vare, the Democratic presidential vote increased from 7,200 in 1924 to over 48,000 four years later, despite the strenuous efforts of the city's then powerful Republican organization to hold the district for Hoover.[15] In Scranton, Pennsylvania, another district where Smith led his party's

15. The 1924 presidential vote in the Pennsylvania 1st was: Democratic 7,229; Republican 59,031; and third-party 6,751. The district's 1928 presidential totals were: Democratic 48,224; Republican 46,578; and third-party 602.

candidates for national office, the total vote for President increased by 59 per cent between 1924 and 1928.[16]

Smith led his party's House ticket in a number of districts with only moderately large Roman Catholic populations. Usually, however, he did not carry such districts. Something more of Smith's differential appeal for various parts of the electorate emerges if the analysis is focused upon those districts that actually had split election results. Smith carried some of these districts while the local Democratic House candidate lost. But in other constituencies with split election results, a Democrat was sent to Congress while Smith went down to defeat. A comparison of two major population indices suggests something of the different types of voters who predominated in the two groups of districts:

	Districts Where Dem. House Nominee Won and Smith Lost	Districts Where Smith Won and Dem. House Nominee Lost
Median % Population Catholic, 1926[17]	3.0	41.3
Median % Population Foreign Born, 1930	6.1	54.7

Among the foreign born and the Roman Catholics, Al Smith was able to win votes that eluded his congressional running mates. Among Protestant, native-born Americans, on the other hand, Democratic House nominees often received support at the polls that was denied to Smith. In no two regions were the contrasts suggested by the above figures more striking than in the South and in New

16. In 1924, the total presidential vote in the Pennsylvania 11th (Scranton) was 62,399. Four years later, 99,269 people voted for President in the district. Many new voters in highly industrialized districts like the Pennsylvania 1st and the Pennsylvania 11th were women from lower-income families. Lubell notes: "Smith . . . made women's suffrage a reality for the urban poor. In better-income families, women started voting in 1920 as soon as they were granted the privilege; but among the urban masses the tradition that a woman's place was in the home still held strong until 1928." Samuel Lubell, *The Future of American Politics* (New York: Harper and Brothers, 1952), p. 40.

17. The number of Roman Catholics in each district reported by the 1926 census of religious bodies is given as a percentage of the district's total population in 1930.

England. And the relationship between the Democratic presidential and congressional vote in those two regions differed sharply, as is underscored by the trend lines in Figure 4.2.

The regional contrast revealed in Figure 4.2 is based on the percentage by which Smith ran ahead of or behind his congressional running mate in individual House districts. In nearly every district in the predominantly Protestant, native-American South, Smith trailed the local Democratic House nomines. In New England, with its large Catholic and foreign-born populations, on the other hand, Smith led his party's congressional candidate in most districts.

Another broad difference between the dominant drift of the 1928 electoral tide in New England and in the South is not brought out by Figure 4.2. In every district in New England, the Democratic share of the presidential vote increased between 1924 and 1928. Even the smallest Democratic presidential swing in the region exceeded 5 per cent.[18] In the South, by contrast, the Democratic portion of the presidential vote declined in all but three of the section's 104 districts. In two of the three districts that departed from this regional trend, the swings to Smith were small—2 per cent or less.[19]

Yet in one southern district, the Lousiana 3rd, Smith did markedly better than Davis had done in 1924: there the Democratic presidential swing was an enormous 29.5 per cent. The voters in this district, which embraced eight parishes in southcentral Louisiana, were no recent arrivals to the United States (the proportion of foreign born was 2.7 per cent). The names of some of the district's parishes—Iberia, Lafourche, and Terrebonne—underscore the antecedents of many of the constituency's voters: Spaniards

18. This finding is based upon analysis of the 1928 presidential swings in 15 New England House districts. Six districts in Massachusetts whose boundary lines were changed between 1924 and 1928, and 11 other New England districts for which no presidential figures are available are excluded from the analysis. All the missing districts, however, were in Massachusetts, New Hampshire, and Rhode Island. Inspection of the returns from individual towns indicates that Smith probably did better than Davis in every district in those states.

19. This finding is based upon a calculation of the presidential swings in 102 of the South's 104 House districts in 1928. The two New Orleans districts for which no presidential figures are available are excluded from the analysis. In nearly half (49) of the South's districts, the swing away from the Democratic presidential ticket was 15 per cent or more in 1928.

and Frenchmen who settled in the area during an entire century before the Lousiana Purchase.

The national traditions of these southern Lousiana settlers differed profoundly from those of the Irish, German, Italians, and Eastern Europeans who came to the United States in successive waves after 1840. Yet, like most members of the later immigrant groups, these earlier settlers were Roman Catholics (the Lousiana 3rd was 69.7 per cent Catholic in 1926). And like many sons and daughters of the post-1840 newcomers, their descendants also were drawn to the banner of Al Smith in 1928. The returns from the Louisiana 3rd offer convincing proof that Smith's appeal was not limited to his coreligionists who came from recent immigrant stock. Between 1924 and 1928, the district's Democratic presidential vote jumped from 54.6 per cent to 84.1 per cent; and the number of people in the constituency who voted for President more than doubled—rising from 9,314 in 1924 to 19,689 just four years later.[20]

In any comparison of the Democratic presidential and congressional vote in 1928, obviously not all of the discrepancy should be attributed to the Democrats' decision to nominate Al Smith. The vote that a party polls for President and for Congressman in a district is the result of a complex equation involving not only the presidential nominees but also the House candidates. In some districts in 1928, it may have been not Al Smith but the local Democratic candidate for Representative who caused many voters to split their ticket at the national level. Nor should it be forgotten that the relative strength of the opposition candidates for Congress and the White House were equally relevant factors in the electoral equation. Even so, a close look at the 1928 returns would suggest that much of the ticket-splitting that year stemmed from Smith's sharply differential appeal to the American electorate.

The findings indicate that the nomination of a major-party presidential candidate may touch off a complex process of alienation and attraction among the nation's voters. In constituencies where the presidential choice alienates many of the party's potential

20. The 1924 presidential vote in the Louisiana 3rd was: Democratic 4,881; Republican 4,058; and others 375. The 1928 presidential totals in the district were: Democratic 16,568, and Republican 3,121. No minor-party presidential votes were reported.

supporters, especially in districts where the party has an incumbent Congressman, the result may be a flood of split-ticket ballots that leaves the presidential nominee weaker than his running mate for the House. But the impact of a presidential candidate's appeal to the electorate is seldom entirely negative. And while the candidate may lose support relative to his party's congressional slate in some constituencies, in other districts he may attract more votes than his party's nominees for the House.

The odds are that the ties of party loyalty that tend to keep each party's presidential and congressional vote in balance were strained more by Al Smith than by most nominees for the Presidency. The point here, however, is that, to some extent at least, every presidential candidate has a unique appeal which evokes a differential response among the electorate. And the net effect of this differential appeal may be to increase the number of voters who split their ticket at the national level. In some elections, it may even become a major source of divergence between the bases of support in the electorate on which the congressional and presidential wings of the same party rest. Consider, for example, the differences in the sources of electoral support for the Republican presidential ticket in 1964 that might have been expected to follow the nomination of each of four different G.O.P. presidential candidates—Nelson Rockefeller, Richard Nixon, William Scranton, or Barry Goldwater.

Differential Appeal of the National Presidential Ticket and the Fate of a Party's Congressional Ticket

THE IMPACT OF THE unique appeal of a presidential candidate on the fortunes of his party's House nominees goes beyond its effect on split-ticket voting. As was indicated in Chapter 1, the swings for a party's presidential and congressional candidates running in the same district tend to move in the same direction. Thus the odds are that a drop in a party's vote for President will be paralleled by a decrease in the vote polled by the party's House nominee. In 1928, Smith's candidacy probably contributed to the defeat of several Democratic House candidates who would have been elected had their party nominated a different presidential standard-bearer.

The violent 1928 revolt against Al Smith in the South, in the

Border States, and in a number of northern districts was accompanied by the loss of a substantial number of Democratic House seats in those constituencies. Even in the Democrats' traditional southern stronghold, the party of Jefferson and Jackson lost five members of Congress. In the Border States, where the G.O.P. was stronger, the consequences of the election for the Democratic party's congressional wing were disastrous. Sixteen Border-State Democratic House candidates went down to defeat. In the North, another dozen formerly Democratic House seats were lost, nearly all in rural and small-town districts.

The great majority of these defeated Democrats were incumbents. Yet, while they were being retired by the voters in districts where Smith made a poor showing, in two urban-industrial districts in the Northeast where Smith ran exceptionally well, the Democrats captured a House seat from the G.O.P.[21] At the same time, in a sizable bloc of big-city districts in the North, Democratic congressional candidates came closer to winning than at any other time in the 1920's. Four years later, nearly all of these House seats were in the Democratic column, and there they stayed throughout the New Deal era.

If Smith had not been the Democratic presidential nominee, the party's congressional losses in 1928 might have been equally severe, or worse. But the odds are that some of the party's gains and losses in the House would have occurred in different districts than they did with Al Smith on the ticket. One can only speculate on the possible result if the Democrats had run a candidate for President who was more palatable to the South and to the Border States in 1928. It is likely, however, that each party's legislative membership also would have been somewhat different, and that the House would have had more Democrats from the South and the Border States and fewer Democrats from northern big-city districts than it actually had when Congress convened in 1929.

Congressmen who are actually on the political firing line are well aware of the effect which the selection of a particular presidential nominee can have on their own chances of electoral survival. A prime example during the 1960 preconvention maneuvering was Repre-

21. Democrats gained House seats in 1928 in the 3rd District of Rhode Island and the 11th District of Pennsylvania.

sentative Charles H. Brown, the Democratic Congressman from the 7th District in Missouri. As the Democratic convention drew nearer, there was much talk that the party which had nominated Al Smith in 1928 might select John F. Kennedy—also a Roman Catholic— in 1960. In Jefferson City, Missouri, however, there were men who had other ideas. A group of Missouri Democratic leaders, it was reported, were "redoubling their efforts in behalf of Senator Stuart Symington for the presidential nomination."[22] Foremost among those leaders was Representative Charles Brown, who was planning a strenuous tour of 15 states to drum up support for his man.[23]

Congressman Brown may well have believed that his fellow Missourian would make a great President, but he also was seriously concerned over the possibility that Senator Kennedy might be the Democratic nominee in 1960. And with good reason. Representative Brown's own chances of reelection in his home district were extremely precarious—in 1956 he won with a paper-thin margin of 50.3 per cent. Even in the Democratic congressional landslide two years later he received only 53.7 per cent of the vote in his district. But more pertinent was the make-up of Congressman Brown's constituency, mostly rural and small-town counties, with few Catholics and a strong strand of Protestant, Bible-belt fundamentalism. In 1928 the voters in these same counties had reacted violently to the Democrats' nomination of Al Smith, rejecting his candidacy by more than two to one. Simultaneously, the local Democratic congressional nominee had also been overwhelmingly defeated,[24] and therein lay Representative Brown's chief fear in 1960. In the November elections, held after Kennedy's nomination, the Democratic presidential ticket once again made a notably poor showing in Congressman Brown's district, polling just 35 per cent of the vote.

22. *The New York Times*, November 1, 1959, p. 56.
23. *Ibid.*
24. Herbert Hoover polled 69.2 per cent of the 1928 vote in the 17 counties which comprised the Missouri 7th in 1960. Between 1924 and 1928, the swing against the Democratic presidential ticket in the area was 12.5 per cent. These 17 counties were scattered among several House districts in 1928. The 1928 district most nearly comparable to the 1960 Missouri 7th was the Missouri 15th. (Five of its seven counties were in the Missouri 7th in 1960.) In 1928, the local Democratic House nominee polled 35.4 per cent of the district's vote. The 1924–1928 swing against the party's congressional ticket was 8 per cent.

Congressman Brown ran a full 10 percentage points ahead of Kennedy; but still he lost, by over 19,000 votes.

Differential Appeal of the Local Congressional Ticket: Edith Nourse Rogers Runs for the House

AS OUR EXAMINATION OF the divergence between the presidential and congressional vote proceeds, one central fact should be kept firmly in mind. The relationship between the vote polled by a party's candidates for the Presidency and for the House depends on the electoral appeal of the party's congressional ticket, as well as on the strength of its presidential standard-bearer. Thus far the analysis has focused on the unique appeal of a particular presidential nominee, and on its effect on his party's vote for President and for Congressman. But by a bit of patient puzzling with the district-by-district voting figures, another broad factor underlying split-ticket voting at the national level can also be discerned.

Throughout the nation's more than 400 congressional districts, there are hundreds of individual House nominees who may induce their constituents to discriminate between the congressional and presidential tickets of their party. In some districts, they may try to do so chiefly by tailoring their policy pronouncements to fit the special requirements of their constituency. But in other districts, the peculiarities of the congressional returns may stem primarily from some personal factor affecting the candidacy of one of the House contestants in the constituency. The discovery that a congressional nominee has transgressed the law, a dislike for his religion, or even unfavorable publicity about the number of relatives whom he has on the public payroll as members of his staff—these and many other personal factors can suddenly acquire political relevance and drive a party's congressional vote well below its presidential tally in individual House districts. Conversely, however, there are other, unusually appealing House nominees who are able to build up such a personal following in their home district that they consistently run well ahead of their party's presidential candidate.

Among notable congressional campaigners of this latter type, few have equaled the remarkable political career of Congress-

woman Edith Nourse Rogers, the Republican Representative from
the 5th District in Massachusetts from 1925 until her death in 1960.
Educated at Rogers Hall School in Lowell, Massachusetts, and at
Madame Julien's School in Paris, Mrs. Rogers served with the
American Red Cross in France during World War I. Subsequently
she was appointed the President's Personal Representative in Care
of Disabled Veterans by Presidents Harding, Coolidge, and Hoover.
In 1925 her husband, John Jacob Rogers, the G.O.P. Representative
from the Massachusetts 5th for some years, died. In the special election to fill the vacant House seat, Mrs. Rogers ran as the Republican
nominee and won, with 71.9 per cent of the vote. Thereafter,
through prosperity and depression, and through good years and
lean years for her party, Mrs. Rogers was reelected, with votes to
spare. In 17 congressional elections from 1926 to 1958, she never
received less than six of every ten votes cast for Congressman in
her district.

This showing alone would be enough to establish Representative
Rogers' prowess as a formidable vote-getter. What is even more
noteworthy about her own vote totals is how she fared at the polls
relative to the G.O.P. presidential nominees in her district. In six
of the eight presidential election years in which Mrs. Rogers won
victories of landslide proportions for the Republican House ticket,
the Democrats' presidential standard-bearer came close to carrying
her constituency. The magnitude and consistency of Representative
Rogers' lead over her presidential running mates between 1928 and
1956—in years of Republican presidential defeat and victory alike—
are brought out by the trend lines in Figure 4.3. In those elections
when the Democrats bothered to run a candidate against her, Mrs.
Rogers' biggest lead over the G.O.P. presidential nominee was 20.3
per cent; her smallest, 5.5 per cent. Yet even these figures fail to
give an adequate picture of some of her more extraordinary
successes at the polls.

In 1928, close to four residents in every ten in the Massachusetts
5th were Roman Catholics; and 62.2 per cent were either foreign
born or of foreign-born or mixed parentage. Many of the district's
voters were stirred by the electoral appeal of Al Smith. Between
1924 and 1928, the total vote for President in the constituency
increased by 38.4 per cent, while the Democrats' share of the

district's presidential poll nearly tripled—jumping from 16,841 in 1924 to 45,469 just four years later. When all the returns were in, Hoover still managed to carry the traditionally Republican constituency, but only by a narrow margin, with 52.8 per cent of the vote. Yet while Herbert Hoover found himself sorely pressed by Al Smith

Figure 4.3—Edith Nourse Rogers and the G.O.P. presidential ticket: The percentage of the two-party vote polled by the Republican congressional candidate and by Republican presidential nominees in the 5th district of Massachusetts in presidential years, 1924–1956

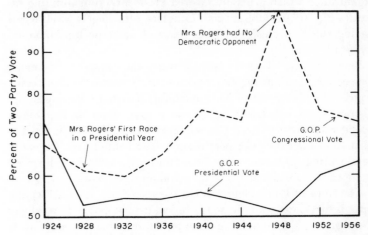

in the district, Representative Rogers defeated her Democratic congressional opponent, Cornelius F. Cronin, with ease. Her share of the district's 1928 House vote was a comfortable 61.1 per cent[25]

In 1944, when Franklin D. Roosevelt held his presidential opponent, Thomas E. Dewey, to 53.6 per cent of the vote in the Massachusetts 5th, Mrs. Rodgers scored another notable victory. This time she ran 19.6 percentage points ahead of her party's presidential nominee. Four years later, when President Truman

25. The 1928 congressional vote in the 5th District of Massachusetts was: Republican 56,004; Democratic 35,713; and others 1. The district's presidential returns were: Republican 50,833; Democratic 45,469; and others 442. The presidential vote in the constituency in 1924 was: Republican 44,315; Democratic 16,841; and third-party 8,722.

came within one percentage point of carrying her district, the local Democrats did not even bother to run a House candidate against her.

These 1948 election results are particularly noteworthy because they underscore the extraordinary personal following commanded by Representative Rogers. Mrs. Rogers was no party maverick. During 1947 and 1948, she voted with her Republican colleagues on 92 per cent of the roll-call votes on which a majority of the Republicans opposed a majority of the Democrats in the 80th Congress.[26] On another analysis of House roll-call votes, undertaken by an organization which generally favored President Truman during his battles with the Republican 80th Congress, Mrs. Rogers was listed as having voted "wrong" on all ten items of domestic legislation examined.[27]

Representative Rogers had gained the support of many Democrats as well as Republicans, but not by voting for Democratic policies. Further proof of her remarkable personal following in her district was forthcoming in 1952 and 1956, years of Republican presidential victory. Even General Eisenhower, the G.O.P.'s champion vote-getter, ran 16.4 percentage points behind Mrs. Rogers in 1952. During his landslide reelection four years later, he still trailed the local congressional ticket by a full 10.1 per cent.

The story of Edith Nourse Rogers' career in the national legislature is dramatic and, it must be added, atypical. Few House members are able to build up such an impregnable personal following as she did. Nevertheless, every presidential year is marked by the achievements of other popular legislative candidates who consistently do better than their party's presidential nominee in their district. And, with equal regularity, the national returns reflect the electoral showing of weak candidates for the House who poll a vote well below that of their party's presidential ticket in their constituency.

26. *Congressional Quarterly Almanac*, Vol. 4, 1948, p. 41.
27. The analysis of House roll-call votes cited was made by Americans for Democratic Action. It covered ten roll-call votes on issues affecting domestic legislation during 1947 and 1948. In nearly every case, a "wrong" vote was a vote against the position favored by President Truman and the majority of the northern Democratic Congressmen in the House. See *A.D.A. World, Special Supplement*, July, 1948, p. 4.

Although a carefully designed study of this aspect of voters' motivations during the course of a campaign would be necessary to demonstrate the point, it is possible that the fate of a party's national presidential ticket is also affected by the idosyncracies of particular congressional candidacies. In districts where a party finds itself saddled with an unappealing House nominee, the deficiency in the quality of its congressional ticket—or in the effort expended by the local party organization—may cost the party's presidential hopeful some votes. On the other hand, in constituencies where the party has an unusually popular House contestant, his presence on the ballot may lend strength to the presidential candidate of his party. In any event, it is clear that there is a wide variation in the personal appeal of the several hundred nominees who compose a party's congressional ticket. And this variety is an element of fundamental importance underlying the partisan divergence between the vote for President and the vote for Congressman in presidential election years.

Partisan Divergence and Ideological Convergence

THE SPECIAL APPEAL of a national presidential nominee may be based both on the candidate's personal attributes and on his policy pronouncements. Fundamentally, it is probably a unique blend of the two. Among House candidates who are able to cultivate special sources of electoral support, both policy considerations and the candidate's personality also may play a role. Edith Nourse Rogers, however, was a Republican whose voting record did not differ greatly from that of most other House Republicans; and the consistently strong races she made in her district afford examples of House contests where the special personal characteristics of a House nominee were probably particularly important. But what of the differences on broad questions of public policy that often appear among congressional candidates of the same party?

As every schoolboy knows, the political views of Congressmen who find themselves on the same side of the aisle in the House can vary profoundly. In the vernacular of American politics, both major parties in the House have their "conservatives," and both have their "liberals." The factors that would tend to limit the effect of these differences on the way individual voters decide upon their choice for Congressman are substantial. Many Representatives come from districts where the bulk of the electorate are oblivious to any subtle differences in the policy stands taken by their Congressman; many constituents are so unfamiliar with their Congressman's record that they do not even know his name.[28] Many voters also approach the voting booth without even the vaguest ideological preconceptions to guide them in their selection of a candidate.[29] Nevertheless, it is at least a plausible notion that a few House candidates, perhaps those of more than average visibility, espouse policy stands which, although they differ from the position taken by a majority of their party colleagues in the House, enhance their appeal in their own district. And this support may help them to win in their district at times when their presidential running mate is unable to carry their constituency.

It has been suggested that often voters in districts that support presidential and congressional candidates of opposite parties are electing national officials who tend to checkmate each other in Washington. Such voters are, in effect, casting their ballot against the positive exercise of governmental power. This result, however, may not always be the consequence of split-ticket voting at the national level.

Some opposition House nominees who are elected in districts carried by a winning presidential candidate may not be bent on opposing most of the President's policies in the House. In fact, opposition Congressmen who are elected in districts where the President himself is unusually strong may actually tend to align themselves with the Chief Executive's supporters in the House. Perhaps some of the partisan divergence found in House districts with split election results masks an ideological convergence between

28. In a 1956 survey by the Survey Research Center of the University of Michigan, 22 per cent of those interviewed gave correctly the name of the party candidate for whom they said they had voted; 43 per cent claimed to have voted for a candidate for Congress on one or the other of the party tickets but could not give his name; and most of the remainder did not vote. V. O. Key, Jr., *Politics, Parties, and Pressure Groups,* Fifth Edition (New York: Thomas Y. Crowell Company, 1964), p. 563.

29. See Angus Campbell, Philip E. Converse, Warren E. Miller, and Donald E. Stokes, *The American Voter* (New York: John Wiley & Sons, Inc., 1960), Ch. 10.

the presidential and congressional candidates whom those districts send to Washington. If true, this similarity in ideology could be an important reason why some Congressmen, but not others, are able to survive an opposition presidential sweep in their district.

If this notion is correct, then Republican Congressmen who survive in Democratic presidential territory should be more likely than most G.O.P. House members to be party mavericks. Conversely, Democratic Congressmen elected in districts where the Republican presidential nominee polls a heavy vote should also be unusually prone to jump the traces of party discipline in the House. Doubtless it would require a lengthy series of analyses testing this relationship to determine all the types of electoral situations to which it is applicable, as well as to specify the conditions in which it does not apply. One such test boring can be made, however, by the use of House voting records drawn from the 80th Congress along with the results of the subsequent general election of 1948.

The Republican-dominated 80th Congress of 1947-1948 frequently found itself at loggerheads with the Democratic President, Harry S. Truman. Yet that Congress will also long be remembered for its passage of several notable pieces of legislation with Administration backing that fundamentally altered the conduct of American foreign policy. Measures such as the Marshall Plan were not without their determined opponents in the House, but it was the area of domestic legislation which contained most of the major issues that sharpened the executive-legislative struggle during this period. Here an embattled Democratic President sought to withstand the determined attempts to shift the nation's domestic policy in a more conservative direction that were made by the first G.O.P. House majority since Franklin Roosevelt. A good many of these attempts, moreover, were successful.

In the election campaign that followed in the fall of 1948, the major points of contention between the Democratic and Republican presidential candidates also concerned issues of domestic legislation rather than foreign policy. The G.O.P. standard-bearer, New York's Governor Thomas E. Dewey, struck a lofty note. Campaigning as a middle-of-the-road Republican, he frequently spoke in generalities, as when in Des Moines, Iowa, he emphasized the country's "need" for a "rudder to our ship of state and a firm hand on the tiller."[30]

Mr. Truman, by contrast, was more specific. Charging that the key issue of the campaign was the record of the "notorious do-nothing Republican 80th Congress," he proceeded to assail that record in pugilistic fashion.[31] The Congress' passage of the Taft-Hartley Labor Act and its failure to support the inflation-control legislation which the President had recommended both came in for heavy attack. So, too, did the Republicans' farm policy. During the autumn, grain prices slid downward. In Dexter, Iowa, Truman cited the legislature's failure to vote funds for additional government grain storage bins and accused the Republicans of having "stuck a pitch fork in the farmer's back."[32]

When the returns were in, President Truman had been reelected, although by a fairly narrow margin; and the Democratic party found itself with a sizable majority in the House of Representatives. In districts carried by President Truman, some 51 Republican incumbents who were up for reelection were swept out of office. On the other hand, 35 G.O.P. Congressmen survived a Truman victory in their constituency.

In Table 4.1, the party regularity of Republican House members in the 80th Congress is related to Truman's strength in their district in 1948. Most measures of party unity, it should be noted, contain inherent limitations. The party-unity index employed in Table 4.1 is no exception. It is based on the percentage of times a House member voted with the majority of his party colleagues on roll-call votes on which a majority of his party's Representatives were opposed by a majority of the opposition Congressmen.

The issues covered by an analysis of this sort may be of great moment or they may be trivial. Nor does such an index indicate anything about the kinds of legislation on which members of the House vote pro or con. Sometimes the majority of a party's legislators may line up in support of a measure benefiting urban minority groups; on another occasion, the bulk of the party's House members may oppose a similar bill. Yet a Representative of that party who

30. Quoted in *The New York Times*, October 15, 1948, p. 15.
31. Quoted in *The New York Times*, September 19, 1948, p. 3.
32. *Ibid.*

consistently voted for legislation favoring urban minority groups would have a party-unity score of only 50 per cent. By itself, a party-unity index may thus reveal little about a Representative's views on specific policy issues or about his underlying political philosophy. It does, however, separate the party regulars from the party mavericks on those issues before the House on which the two major parties took conflicting positions.

Table 4.1—Congressmen Reelected in Districts where the Opposition's Presidential Candidate Is Strong Tend to Be Party Mavericks: Average Party-Unity Score of Republican Representatives in the 80th Congress Who Were Reelected in 1948 and Truman's Share of the Two-Party Presidential Vote in their District

District's Democratic Presidential Percentage in 1948	Number of Districts Won by an Incumbent Rep. House Member in 1948	Average Party-Unity Score of Winning Incumbent Rep. House Members[a]	Number of Winning Incumbent Rep. House Members With a Party-Unity Score Below 80	% of Winning Incumbent Rep. House Members With a Party-Unity Score Below 80
5–29.9	2	98.0	0	0.0
30–34.9	7	95.0	0	0.0
35–39.9	24	94.0	1	4.2
40–44.9	35	90.4	1	2.9
45–47.4	20	90.4	2	10.0
47.5–49.9	18	86.6	4	21.1
50–52.4	18	86.3	3	17.6
52.5–54.9	7	78.7	2	25.0
55–59.9	7	81.6	1	14.3
60–64.9	3	69.0	3	100.0
Total	141		17	

[a] The index of party unity used in this table appears in the *Congressional Quarterly Almanac*, Vol. 4, 1948, pp. 40–43. The party-unity score indicates the percentage of times a Representative aligned himself with the majority of his party's House membership on roll calls on which a majority of one party was opposed by a majority of the other party. In the computation of the index, only roll calls on which the Representative actually voted or publicly committed himself were considered. Roll calls from which a Representative was absent and did not announce his stand were excluded.

The voting records of Republican Representatives analyzed in Table 4.1 cover a period of nearly two years before the 1948 general election. Yet the likelihood that G.O.P. Congressmen would vote with the majority of their colleagues in the House varied markedly with the number of potential Truman voters in their districts. To state the finding another way, Republican Congressmen from districts that President Truman was to carry in 1948 were more likely to be party mavericks than were their fellow partisans from indisputably Republican territory. G.O.P. Representatives from districts that Governor Dewey carried with over 52.5 per cent of the vote aligned themselves with the majority of their party's legislators more than nine times out of ten. Republican House members from districts where President Truman polled between 52.5 and 60 per cent of the vote, by contrast, wore their Republicanism more lightly. They could be counted on by their party leaders about four fifths of the time.

The reelection of three Republican incumbents in districts where the Truman vote exceeded 60 per cent is even more noteworthy. These Congressmen may definitely be regarded as G.O.P. mavericks, for they voted with the Democrats on nearly a third of the issues on which a majority of Republicans opposed a majority of Democrats in the House. Broadly speaking, the data in Table 4.1 suggest that the G.O.P. House leadership encountered real insurgency only among Republican Representatives who came from districts where the opposition's presidential ticket was exceptionally strong. And even these House members lined up with their party colleagues about two thirds of the time. Nevertheless, their voting records still placed them among the most unreliable Republicans in the House.

Congressmen who manage to get reelected in districts where the opposition's presidential candidate is strong may tend to be party mavericks. But on what kinds of issues do they disassociate themselves from the bulk of their party colleagues in the House? And when they do revolt, do they find themselves in agreement with the presidential wing of the opposition party? Here again, the voting records of House members in the 80th Congress and the returns from the subsequent general election of 1948 provide findings that bear on our inquiry. In Table 4.2, the support which President Truman was able to command among northern Congressmen who were reelected in 1948 is related to Mr. Truman's strength in their district in that year.

A word or two about the method of analysis employed in the table may be in order. The House voting records of both Republican and Democratic Representatives outside the South and Border States are examined, and the data used cover ten key votes on domestic legislation which Americans for Democratic Action felt were particularly important in 1947 and 1948. Among the issues involved were tax policy, a displaced persons bill, anti-inflation legislation, rent control, public housing, social security legislation, appropriations for the Tennessee Valley Authority, and antitrust

Table 4.2—Partisan Divergence and Ideological Convergence in 1947–1948: Republican and Northern Democratic Representatives Who Were Reelected in 1948; Their Relative Support for President Truman's Position on Domestic Legislation during the 80th Congress; and the Truman Strength in their District in 1948

DISTRICT'S DEMOCRATIC PRESIDENTIAL PERCENTAGE IN 1948	PERCENTAGE SUPPORT FOR TRUMAN ON 1947–1948 DOMESTIC ISSUES BY HOUSE MEMBERS REELECTED IN 1948[a]		NUMBER OF HOUSE MEMBERS	
	Rep.	Northern Dem.	Reps.	Northern Dems.
0–4.9	—	—	—	—
5–29.9	0.0	—	2	—
30–34.9	1.4	—	7	—
35–39.9	4.8	—	24	—
40–44.9	6.8	—	35	—
45–47.4	7.9	100.0	20	1[b]
47.5–49.9	9.1	50.0	18	1
50–52.4	13.6	80.0	18	1
52.5–54.9	16.4	86.8	7	8
55–59.9	16.2	92.7	7	11
60–64.9	43.7	92.4	3[c]	10
65–69.9	—	94.9	—	9
70–94.9	—	96.3	—	9
Total			141	50

[a] The index of Truman support used in this table is based on a roll-call vote analysis prepared by Americans for Democratic Action in 1948. A.D.A. examined each Representative's voting record to determine the number of "correct" and "incorrect" votes he recorded on ten important House roll calls in 1947 and 1948. A "correct" vote was one that A.D.A. considered "in harmony with liberal policies." An "incorrect" vote was one that A.D.A. considered "contrary to liberal policies." In every case, a "correct" vote coincided with the stand taken by the President or by most of his staunchest supporters in the House. The issues covered included tax policy, a displaced persons bill, anti-inflation legislation, rent control, public housing, social security legislation, appropriations for the Tennessee Valley Authority, and antitrust legislation. For the index, and for a discussion of the background of the roll calls analyzed, see A.D.A. World, Special Supplement, July, 1948, pp. 2–4.

[b] The Democratic Congressman in this unit was Frank Havenner of the 4th District in California. The district's 1948 Wallace vote was 6.8 per cent. The Wallace and Truman vote together accounted for more than half of the constituency's total vote for President.

[c] In addition to the three Republicans in this unit, one other non-Democratic Congressman was reelected in a district where Truman polled over 60 per cent of the vote. He was Vito Marcantonio, the American Labor Party Representative from New York's 18th District. Although he opposed the President on most foreign policy issues, Marcantonio supported Truman on every issue of domestic legislation included in the A.D.A. roll-call analysis. If his domestic voting record is grouped with that of the other three non-Democratic Representatives who won in districts where Truman polled over 60 per cent of the vote, the group's index of Truman support rises to 56.3.

legislation.[33] On each of the roll calls considered, a vote which A.D.A. termed "correct" coincided with the stand favored by the Truman Administration at the time. A Representative's percentage of A.D.A. "correct" votes thus constitutes a sort of rough index of the House member's support for Mr. Truman on issues of domestic legislation before the 80th Congress.[34]

The members of the 80th Congress were elected in 1946, the year of the G.O.P. midterm congressional sweep. In the 1948 contest covered by the data in Table 4.2, however, the Democratic tide was running higher in nearly every district in the country. As a result, only two northern constituencies where Truman polled less than 50 per cent of the two-party presidential vote had incumbent Democratic Congressmen who could be reelected. One of these Democrats from districts where Truman was weak, Congressman Harold Donohue from the 4th District in Massachusetts, backed the President on only half the roll calls analyzed—far less often than most Democratic Congressmen from the North. The other House member in this category was Frank Havenner from the 4th District in California. He supported President Truman on all ten roll-call votes, but his district included a sizable number of 1948 Wallace voters, and the Truman voters plus the Wallace voters actually constituted an anti-Dewey majority in the California 4th in 1948. Among Democratic Congressmen from the remaining House districts where Truman's vote was larger, support for the Truman program tended to increase as Truman's strength grew.

Over-all, there were very few northern Democratic Representatives from districts where their party's President ran poorly in

33. For a detailed discussion of the votes included in the A.D.A. roll call analysis, see *A.D.A. World, Congressional Supplement,* July, 1948, pp. 2–4.

34. It should be emphasized that roll-call votes alone may reveal little about the full range of a legislator's activities on Capitol Hill. They may, for example, indicate nothing about a member's actions behind the scenes or about his attitudes on issues that never reach the floor of the House. Nevertheless, the fact that they are public in character makes them important items of political data; for they are a major part of the record to which a Congressman publicly commits himself which may be used for or against him in a campaign. For a fuller discussion of the use of roll-call analyses in the study of legislative behavior, see David B. Truman, *The Congressional Party, A Case Study* (New York: John Wiley and Sons, Inc., 1959), pp. 12–13.

1948. Republican Congressmen who managed to survive in opposition presidential territory, on the other hand, were more numerous, and their voting record in the House also shows a tendency to vary with the Truman strength in their constituency. For his domestic program the President received less than one vote of every 20 recorded by G.O.P. Congressmen from districts where Truman polled under 40 per cent of the vote in 1948. Thereafter, the amount of support that Republican House members gave the Truman domestic policies went up as the President's own strength in their district increased. G.O.P. Congressmen who survived in districts which Truman carried with between 50 and 60 per cent of the vote supported the Democratic Chief Executive about a sixth of the time during the 80th Congress. Those who managed to get themselves reelected in districts that Mr. Truman swept with over 60 per cent of the vote had, on the average, backed the President's policies on more than four of every ten domestic roll calls.

In constituencies where the Democratic President drew over 60 per cent of the vote, only three Republicans—all incumbents—were elected to the House. One of these, Jacob Javits, was an urban liberal who was first elected to Congress by a narrow margin in the 1946 Republican landslide. Representative Javits came from New York's 21st District on Manhattan's upper West Side, and on domestic issues his voting record was almost indistinguishable from that of a northern big-city Democrat. On the House roll calls analyzed in Table 4.2, he voted against President Truman's stand only once.

The other two Republican Congressmen who were reelected in districts where there was a Truman sweep represented vastly different constituencies—a pair of farm districts in the northwestern and southwestern corners of Minnesota. The Representatives in question were Harold Hagen, from the Minnesota 9th, and H. Carl Andersen, the Congressman for Minnesota's 7th District. Both were more old-fashioned agrarian radicals than exponents of the new urban liberalism of the Javits type, and their collective support for President Truman on just over a fifth of the domestic roll calls analyzed fell far short of Mr. Javits' record of Truman support. Nevertheless, the backing they gave the Democratic President still exceeded that of every other Republican in the House except the New Yorker.

The data in Table 4.2 make one thing clear. Republican Congressmen who carried districts where President Truman was strong in 1948 had seen fit to associate themselves with at least some of the Truman policies. But is there any evidence that these Representatives fared better at the polls than did G.O.P. Congressmen from banner Truman districts who had been less generous in their support for the President? In Table 4.3, the voting record of Republican incumbents who were swept out of office in 1948 is compared

Table 4.3—Republican Representatives Who Won and Lost in 1948; their Relative Support for President Truman's Position on Domestic Legislation during the 80th Congress; and the Truman Strength in their District in 1948

DISTRICT'S DEMOCRATIC PRESIDENTIAL PERCENTAGE IN 1948	PERCENTAGE SUPPORT FOR TRUMAN ON 1947–1948 DOMESTIC ISSUES BY HOUSE MEMBERS SEEKING REELECTION IN 1948[a]		NUMBER OF HOUSE MEMBERS WHO	
	Rep. Incumbents Who Won in 1948	Rep. Incumbents Who Lost in 1948	Won	Lost
0–4.9	—	—	—	—
5–29.9	0.0	—	2	—
30–34.9	1.4	—	7	—
35–39.9	4.8	—	24	—
40–44.9	6.8	11.1	35	2
45–47.4	7.9	0.0	20	1
47.5–49.9	9.1	8.3	18	9
50–52.4	13.6	4.5	18	14
52.5–54.9	16.4	9.0	7	16
55–59.9	16.2	7.2	7	16
60–64.9	43.7	12.2	3	5
Total			141	63

[a] The index of Truman support used in this table is identical to that in Table 4.2.

with the record of G.O.P. House members who survived the Republican debacle. These vote indices for both groups of Congressmen are in turn related to the Truman strength in their district. Although the number of cases analyzed is fairly small, it still should be possible to squeeze some meaning from the figures.

In districts where President Truman lost, both the Republican incumbents who were reelected and those who lost had given about the same amount of support to the Truman program. In the constituencies the President carried, however, the Republican

Congressmen who won were more sympathetic to the Democratic chieftain's policies than were their party colleagues who were swept out of office with the Democratic presidential tide. In districts where Truman garnered between 50 and 60 per cent of the vote, the differences between the voting records of the two groups of Representatives, though suggestive, are not great. The case of the Republican Representatives who had the unenviable task of running in districts where Truman drew over 60 per cent of the vote, however, is more clear-cut. The three G.O.P. Congressmen who managed to survive in these constituencies had supported the President's domestic program much more frequently than their five defeated party colleagues. Where Truman was very strong, in short, Republican House members who favored some of the President's domestic policies had a better chance of being reelected than the President's more resolute opponents.

The data on Table 4.3 are based on the House voting records of Republicans and northern Democrats, nearly all of whom came from states that had at least the rudiments of a two-party system. A more general picture of the relationship between Truman's strength and the ideological coloration of House members from all parts of the country emerges from Table 4.4. There the domestic voting records of the entire Democratic membership in the House are related to President Truman's share of the two-party presidential vote in their district. Once again the data are drawn from the 80th Congress and the subsequent election of 1948.

Broadly speaking, the southern Democrats supported the President on about half the domestic roll calls analyzed; while the northern Democrats backed him about nine times out of ten. Even the southerners' support for Mr. Truman, it should be noted, was much more generous than that of any significant group of Republicans in the House. Border-State Democrats, whose support for Truman stood midway between that of their northern and southern colleagues, reflected the mingling of southern and northern cultures which condition the politics of their region.[35]

That the southern Democrats backed Truman's domestic program less enthusiastically than their northern counterparts in 1947-

35. John H. Fenton, *Politics in the Border States* (New Orleans: The Hauser Press, 1957), pp. i and 1.

1948 is no surprise. What is of interest in Table 4.4, however, is that the southerners who came from districts where Truman trailed his G.O.P. opponent had unusually low records of Truman support. The President had some staunch adversaries who represented constituencies where he ran ahead of Dewey.[36] Most of these

Table 4.4—Partisan Divergence and Ideological Convergence in 1947–1948, a Regional Analysis of the Democrats: Democratic Representatives from Northern, Southern, and Border-State Districts Who Were Reelected in 1948; Their Relative Support for President Truman's Position on Domestic Legislation during the 80th Congress; and Mr. Truman's Strength in their District in 1948[a]

DISTRICT'S DEMOCRATIC PRESIDENTIAL PERCENTAGE IN 1948	PERCENTAGE SUPPORT FOR TRUMAN ON 1947–1948 DOMESTIC ISSUES BY DEMOCRATIC HOUSE MEMBERS REELECTED IN 1948 IN THE:			NUMBER OF HOUSE MEMBERS		
	North	Border States	South	N	BS	S
0–4.9	—	—	58.2	—	—	6[b]
5–29.9	—	—	—	—	—	—
30–34.9	—	—	—	—	—	—
35–39.9	—	—	—	—	—	—
40–44.9	—	—	—	—	—	—
45–47.4	100.0	—	35.0	1[c]	—	2[d]
47.5–49.9	50.0	—	27.2	1[e]	—	2[f]
50–52.4	80.0	50.0	40.0	1	2	2
52.5–54.9	86.8	—	50.0	8	—	2
55–59.9	92.7	65.0	55.3	11	2	9
60–64.9	92.4	77.6	51.3	10	5	8
65–69.9	94.9	88.9	54.6	9	3	4
70–94.9	96.3	60.0	52.6	9	2	48
Total				50	14	83

[a] The index of Truman support used in this table is identical to that in Table 4.2.
[b] The six Democrats in this unit were reelected in Alabama in 1948. President Truman's name did not appear on the state's ballot that year.
[c] Frank Havenner won California's 4th District.
[d] The southern Democrats in this unit were Burr P. Harrison of Virginia's 7th District (northwestern part of the state, including Winchester), and Dwight L. Rogers of the 6th District in Florida (Palm Beach).
[e] Harry R. Sheppard won in the 21st District of California.
[f] The southern Democrats in this unit were Howard W. Smith of Virginia's 8th District (northeastern corner of the state), and Hamilton C. Jones from the 10th District of North Carolina (Charlotte).

36. Slightly over a fifth (17 in 77) of the southern Democrats who stood for reelection in districts where Truman was stronger than Dewey deserted their President on at least 60 per cent of the domestic roll calls analyzed. In some of these districts, Truman lost to the Thurmond States' Rights ticket although he ran ahead of Dewey. In the four constituencies where Truman trailed the G.O.P. presidential nominee, on the other hand, all of the Democratic Representatives had opposed their President at least six times out of ten.

Congressmen came from black-belt districts with large Negro populations—constituencies where there was a large third-party presidential vote for Thurmond in 1948. But taken as a group, the southern Democrats from districts where Truman was weaker than Dewey had the lowest record of Truman support of any group of southerners in the House.

A look at the Congressmen from districts where Dewey outpolled Truman should suffice to establish the conservatism of the group. They were: Dwight L. Rogers of Florida, Hamilton C. Jones from North Carolina, and Burr P. Harrison and Howard W. Smith of Virginia. Congressman Rogers' 6th District in Florida contained Fort Lauderdale, West Palm Beach, and much of the Atlantic Coast resort area above Miami. Representative Jones came from the North Carolina 10th, a district that included the thriving business center of Charlotte; while Congressman Harrison represented a cluster of counties in northwestern Virginia. Representative Smith, of House Rules Committee fame, came from the Old Dominion's northeastern corner, with its burgeoning Washington suburbs.

All of these gentlemen except Harrison represented some of the most rapidly growing urban areas in the South, and all were impeccably conservative. Within four years, two of the three from districts with a large urban population had been displaced by a Republican.[37] Even in 1948, however, the dominant sentiment in these constituencies was reflected fairly accurately in majorities for a conservative Democratic Congressman and the G.O.P. presidential nominee.

The preceding analyses suggest that a Congressman who is reelected in opposition presidential territory may have much in common with the opposition's candidate for the White House. In

37. It is fair to say that one of these Representatives, Howard W. Smith, was displaced by a Republican, although he was not defeated by a G.O.P. House aspirant. Throughout the 1940's the Republican congressional vote in his constituency mounted steadily. Before the 1952 election, a sympathetic state legislature redrew the 8th District's boundary lines in a way that benefited "Judge Smith." The redistricting excluded from his constituency the Washington suburbs, which had provided most of the anti-Smith votes, and left him secure in the new 8th District farther south. The area around Washington, which now composed the new Virginia 10th District, promptly elected a Republican. Congressman Jones' district, the North Carolina 10th, also elected a G.O.P. Representative in 1952.

fact, the ideological orientation of a Congressman in such a district may have an important bearing on his own chances of electoral survival. But what of a Congressman's response to the electoral verdict in his constituency, after the ballots have been counted? Often a Representative may find it difficult to gauge exactly how strong an opposition President really is in his district. In 1948, for example, the number of Congressmen who anticipated in May that

Table 4.5—Partisan Divergence and Ideological Convergence in 1948–1949: Republican and Democratic Representatives' Relative Support for President Truman's Position on Domestic Legislation during the First Session of the 81st Congress in 1949 and Mr. Truman's Strength in their District in 1948

DISTRICT'S DEMOCRATIC PRESIDENTIAL PERCENTAGE IN 1948	PERCENTAGE TRUMAN SUPPORT ON 1949 DOMESTIC ISSUES BY HOUSE MEMBERS ELECTED IN 1948[a]		NUMBER OF HOUSE MEMBERS	
	Republicans	Northern Democrats	R	ND
0–4.9	—	—	—	—
5–29.9	11.7	—	3	—
30–34.9	13.5	—	7	—
35–39.9	12.9	—	27	—
40–44.9	18.0	78.4	41	2[b]
45–47.4	21.4	95.8	27	4
47.5–49.9	22.6	96.4	25	12
50–52.4	32.7	97.6	19	12
52.5–54.9	27.3	97.2	7	24
55–59.9	27.0	91.4	8	23
60–64.9	59.8	95.8	3[c]	15
65–69.9	—	94.6	—	8
70–94.9	—	97.1	—	11
Total			167	111

[a] The index of Truman support used in this table is based on a roll-call vote analysis that appeared in the New Republic in November, 1949. The New Republic examined each Representative's voting record to determine the number of "progressive" and "anti-progressive" votes he recorded on 13 important House roll calls concerning domestic legislation in 1949. In every case, a vote which the New Republic considered "progressive" coincided with the stand taken by the President or by most of his staunchest supporters in the House. The issues covered included rent control, public housing, legislation to broaden the coverage of the social security system, a veterans' pension plan, the Brannan farm plan, anti-poll-tax legislation, a natural-gas act, strengthening the Clayton Act, increasing the minimum wage, the basing-point system, and the Taft-Hartley Labor Act. For the index, and for a discussion of the background of the roll calls analyzed, see The New Republic, November 14, 1949, pp. 17–32, and especially p. 26.

[b] The two Democrats in this unit were Robert T. Secrest from the 15th District in Ohio, and Edward H. Kruse, Jr., from Indiana's 4th District.

[c] The Republicans in this unit were Jacob Javits of New York's 21st District, H. Carl Andersen from the 7th District in Minnesota, and Harold G. Hagen from Minnesota's 9th District. The American Labor party's Vito Marcantonio also was elected in a district where Truman polled over 60 per cent of the vote in 1948. If his 1949 domestic voting record is grouped with that of the three Republicans in this unit, the group's index of Truman support rises to 67.8.

Truman would run as strongly as he did in November must have been small indeed. Immediately after the election, however, there was less room for doubt. In these altered circumstances, opposition Congressmen who had just survived in districts where President Truman was unusually strong might be expected to be somewhat more prone to support the Chief Executive.

This expectation is borne out by the data in Table 4.5, which focuses attention on the first session of the new 81st Congress that convened shortly after the 1948 election. The data cover the voting records of all Republican and Democratic House members outside the South and the Border States. Once again, the frequency with which a member recorded votes that a liberal organ called "correct" on important domestic roll calls has been determined, and once again, a "correct" vote coincided with the stand taken by the Truman Administration.

The voting record of the Republican Congressmen is of particular interest. Those who came from districts that President Truman had carried gave the Administration substantially more support than their colleagues from the Dewey strongholds. The voting record of the few Republicans who survived in districts where Truman polled over 60 per cent of the vote is unusually note-worthy. On the average, they supported the Democratic President on six of every ten domestic roll calls. The only other non-Democrat who won in a constituency where Truman polled over 60 per cent of the two-party vote—Representative Vito Marcantonio of New York's 18th District—supported the President on nine of the ten roll calls.

The variation in the pattern of Truman support among northern Democrats is less clear-cut. For one thing, no Democrat was elected in a district where Dewey got over 60 per cent of the vote, and the Democrats from the North who won in districts Truman lost by margins of under 5 per cent stuck by the President fairly well. The two Democrats from constituencies where Truman's strength was below 45 per cent, however, were less reliable Administration supporters. One of these, Representative Edward Kruse, Jr., from Indiana's 4th District, disassociated himself from the President on 18.2 per cent of the 1949 roll calls analyzed. In 1950 he was defeated.

The other Representative from a district where Truman was weak,

Robert T. Secrest, broke with the President on a quarter of the first-session roll calls studied. In the second session, he deserted Truman's policies even more frequently, but his subsequent political career was happier than that of Mr. Kruse. Congressman Secrest, who defeated a G.O.P. incumbent in 1948, had also represented the 15th District in Ohio from 1933 to 1942. He had a large personal following in his constituency to supplement his occasional espousal of conservative domestic policies. Reelected in 1950, he was so well entrenched by 1952 that he was again sent to Washington despite an Eisenhower landslide in his district. The 1952 returns in the Ohio 15th were: Eisenhower (Republican) 62.3 per cent; and Secrest (Democrat) 64.3 per cent. It was not until 1954, a year when the G.O.P. generally lost ground, that the Republicans finally won back the district; and that was only after Representative Secrest had resigned his House seat to accept an appointment on the Federal Trade Commission. Ohio's senior Republican Senator, John W. Bricker, reportedly helped the Democrat obtain the President's nomination to the post.[38]

There is a lesson to be drawn from the career of Mr. Secrest. On occasion, an element of ideological convergence may help explain split election results in northern districts with majorities for a Democratic Congressman and a G.O.P. President. But it may also work the other way. In 1948-1949, ideological convergence and partisan divergence in the North were more likely to crop up in districts that supported President Truman and a Republican Congressman.

There are definite limitations on the amount of ideological convergence that appears in Table 4.5 and in the preceding analyses. Outside the South and the Border States, virtually every Democratic Congressman gave Truman more support than almost any Republican, regardless of Mr. Truman's strength in his district. Representatives who find themselves in opposition presidential territory may break with their party colleagues on some issues. But very few of them are opposition Congressmen in disguise. The analysis has also focused exclusively on the amount of agreement on issues of domestic legislation that exists between candidates of opposite parties. The candidates' stands on problems of foreign policy have

38. *Congressional Quarterly Weekly Report*, week ending July 2, 1954, p. 829.

not been considered. Even when these necessary qualifications are made, however, it seems clear that ideological convergence was an important factor underlying some of the split-ticket voting at the national level in 1948. To determine whether it is a significant factor in other elections and in other conditions, a good many additional analyses would be required.

Partisan Divergence, Ideological Convergence, and the National Party System

VOTERS IN DISTRICTS WITH split election results may not always support candidates for national office who continually oppose each other on questions of governmental policy. Yet it is possible that the peculiarities of the choice offered by the presidential and congressional tickets of opposite parties in such districts are even greater than this finding alone would suggest. In 1948 President Truman ran on a platform of domestic liberalism. At the same time, he charged that his Republican opponent's commitment to liberal domestic policies was less wholehearted. On issues of foreign policy, by contrast, both Truman and Dewey took an international-ist position, and most of the political debate between the two men was concerned with domestic problems. During the autumn campaign, when grain prices began to sag, President Truman charged that the drop was a result of Republican farm policies, and he predicted worse to come if the G.O.P. should win the election. In November the electorate in two Minnesota districts which returned Republican Congressmen to Washington gave Truman more than 60 per cent of their vote for President. Both Republican Congressmen from these districts had given Truman more support than nearly all of their party colleagues in the 80th Congress.

In the neighboring state of Wisconsin, two other G.O.P. lawmakers with moderately liberal domestic voting records also won handily in farm districts which supported Mr. Truman. They were Representative Alvin O'Konski, of the Wisconsin 10th, and Congressman Merlin Hull, from Wisconsin's 9th District.[39] Representatives

39. Truman polled 55.2 per cent of the two-party presidential vote in the Wisconsin 10th. In the Wisconsin 9th his vote was 53.9 per cent. Representative O'Konski won with 56.9 per cent of his district's two-party House vote. Congressman Hull had no Democratic opponent. When in 1950 a Democrat ran against him, Hull received 70.8 per cent of the vote.

O'Konski and Hull of Wisconsin and Andersen and Hagen from Minnesota had much in common. All four were maverick Republicans, and all four were old-fashioned agrarian radicals in the Populist, Progressive, Farmer-Labor party tradition. In 1947-1948, they supported President Truman on an average of 30.8 per cent of the domestic roll calls analyzed earlier in this chapter. In 1949, after the election, their backing for Truman's stand on domestic issues rose to 56 per cent. Throughout the period between 1947 and 1949, their over-all average of support for the Democratic President was 44.9 per cent—higher than that of any other group of Republicans in the House.

The districts which sent O'Konski, Hull, Andersen, and Hagen to Washington had a long tradition of supporting Congressmen who voted for liberal domestic welfare measures—especially those affecting rural interests. But the four constituencies also had a lengthy history of isolationism. As has been pointed out, the ideological convergence discerned in the preceding analyses concerned domestic problems exclusively. On five major votes on foreign policy, the four maverick Republicans departed sharply from the Truman position.[40] From 1947 to 1949, they supported Truman on only 21.1 per cent of the foreign policy measures the Democratic President insisted were necessary if the United States were to play her proper role in the world. Their support for internationalism was well below that of most other G.O.P. members of the House.

The odds are that issues of domestic policy were more salient

40. The five roll calls on which this calculation is based involved the following foreign policy issues: interim economic aid for Europe and China, December 15, 1947; the Foreign Assistance Act of 1948 (the Marshall Plan), March 31, 1948; extension of the Reciprocal Trade Agreements Act, May 26, 1948; extension of the Reciprocal Trade Agreements Act, February 9, 1949; and continuation of the Marshall Plan, April 12, 1949. O'Konski and Hull had no votes on the five roll calls in favor of the internationalist position taken by the Administration. Hagen recorded only one internationalist vote—for interim economic aid to Europe and China in 1947. Andersen, who supported the Administration's economic aid programs but opposed the Administration on extension of the Reciprocal Trade Agreements Act, recorded three internationalist votes. For details on the legislative background of the roll calls analyzed and for the Representatives' voting records, see *A.D.A. World, Special Supplement,* July, 1948, pp. 2-4, and *The New Republic,* November 14, 1949, pp. 26-29.

than foreign policy considerations for most voters in 1948. The United States was not at war; and domestic concerns such as sagging agricultural prices probably had a greater immediacy to most midwestern farmers than complex questions of foreign policy.[41] Moreover, between the presidential wings of both parties there was little to choose on those issues. Both Truman and Dewey were internationalists. But by voting for Truman and for an isolationist, maverick G.O.P. Congressman, the electorates in the 9th and 10th Districts of Wisconsin and the voters in the 7th and 9th Districts of Minnesota were able to record votes for domestic liberalism and for isolationism.

Broadly speaking, these returns were a commingling of partisan divergence and ideological convergence on domestic issues, coupled with a sharp ideological divergence on questions of foreign policy. Moreover, by voting for an isolationist, maverick G.O.P. Congressman, those voters with isolationist inclinations in these constituencies were able to opt for an isolationist position on foreign policy that was denied them by the national presidential choices. This kind of choice was made possible by the flexibility of a party system that enables voters to express their preferences at two points at the national level.

These general findings open up additional lines of speculation about some of the forms that may be taken by partisan divergence and ideological convergence at the national level. On rare occasions, as the case of Mr. Javits suggests, a Congressman may be elected who is in agreement with the opposition's presidential nominee on most issues of the day, including questions both of domestic and of foreign policy.[42] But perhaps in other districts with split election

41. In the Survey Research Center's study of the 1948 election, based on a small national probability sample of the adult population, Angus Campbell and Robert L. Kahn concluded that "foreign policy played no great part in voters' thinking about the election" and that "voting behavior was probably largely independent of attitudes toward foreign policy." (p. 57.) They also noted that, although "many of Truman's voters said, in one way or another, that they were for the same policies as Truman," Truman's foreign policy was rarely mentioned. (p. 52.) Angus Campbell and Robert L. Kahn, *The People Elect a President* (Ann Arbor: Institute for Social Research, The University of Michigan, 1952).

42. Even Representative Javits declined to support President Truman in 1948 and 1949 on an old issue which had traditionally divided the parties—the tariff.

results, the voters may support a Congressman who agrees with an opposition President on one cluster of issues while opposing him on other issues. If this line of reasoning is correct, then the nature and content of the ideological convergence in such districts may vary with the saliency of specific issues in the constituency. In several farm districts where there was partisan divergence in 1948, issues of domestic policy were probably paramount. Election results in these constituencies featured Democratic presidential majorities and Republican House victories.

In some districts, however, issues of foreign policy may become salient, and a different pattern of partisan divergence may prevail. The 1944 returns in New York's 29th District, an area that included some of New York City's more fashionable suburbs, provide a case in point.[43] The voters in the 29th returned a heavy majority for Thomas E. Dewey against Franklin Roosevelt in 1944, and normally they would have been for a G.O.P. Congressman as well. But their Republican Representative was Hamilton Fish, one of the few unreconstructed isolationists left on the East Coast at a time when sentiment on that issue was moving the other way. Several of New York City's more distinguished newspapers singled out Fish for special attack, and some regular Republicans joined in the assault. When the returns were in, Fish had been defeated by an internationalist Democrat, even though Dewey swept his district with 62.2 per cent of the vote. Two years later, an internationalist Republican won back the House seat and began a lengthy career as the district's Representative.[44]

This 1944 New York result was essentially a vote for internationalism and domestic conservatism. It thus was unlike the 1948 farm district returns. Many of the New York 29th's normally Republican voters were prepared to support a Democratic House candidate in order to defeat an isolationist G.O.P. Representative. These New York returns also differed from the 1948 midwestern results in that

43. In 1944, the New York 29th included Delaware, Orange, Rockland, and Sullivan counties.
44. Katharine St. George was the Republican Representative elected in the New York 29th in 1946. She served in the House until her defeat in the face of the Johnson presidential landslide in 1964.

they involved a G.O.P. presidential victory and a Democratic House triumph. Yet both types of results illustrate some of the different forms which partisan divergence and ideological convergence can take, as the saliency of issues varies from district to district. With more refined methods of analysis, perhaps other variations on this basic pattern could be found.

The likelihood that a particular constituency will split its results can also change in response to the altered circumstances which accompany different elections. Perhaps what can happen is that in a new electoral contest a whole new set of issues or the appeals of different candidates—or some combination of the two—may become paramount. And when this occurs, the partisan divergence which prevailed in a constituency at an earlier election may be wiped away entirely.

Here again the four Minnesota and Wisconsin districts with maverick Republican Representatives in 1948 are instructive. The circumstances of the 1952 election campaign differed sharply from the 1948 contest's setting. In 1952 the nation's economy was booming, and even the farmers seemed to be sharing in the general prosperity. At the same time, however, the frustrating conflict in Korea was in its third year.[45] During the campaign, General Eisenhower explicitly disavowed isolationism. But his promise in Detroit to "go to Korea" if elected, and his declaration in Champaign, Illinois, that it should be "Asians against Asians" if there had to be war in the Far East were skillfully attuned to the nation's *malaise*

---

45. The authors of the Survey Research Center's study of the 1952 election reported that foreign policy was a major issue in 1952 and that "foreign affairs were almost exclusively an area favorable to the Republicans." (p. 46.) "The Korean War, the loss of China to the Communists, the Soviet threat in Europe, and the general frustrations of the period of cold war moved the American electorate to a degree quite unknown in 1948. Foreign policy became a dynamic component of total public motivation in 1952 in a manner which contrasted sharply with the 'bipartisan era' of 1948." (p. 175.) They also noted that, whereas neither presidential candidate was seen as an inspiring leader by the voting population in 1948, General Eisenhower had a strong personal appeal in 1952, and that "a central aspect of his appeal was his presumed ability to do something personally about Korea and the cold war." (p. 67.) Angus Campbell, Gerald Gurin, and Warren E. Miller, *The Voter Decides* (Evanston, Illinois: Row, Peterson and Company, 1954).

over a struggle that seemed to be dragging on endlessly in the Western Pacific.[46]

The shift of the presidential vote in the four constituencies that had elected an isolationist Republican Congressman while supporting Truman in 1948 was particularly violent. The swings to the Republican presidential ticket in these districts ranged from 14.1 per cent to 21.6 per cent—the largest shift of sentiment recorded in any district outside the South. Eisenhower's 1952 strength in these constituencies was still below his showing in neighboring farm districts where historically the strain of agrarian radicalism was less strong. Nevertheless, in all four farm districts where Truman polled a heavy vote, both the G.O.P. presidential nominee and his congressional running mate now received comfortable majorities. Fundamentally, many voters in these districts had, by the 1940's, come to lean toward Democratic domestic policies, particularly when there were visible signs of economic hardship in their area. On issues of foreign policy, and particularly on questions of peace and war, however, the Democratic party was suspect. Korea was but a sequel to World War I and World War II—all fought under Democratic Presidents. In 1956, when farm income was again a problem and the United States was once again at peace, even General Eisenhower's personal popularity failed to prevent the G.O.P. presidential vote from slipping in these four constituencies.

It would require a lengthy series of analyses (and detailed survey data on the attitudes and perceptions of voters in individual House districts) to explore fully the relationship between voters' preferences and the success of particular candidates for President and for Congress in districts with split election results. Yet the aggregate election results themselves, and such collateral data as can be brought to bear on the problem, support the supposition that there are certain broad patterns in the returns. The nature of the ideological convergence that may sometimes be discerned in districts with split election results varies with the circumstances of particular

46. See, for example, other passages in General Eisenhower's Champaign speech: "We must avoid, ladies and gentlemen, the kind of bungling that led us into Korea and could lead us into others. The young farm boys must stay on their farms; the students must stay in school." This passage and the one cited above are quoted in *The New York Times*, October 3, 1952, p. 16. General Eisenhower's Detroit speech is quoted in *The New York Times*, October 25, 1952, p. 8.

election campaigns. It also may change in response to the saliency of specific issues in individual districts. In at least some presidential years, however, split results occur that are accompanied by a measure of ideological similarity between presidential and congressional nominees of opposing parties who win in the same district. At times, moreover, the peculiarities of the electoral situation in these districts may offer the voters a policy alternative at the congressional level that the major-party presidential candidates fail to provide.

CHAPTER 5

Minor Parties and the

Presidency and Congress

Among nations where genuine electoral competition is permitted, the United States is one of the relatively few countries where there are only two major political parties. Nevertheless, every four years some American voters spurn the alternatives offered by the major parties to support minor-party or independent candidates for national office. In most elections the number of such voters is small. Yet periodically the vote polled by minor-party movements in the United States has risen to impressive proportions.

The occasions when large segments of the electorate have become so disenchanted with one or both of the major parties that their discontent has spilled out through the mechanism of a third party have provided some of the most colorful episodes in American politics. The image of the Populist spellbinder, Mary Elizabeth Lease, exhorting the farmers of Kansas to "raise less corn and more Hell";[1] the vision of an embattled Theodore Roosevelt standing at Armageddon to finish his speech after having been shot in the

---

1. Quoted in John D. Hicks, *The American Nation,* Second Edition (Cambridge: The Riverside Press, 1949), p. 248.

chest; and the memory of a solemn Robert M. La Follette inveigh-
ing against the "interests" in a futile bid for the Presidency—all
these are integral parts of the American political tradition.

To consider all aspects of the role of minor parties in the American
political system, a lengthy discussion would be required. The objective here, however, is narrower in scope, *viz.*, to estimate and to
assess the amount of ticket-splitting at the national level occasioned
by the intervention of minor-party and independent candidates for
President and for Congressman. An increase in support for minor-
party presidential and House nominees does not necessarily swell
the ranks of the split-ticket voters. If everyone who supported a
third-party presidential candidate also voted for a House nominee
of the same minor party, the number of straight-ticket voters would
be unchanged by the success of third-party appeals.

In practice, however, an upsurge of minor-party activity in the
American political system has usually been accompanied by
increased ticket-splitting. In many districts, the voters may have
the option of voting for several minor-party presidential candidates;
but they may not be able to support even one minor-party candidate
for the House unless they resort to the usually futile expedient
of casting a write-in vote. In other districts, a House candidate
who is unaffiliated with either of the major parties may offer himself for the public's commendation; but there may be no presidential nominee on the ballot for whom the citizen who is dissatisfied
with both major parties can vote. Yet even in districts where a minor
party offers a complete national ticket, the electorate is likely to
grant its favors with selectivity. For the odds are that the minor-
party presidential candidate will poll more votes than his congressional running mate, or *vice versa.*

These propositions require evidence to support them, evidence
that will be supplied in subsequent pages; but this much is clear.
Both third-party movements that poll more votes for President than
for Congressman and minor parties whose House ticket runs far
ahead of the party's presidential slate induce some voters to split
their ticket for President and Congressman. Both divert votes that
might otherwise have gone to one of the major-party nominees.
The net effect of their differential impact on the presidential and
congressional wings of the major parties is to widen the gap between

the number of votes polled by each major party's presidential and congressional tickets.[2]

By analyzing third-party votes for President and Congressmen together, it is possible to distinguish between the impact that minor-party movements have at the two points within the American electoral system at which the voter can express his preferences for national policies and candidates. Such an inquiry should reveal something about the nature and function of different types of third-party movements. Yet by highlighting the way in which minor parties siphon off votes from the major-party presidential and congressional wings, it should also provide insights into how the major parties themselves play their central role in the American political system.

General Impact of Minor-Party Candidacies on the Presidency and the Congress

TICKET-SPLITTING ASSOCIATED WITH minor-party candidacies shows up most dramatically in House districts with split election results that are carried either by a minor-party presidential candidate or by a third-party congressional nominee. Sometimes a minor-party House candidate wins while a major-party presidential nominee carries his district. In 1948, the voters in New York's 18th District reelected Representative Vito Marcantonio, the American Labor party nominee, after a heated, three-way contest. Yet President Truman carried Marcantonio's East Side Manhattan constituency in 1948 with more than 18,000 votes to spare.[3]

2. Some voters who split their ballot to support a minor-party nominee, it should be noted, might have voted a split ticket even if there had not been a minor-party candidate on the ballot. And some voters, perceiving a third-party threat to the party with which they normally feel identified, may rally to the support of a major party that might not otherwise have received their unqualified backing at the polls. The inquiry here focuses only on ticket-splitting directly associated with the intervention of a third party. It removes none of the mystery about how the electorate might have divided their votes between the major parties if no third-party candidates had appeared.

3. The 1948 congressional vote in New York's 18th District was: Republican (with Liberal party support), 30,899; Democratic, 31,211; and American Labor party, 36,278. Of the total House vote, Representative Marcantonio received 36.9 per cent. The district's presidential totals were: Democratic and Liberal parties, 49,253; Republican, 30,986; and third-party (mostly Wallace votes cast on the American Labor party line), 19,238.

In recent years minor-party or independent House candidates have failed to generate much support.[4] But between 1920 and 1952 at least one district was carried by a minor-party or independent House nominee in every presidential year (Figure 5.1). Elections when minor-party or unpledged presidential electors have carried

Figure 5.1—Congressional districts with split election results involving major- and minor-party candidates for President and Representative: Districts carried by minor-party presidential nominees and districts carried by minor-party congressional nominees, 1920–1964

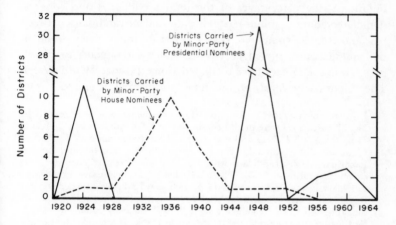

one or more House districts, by contrast, have been more sporadic. Between 1920 and 1964, this occurred in 1924, 1948, 1956, and 1960.

In 1924, Senator Robert M. La Follette, the Progressive presidential nominee, won at least eight districts in Wisconsin, two districts each in North Dakota and Minnesota, and one district in California. Only the two Minnesota districts, however, elected minor-party House candidates who were closely associated with La Follette's presidential candidacy. All the rest sent major-party Congressmen

4. One exception occurred in 1958 in the 5th District of Arkansas (Little Rock), where Dale Alford ran as an independent and defeated Congressman Brooks Hays, a conspicuous southern moderate during the Little Rock integration crisis.

to Washington.[5] The 1948, 1956, and 1960 revolts of some southern voters who opposed both the national Democratic and the Republican presidential nominees had even less effect on the major-party House tickets. In all three years, minor-party or unpledged electors presidential movements carried districts in the South that remained Democratic in the balloting for Representative.[6]

Something more of the differential impact of minor-party candidacies on the Presidency and the Congress emerges if one probes behind the relatively few districts that are actually carried by a third-party candidate to examine the total number of popular votes polled by minor-party movements for President and for Congressman. In Figure 5.2, the percentages of the total presidential and congressional vote going to minor-party or independent candidates between 1920 and 1964 are compared. Both support for minor-party presidential candidates or unpledged electors slates and support for third-party House nominees have oscillated violently since World War I. The minor-party share of the total presidential vote has varied

5. Districts which elected major-party House candidates and were carried by La Follette in 1924 were the Wisconsin 2nd, 3rd, 6th, 7th, 8th, 9th, 10th, and 11th; the North Dakota 2nd and 3rd; and the California 2nd. In the two Minnesota districts that La Follette carried, the 7th and the 9th, Farmer-Labor party House candidates won. The Minnesota Farmer-Labor party was closely identified with La Follette's Independent Progressive presidential candidacy in 1924. Of the other 11 districts that La Follette carried, 10 sent Republican Representatives to Washington and one elected a Democrat. It should be noted that La Follette's strength has been analyzed only in districts for which the 1924 presidential returns are available. It is possible that in one or two additional districts not covered by the analysis, particularly the Wisconsin 4th (Milwaukee), both La Follette and a minor-party House nominee also won.

6. The 31 southern districts that elected Democratic House candidates but supported Governor J. Strom Thurmond's third-party presidential candidacy in 1948 included all of the districts in Louisiana, Mississippi, Alabama, and South Carolina, and the 10th District in Tennessee (Memphis). In Louisiana, Mississippi, Alabama, and South Carolina, as has been noted, Governor Thurmond was listed on the ballot as the regular Democratic presidential nominee. In Alabama, electors pledged to President Truman did not even appear on the ballot. It is thus debatable whether the Louisiana, Mississippi, Alabama, and South Carolina constituencies that elected Democratic House candidates and supported Thurmond when he was running as the Democratic presidential standard-bearer should be included in our total of districts with split election results. The odds are, however, that at least some of these districts would have supported Thurmond over Truman even if Thurmond had been listed on the ballot as a third-party States' Rights candidate.

from a high of one in every six ballots cast in 1924 to a low of one in every 200 votes in 1952 and 1964. The vote for minor-party House candidates has never been as large as the vote polled for President by Senator La Follette in 1924. Nevertheless, the showing made by minor-party and independent congressional nominees has also fluctuated widely from year to year—from one vote in every 19 cast for Congressmen in 1920 to one vote in every 467 in 1956.

Figure 5.2—Percentage of the total presidential vote polled by minor-party candidates and the percentage of the total congressional vote polled by minor-party candidates, 1920–1964

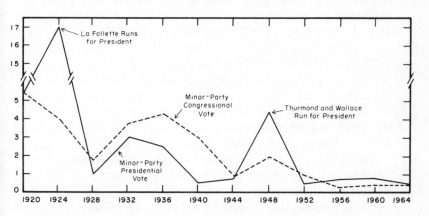

These minor-party presidential and congressional totals seldom fluctuate together. In 1924 the share of the total presidential vote for minor-party candidates was three times as large as it had been four years before. During the same period the minor-party congressional vote fell by more than a quarter. Between 1932 and 1936, third-party presidential candidates also improved on their earlier electoral showing, while the number of votes for House candidates who were not on the Democratic or Republican tickets fell.

Yet, even when the minor-party presidential and congressional vote did rise and fall together, the chances were that the discrepancy between the two minor-party vote totals would be large. Thus, between 1920 and 1964 the minor-party House vote, stated as a percentage of the third-party presidential vote, varied as follows: [7]

1924	22%	1944	116%
1956	30	1932	123
1948	34	1936	159
1960	39	1928	168
1964	91	1952	178
1920	93	1940	525

Between 1920 and 1964 the ratio between the minor-party House vote and the third-party presidential total has varied from just over one to five to more than five to one. These ratios, moreover, are based on the minor-party totals in the country as a whole. In individual House districts, where a minor party may run a candidate for President or for Congressman, but not for both, the discrepancy is even larger.

These figures afford striking evidence of the extent to which third-party votes are likely to be split-ticket votes, but they can easily be misconstrued if some other facts are not kept in mind. In most elections, the minor-party share of the total vote for President and for Congressman is relatively small. In the twelve elections covered by the data in Figure 5.2, the median minor-party House vote was 1.4 per cent of the total; for third-party presidential candidates it was 1.8 per cent. Nevertheless, most of the limited success that minor-party movements do enjoy serves to swell the ranks of the split-ticket voters by siphoning off support disproportionately from the major-party presidential and congressional tickets. And in an occasional election, such as 1920, 1924, or 1948, third-party candidacies have accounted for a substantial portion of the total vote.

In Table 5.1, both the total number of districts with split election results since World War I and the number of districts in which a third-party candidate was one of the winners are listed. As a glance at the figures in the right-hand column will make clear, about one in twelve of the districts which returned a mixed verdict between

---

7. In these computations, votes for independent or unpledged presidential electors are included with the minor-party presidential totals. Votes for independent House candidates are included with the minor-party House totals.

1920 and 1964 were carried by minor-party presidential or congressional nominees. In another group of districts with split results, the outcome also may have been influenced by the intervention of third-party candidates. In these constituencies, the minor-party vote exceeded the difference between the vote totals received by the major-party candidates.

Table 5.1—*Congressional Districts with Split Election Results and the Impact of Third-Party Candidacies, 1920–1964ᵃ*

Year and Number of Districts Analyzed		No. With Split Results of all Kinds	No. Won by Presidential and House Candidates of Opposite Major Parties	No. Won by a Major-Party Presidential & a Minor-Party House Nominee	No. Won by a Minor-Party Presidential & a Major-Party House Nominee	Total No. of Split Results Involving Minor-Party Candidacies	Per Cent of Total No. of Split Results
1920	344	11	11	0	0	0	0.0
1924	356	42	30	1	11	12	28.6
1928	359	68	67	1	0	1	1.5
1932	355	50	45	5	0	5	10.0
1936	361	51	41	10	0	10	19.6
1940	362	53	48	5	0	5	9.4
1944	367	41	40	1	0	1	2.4
1948	422	95	63	1	31	32	33.7
1952	435	84	83	1	0	1	1.2
1956	435	130	128	0	2	2	1.5
1960	437	114	111	0	3	3	2.6
1964	435	145	145	0	0	0	0.0
Total	4668	884	812	25	47	72	8.1

ᵃ The data in this table cover all House districts which returned pluralities for presidential and congressional candidates of different parties between 1920 and 1964, including districts with results split between opposite major parties and districts with results split between a major-party candidate and a minor-party candidate. Districts for which no presidential figures are available are not covered by the data.

The process by which minor-party candidacies siphon off votes from the major-party tickets or activate voters who might not otherwise have gone to the polls is complex. Sometimes when a major party is deserted by a bloc of voters who are attracted to a minor-party nominee, other voters may come to its support. Samuel Lubell has argued: "No third party . . . is ever a complete liability. If it diverts votes, it also adds votes in counterattraction."[8] Even in districts where most of the minor-party candidate's vote

8. Samuel Lubell, *The Future of American Politics* (New York: Harper & Brothers, 1952), p. 203.

was probably drawn from just one of the major parties, there is still no certainty that the major party would have made a better showing in these districts if the minor-party nominee had not appeared on the ballot. Even so, in at least some of the districts with split election results where one of the winners obtained only a plurality, the outcome would have been different in the absence of a minor-party intervention.[9]

Table 5.2—Congressional Districts with Split Election Results Where the Minor-Party Vote Exceeded the Difference Between the Major-Party Vote Totals, 1924–1964

Year and Number of Districts Analyzed		No. With Results Split Between Major-Party Candidates[a]	No. Where the Minor-Party Vote Exceeded the Difference Between the Major-Party Vote for:		Total No. of Districts Affected[b]	Per Cent of Total No. of Districts With Split Results
			Cong.	Pres.		
1924	356	30	3	20	21	70.0
1928	359	67	2	1	3	4.5
1932	355	44	10	9	18	40.9
1936	361	41	6	6	11	26.8
1940	362	48	2	1	3	6.3
1944	367	40	0	3	3	7.5
1948	422	63	7	22	23	36.5
1952	435	83	2	1	3	3.6
1956	435	128	1	6	7	5.5
1960	437	111	0	5	5	4.5
1964	435	145	1	0	1	0.7
Total	4324	800	34	74	98	12.3

[a] In some of the districts listed as having had election results split between the two major parties in 1948, Governor Thurmond appeared on the ballot as the regular Democratic presidential nominee.
[b] In some cases, the totals in this column are smaller than the sum of the districts where the minor-party vote exceeded the difference between the major parties' vote for Congressman and for President. This is because some districts where the minor-party vote exceeded both the major-party presidential vote difference and the major-party congressional vote difference are listed twice.

Between 1924 and 1964, the results in about one of every eight districts won by opposite major-party candidates might not have been split if no third-party candidate had entered the race (Table 5.2). In about a third of these districts, the margin separating the major-party candidates was narrow. Here the split-ticket voting

9. It is equally possible, of course, that some districts that did not have split results might have returned a mixed verdict if the minor-party votes cast in those districts had been divided unequally between the major-party nominees.

attributable to third-party appeals, though potentially decisive to the outcome in the district, was negligible. In the other districts, however, either the minor-party presidential vote or the minor-party House total exceeded 5 per cent.

These data indicate, in summary form, the impact that votes cast for minor-party candidates can have on partisan divergence at the national level. Although the great majority of districts are unaffected by third-party activities, about a twelfth of all districts with split results between 1920 and 1964 were carried either by a third-party presidential candidate or by an independent or minor-party House nominee. In about an eighth of the remaining districts which returned a mixed verdict, minor-party candidates occupied a balance-of-power position between the major-party adversaries. And in many other districts where the results were less clearcut, the appearance of minor-party candidates for President and Representative undoubtedly led to increased split-ticket voting.

Types of Minor-Party Candidacies for National Office

MINOR-PARTY VOTES USUALLY mean split-ticket votes. Yet some minor parties are supported almost exclusively by split-ticket voters; others are not. And the various political groups that go under the name "minor party" differ widely both in their structure and in their function in the nation's political system.

The most dramatic American minor-party movements have been the periodic explosions of discontent with both major parties that have given a Theodore Roosevelt or a Robert M. La Follette vote totals that could be counted in the millions. Episodic but short-lived movements of protest such as these have, on occasion, erupted with almost volcanic intensity. Broadly speaking, they have been of two types. Some have been primarily parties of economic protest. Sometimes they enlist their support mainly from the ranks of one of the old, established parties; but they may also draw votes from both former Democrats and former Republicans. The Populist revolt before the turn of the century and the La Follette Progressive movement are both notable examples of minor parties of economic protest. Yet periodically a second type of episodic protest movement has also made its appearance. Such minor parties have marshalled their electoral support largely from former backers of one of the two major parties. They seem, in short, to serve as a vehicle for voters who wish to secede at least temporarily from one of the major parties, but who are as yet unprepared to join their traditional adversaries in the other major party.

Much of the leadership of these secessionist movements may also have been conspicuously associated with one of the major parties in the past. And many of these leaders may endeavor to return to the fold once the events that generated their party apostasy have spent their force. In any event, their political origins are plain for all to see. The 1948 schism from the Democratic party of the Wallace Progressives, the Thurmond States' Righters, and the desertion of the regular Republican presidential nominee by the Theodore Roosevelt Progressives in 1912 offer notable examples of this type of episodic protest movement.[10]

Most minor-party movements that have rolled up the largest vote totals since the Civil War have been spearheaded either by parties of economic protest or by secessionist parties. These two types of third parties differ in important respects—in their electoral support, in the sources of their leadership, and sometimes even in the motives that bring them into being. Yet, in their role in the party system as a whole, both types of minor parties appear to be fundamentally similar.

The ties that link these economic protest and secessionist parties to the Republican and Democratic parties suggest that basically both types of minor parties are an integral part of America's fundamentally two-party system. Both reflect the inability of one or the other major party to cope with the issues of the day in a way that will

10. In their origins and purposes, the recent unpledged or independent presidential electors movements backed by groups in the South who have been unwilling to support the national Democratic presidential ticket bear a close resemblance to earlier southern secessionist party movements. In 1948 Thurmond's third-party presidential candidacy did well only in those southern states where Thurmond appeared on the ballot as the Democratic presidential nominee. In later years, many southern Democrats who had been dissatisfied with the national Democratic party seemed to have turned to the independent electors expedient because Thurmond's 1948 third-party presidential movement failed to work. Had not Barry Goldwater voted against the Civil Rights Act and been nominated by the Republicans in 1964, however, there might well have been another major effort, led by Alabama's Governor George Wallace, to launch a third-party movement in the South.

maintain party unity. Both highlight a failure of one of the major parties to win potential converts from the enemy camp; and both divert votes that might otherwise have gone to the major parties.

Sometimes these minor parties may serve as way stations for groups of voters *en route* to changing their major-party affiliation. In such cases, their appearance may be the harbinger of an important major-party realignment. Sometimes, however, the voters and leaders of these minor-party movements may return to the party they have normally supported. Nevertheless, the odds are that the balance of power among the forces contending for control of the party which they left will have been changed by their walkout. As Samuel Lubell has noted, the momentary eruptions of these types of minor parties shed "penetrating light on the inner torments of the major party."[11]

Secessionist parties and parties of economic protest are dramatic, quick to burn with brilliance in the American political constellation, and almost as quick to burn themselves out. Sometimes they roll up quite large and, to established political leaders, no doubt, quite frightening vote totals. Yet, impressive as their occasional outbursts of electoral activity may be, these most colorful of the minor-party movements are usually woefully lacking in any continuous, year-round organizational substructure at the precinct and congressional district level.

In a third and quite different category are the well-organized and much longer-lived minor parties that have been important factors in individual states during different phases of their political history. In years gone by, the Minnesota Farmer-Labor party and the Wisconsin Progressive party were the most important parties to oppose the local Republicans in their states. Like the larger national, episodic dissident party movements, the Minnesota and Wisconsin minor parties pointed to the incapacity of the state Republican organizations to maintain party unity within their states' borders. But their success also reflected the unwillingness of the dissidents to work through the Democratic party in their states.

In this respect, these Minnesota and Wisconsin state minor parties resembled the national secessionist parties. They also exhibited a partial kinship with the national parties of economic protest.

11. Lubell, *op. cit.*, p. 205.

Nevertheless, their persistent electoral and organizational strength at the county and precinct level, coupled with the localization of that strength within the borders of an individual state, differentiates them sharply from the episodic regional or national parties of secession and economic protest.

During the 1930's, both the Minnesota Farmer-Labor party and the Wisconsin Progressive party were so strong in their areas that they could win even the supreme political prize in the state, the governorship, without benefit of an alliance with any other party. Other state minor parties, however, have had more modest objectives, and more modest support among the electorates to which they appeal. Parties such as the American Labor party and the Liberal party in New York have often allied themselves with one of the major parties, and sometimes the votes cast on the Liberal or the American Labor party line have meant the difference between victory or defeat for the major-party candidates concerned. But before they agree to make common cause against the enemy, these minor parties are likely to try to extract concessions from their major-party allies on both candidates and policies at the state, congressional, and local levels. The Liberal party, and, when it was a potent force in the Empire State's politics, the American Labor party have usually not tried to elect candidates by themselves. But, like the Minnesota and Wisconsin parties with more ambitious objectives, these state minor parties find that their effectiveness is greatly enhanced by maintaining an organization year-in and year-out, from precinct committeemen to state chairman.

Marxist, or doctrinal parties constitute still a fourth type of minor party which may appear on American ballots on election day. Both the theoretical underpinnings and the events that first gave rise to most doctrinal party activity were of European origin; and, except on rare occasions, the vote totals amassed in the United States by the Socialist Workers party, the Communist party, the Socialist Labor party, or even by the Socialist party have not been impressive. Yet, if their impact on the course of events has been slight, doctrinal parties have, in the past at least, contrived to place candidates on the ballot fairly regularly in many parts of the country. In a more fundamental sense, however, these parties exist outside the American party system. Even the most severe domestic crises have seldom resulted in many lasting conversions of American voters to the ranks of the nation's doctrinal parties.

Parties of economic protest and secessionist parties that spring to prominence intermittently, and state minor parties and doctrinal parties whose electoral activity is less sporadic have all run candidates for national office.[12] In addition, still another type of candidate unaffiliated with either major party, the independent, may appear on the ballot in individual House districts. The burden of the argument thus far is that the number of popular votes cast for these third-party presidential candidates and for minor-party House aspirants are often vastly unequal. In the presidential elections since 1920, the third-party House vote has varied from 22 per cent to 525 per cent of the minor-party presidential vote. The comparable figures for the major-party congressional and presidential totals are 92 per cent to 107 per cent.

One of the principal reasons for this discrepancy is that individual minor parties differ sharply in their relative ability to poll votes for President and for Congressman. Some types of third-party movements, in short, tend to draw the bulk of their support at the presidential level, leaving the balloting for Representatives relatively untouched. Others attain their greatest impact on the national party system in the races for Congress. Yet though they may defeat both the Republican and the Democratic nominees for the House in an occasional congressional district, their drawing power in the presidential contest is negligible. And the discrepancy between the minor-party popular vote totals for President and for Congressman varies according to whether one type of minor-party movement or another type is more successful. By examining the impact of these different types of minor-party movements on the balloting both for President and for Congressman—and not just their showing in presidential elections alone, a fuller picture of the nature and function of minor-party movements in the American political system can be obtained.

12. Throughout this section dealing with the general nature of American third-party movements, I have drawn heavily on the treatment of minor parties by Professor V. O. Key. See V. O. Key, Jr., *Politics, Parties, and Pressure Groups*, Fifth Edition (New York: Thomas Y. Crowell, 1964), Ch. 10.

Types of Minor-Party Movements and their Impact on the Presidency and the Congress

IN AT LEAST 72 districts that had split election results between 1920 and 1964, candidates put up by the major parties were defeated

Table 5.3—Congressional Districts with Split Election Results Which Were Carried by a Minor-Party Candidate and the Type of Minor-Party Movement Whose Candidate Was Successful, 1920–1964[a]

Type of Minor Party	Districts Carried for Congressman but not for President	Districts Carried for President but not for Congressman
I. Episodic Parties of Economic Protest	None	Wisconsin 2, 3, 6–11. North Dakota 2, 3. California 2. (La Follette in 1924[b]).
II. Episodic Secessionist Parties	None	Alabama 1–9. Louisiana 1–8. Mississippi 1–7. South Carolina 1–6. Tennessee 10. (Thurmond in 1948[c]). South Carolina 1, 2. (Byrd in 1956[d]). Mississippi 3–5. (Unpledged Democratic electors in 1960[e]).
III. Persistent State Minor Parties	Minnesota 8. (Farmer-Labor in 1924). Minnesota 7. (Farmer-Labor in 1928). Minnesota: 5 seats at Large (Farmer-Labor in 1932). Minnesota 7–9. (Farmer-Labor in 1936). Wisconsin 1–3, 7–10. (Progressive in 1936). Wisconsin 2, 9, 10. (Progressive in 1940). Minnesota 9. (Farmer-Labor in 1940). Wisconsin 9. (Progressive in 1944). New York 18. (American Labor party in 1948).	None

| IV. Persistent Doctrinal Parties | None | None |

| V. Independent Candidacies Limited to One District | Tennessee 5. (J. Percy Priest in 1940). Ohio 9. (Frazier Reams in 1952). | None |

ᵃ The data in this table cover all districts for which presidential figures are available from 1920 to 1964. Districts for which no presidential figures are available are excluded from the analysis. Socialist Congressmen were elected in districts for which the presidential returns are missing in New York City and Milwaukee during the 1920's.

ᵇ La Follette ran as an Independent Progressive in Wisconsin, a Nonpartisan in North Dakota, and a Socialist in California.

ᶜ Thurmond ran as the Democratic presidential nominee in Alabama, Louisiana, Mississippi, and South Carolina. He appeared as the States' Rights party candidate in Tennessee.

ᵈ Senator Harry F. Byrd was an Independent write-in candidate in South Carolina.

ᵉ After the election the unpledged Democratic electors in Mississippi agreed to support Senator Harry F. Byrd.

either by a minor-party presidential nominee or by a third-party or independent House candidate. Table 5.3 lists the types of dissident party movements to which these candidates belonged and indicates which types were more successful in winning individual districts for President or for Congressman. By a close reading of the table, one can bring into focus the relative impact of the major types of American third-party movements on the Presidency and on the Congress.

In 1924, 1948, 1956, and 1960, parties of economic protest and secessionist parties carried some 47 districts for President. In all these districts, however, Republican or Democratic congressional candidates were elected on the same day.[13] These successes by minor-party presidential movements have clearly been episodic. In four elections over a 44-year period they generated enough support to outpoll the major-party presidential candidates in several House districts. In the eight other presidential elections between 1920 and 1964, however, not a single district returned a plurality for a minor-party presidential nominee.

The success of third-party and independent movements in elect-

13. In addition to the 47 districts with split election results which were carried by a third-party presidential nominee and are listed in Table 5.3, two districts not included in the table were also carried by a minor-party presidential movement between 1920 and 1964. The districts in question were won by Senator La Follette in 1924. Both, however, were also carried by minor-party House candidates closely associated with the Wisconsin Senator's presidential candidacy.

ing an occasional Representative, by contrast, has been more consistent—although the number of successful minor-party candidacies has varied from year to year. Between 1924 and 1952, at least one third-party or independent Congressman was elected in every presidential election year. The likelihood that one of these minor-party candidates would win depended, in part, on the magnitude of the wave of economic protest which was sweeping the nation. Thus, the number of successful minor-party congressional aspirants rose from one in the boom year of 1928 to a peak of ten in the depression year of 1936.[14] By 1944, third-party representation in the House had shrunk once again to a solitary Congressman. Even in good times, however, an occasional minor-party or independent nominee has been able to best his major-party opponents in contests within an individual House district.

There is also a clear-cut difference between the type of third-party candidates who have carried districts for President and the type of minor-party movements that have succeeded in electing House members (Table 5.3). Secessionist and economic protest parties have enjoyed their greatest success in carrying districts for President. State minor-party and independent candidates, on the other hand, have been most successful in the contests for Representative. In districts covered by the data in Table 5.3, victory eluded the candidates of the doctrinal parties at both the presidential and the congressional level.

This contrast can be pushed further. Both secessionist parties and parties of economic protest, as has been noted, spring into being periodically, but then usually disintegrate almost as spontaneously as they originated. And, although in the Populist uprising in the 1890's, some economic protest party House candidates were elected, in the 20th century they have been notoriously weak at the congressional level. Between 1920 and 1964, the dramatic, episodic third-party movements that carried a substantial number of House districts for President did not elect a single Congressman.

This differential impact on the Presidency and on the Congress

14. In 1936 three third-party or independent House candidates also won in districts for which no presidential returns are available and hence not covered by the data in Table 5.3. The actual total number of minor-party or independent Representatives elected in 1936 was 13.

is also reflected in the number of popular votes polled by secessionist and economic protest parties for President and Congressmen throughout the country. The bar graphs in Figure 5.3 underscore a marked discrepancy between the number of presidential and congressional votes attracted by three of the most conspicuous third-party movements of this type—the La Follette and the Wallace

Figure 5.3—Popular votes polled for President and for Representative by the La Follette Progressive, the Thurmond States' Rights, and the Wallace Progressive Third-Party Movements, 1924 and 1948[a]

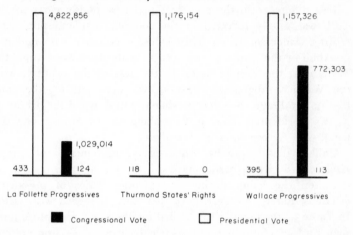

La Follette Progressives   Thurmond States' Rights   Wallace Progressives

■ Congressional Vote   □ Presidential Vote

[a] The figures immediately above the base lines indicate the number of districts in which the parties ran candidates for President and for Congressman.

Progressives, and the Thurmond States' Righters. In 1924, the vote for minor-party House candidates associated with La Follette's campaign was about a fifth as large as the Wisconsin Senator's presidential poll. In the 1948 returns, no States' Rights congressional votes were reported to match the more than one million votes polled by J. Strom Thurmond for President.

The showing made by Henry Wallace's Progressive movement in 1948 was somewhat different. As the data in the right-hand section of Figure 5.3 indicate, the movement's congressional vote was two thirds the size of Wallace's presidential total. But the lion's share of the House votes was contributed by one of the established state minor parties that associated itself with Wallace's third-party presidential bid. In New York State, both Wallace and the House nominees allied with his candidacy appeared as the candidates of the American Labor party. Although now defunct, in 1948 the ALP had been fighting elections continuously for more than a decade and had a well-developed organization in several parts of the state, particularly New York City. In contrast with the situation in most other states, the Progressive movement in the Empire State was not merely the result of several months of improvised and hurried organization.

This difference in the organizational base of the party in New York was amply reflected in the congressional and presidential returns. American Labor party House candidates, who ran in all but nine of the state's 45 districts, actually drew more votes than Wallace in the Empire State. In the rest of the country, where the Wallace Progressive organizations were put together more hastily, the Progressives' congressional poll dragged far behind the party's presidential showing (with about 260,000 House votes compared with 647,000 votes for President).[15]

Unlike these episodic minor-party movements of protest, America's doctrinal parties have diligently sought to place candidates on the ballot during an extended series of presidential elections. Rarely, however, have they been rewarded with victory. In Table 5.4 the popular vote polled for President and for Congressman by four of the nation's doctrinal parties since 1920 are compared. Most of these parties failed to run enough House candidates to give much meaning to comparisons between the presidential and congressional totals. Nevertheless, the showing made by the Socialist party, which once made a determined effort to put congressional candidates on the ballot, merits closer scrutiny.

In the days when the Socialist vote was considerable, the ratio of House votes to presidential votes polled by the party was much higher than similar ratios for secessionist parties and parties of

15. Most of the congressional votes that the Progressives received outside New York came from California. There many of the votes were cast in congressional districts where one of the major parties failed to run a candidate for the House. The odds are that if the voters in those districts had had the opportunity to vote for a major-party House nominee of their choice, the Progressive congressional vote outside New York would have been even smaller.

Table 5.4—A Comparison of the Presidential and Congressional Vote Polled by Candidates of the Socialist, Prohibition, Communist, and Socialist Labor Parties, 1920–1964

Party and Year[a]	Total House Vote	Total Presidential Vote	Party's House Vote as a Percentage of Its Presidential Vote	Number of Districts Contested for Congressman
Socialist				
1956	1,743	846	206.0	2
1936	172,504	187,720	91.9	136
1920	637,961	897,704	71.1	199
1928	187,578	267,420	70.1	83
1932	487,506	884,781	55.1	164
1944	28,294	79,010	35.8	34
1952	4,892	19,685	24.9	4
1940	19,782	99,557	19.9	30
1948	20,473	139,588	14.7	42
1960	2,350	0	—	1
Prohibition				
1940	62,504	57,812	108.1	47
1928	15,044	20,106	74.8	20
1932	53,194	81,869	65.0	22
1952	38,664	72,769	53.1	51
1924	29,885	57,520	52.0	15
1944	35,782	74,758	47.9	50
1920	66,527	182,711	36.4	33
1948	32,648	103,718	31.5	43
1936	11,568	37,847	30.6	19
1956	12,298	41,937	29.3	20
1960	6,548	46,203	14.2	25
1964	734	23,267	3.2	1
Communist				
1940	95,173	46,251	205.8	50
1936	100,998	80,159	126.0	72
1932	57,274	102,991	55.6	75
1924	2,702	36,386	12.1	9
1928	4,404	48,770	5.5	14
Socialist Labor				
1940	6,403	9,458	67.7	12
1928	8,689	21,603	40.2	7
1920	11,192	31,084	36.0	7
1924	12,666	36,428	34.8	9
1932	4,238	33,276	12.7	7
1936	1,303	12,777	10.2	16
1956	2,217	41,159	5.4	5
1944	340	45,189	0.8	7
1952	177	30,376	0.6	1
1948	48	29,189	0.2	3
1960	5,816	47,522	12.2	3
1964	1,476	45,186	3.3	5

[a] In instances where presidential years between 1920 and 1964 are omitted, there was no presidential or House vote for the indicated minor party in that year.

economic protest. Before 1940, Socialist House candidates throughout the country polled upwards of two thirds of the total Socialist presidential vote. Even this ratio, like the ratio between congressional and presidential popular votes for most minor parties, was affected by the fact that Socialist presidential candidates appeared in more districts than did Socialist House nominees. In several states where the party ran a full congressional slate, the amount of straight-ticket voting at the national level by Socialist voters approached, if it did not exceed, the party loyalty of the major parties' supporters. In New York in 1920, for example, the Socialist House vote was 107 per cent of the party's state presidential poll. In 1928 it was 97 per cent.[16] This showing was probably related to the fact that, in the past, at least, the Socialist party has had considerable organizational strength at the precinct, township, ward, and county level in a few areas of the country.

In districts for which presidential returns are available between 1920 and 1964, not a single doctrinal party candidate was successful. In 1920 and 1924, however, Socialists did elect Representatives in two big-city districts not covered by the data in Table 5.3. They were Meyer London in New York's 12th District in 1920 and Victor L. Berger, from the Wisconsin 5th District in Milwaukee in 1924. In 1924, Fiorello La Guardia, running on the Socialist and the Progressive tickets in a three-way race with a Republican and a Democrat in New York's 20th District also was elected; but his victory almost certainly stemmed in part from his strong personal following among his constituents.[17]

16. The Socialist congressional vote in New York state in 1920 was 217,766. The party's state presidential total was 203,201. Similar figures for 1928 were 103,700 and 107,332.

17. In 1922, when La Guardia ran for the House as a Republican, the Socialist congressional vote in the New York 20th District was 24.2 per cent of the total. When, two years later, La Guardia ran as the Socialist and Progressive nominee, the vote for the Socialist-endorsed candidate jumped to 43.0 per cent in a three-way fight with the Democratic and Republican contenders. In 1926, when La Guardia again ran as a Republican (again with Progressive party endorsement), the Socialist congressional vote in the district dropped to 5.5 per cent. Berger was elected in a straight fight with a Republican and London won a straight fight with a Democrat. Nevertheless, the success of all three of these minor-party candidates was based on substantial third-party congressional strength which had manifested itself persistently in their districts for a number of years before 1920 and 1924.

The most significant of the doctrinal parties once polled votes in almost equal measure for its presidential and congressional tickets. The performance of state minor parties in House elections, by contrast, has far outstripped their showing for President. In the districts with split election results listed in Table 5.3, 23 of the 25 House candidates who were elected without benefit of a major-party nomination ran on the tickets of parties that had considerable strength in their own states. All 23 represented parties which had put candidates on the ballot over a number of years, and all but one were the nominees of either the Farmer-Labor party in Minnesota or the Progressive party in Wisconsin.

In their heyday, the Farmer-Labor party and the Progressive party had such strong local and state organizations that they enjoyed a kind of major-party status for most elections in Minnesota and Wisconsin. The other state minor-party congressional success, that of Representative Vito Marcantonio on the American Labor party ticket in New York in 1948, was of a slightly different order. The ALP was never so strong in the Empire State as the Farmer-Labor and Progressive parties once were in Minnesota and Wisconsin, and Marcantonio's 1948 campaign was undoubtedly helped by the fact that he was an incumbent. (He had been elected two years earlier when he secured both the ALP and the Democratic party nominations.) Still, to Representative Marcantonio's personal following in the district, the ALP was able to contribute the considerable organizational strength in the New York 18th that it had built up over the years.

Yet all of the state parties which elected an occasional Congressman and had a strong organizational base in their own localities produced very few presidential votes. Except in 1948 when the ALP rode the crest of the Wallace secessionist movement, the presidential showing made by these parties independently has been infinitesimally small. The more robust of the state minor parties sometimes have not even bothered to run a candidate for the nation's highest office. The smaller minor parties, like the Liberals and the ALP in New York, have usually endorsed one of the major-party presidential nominees. Yet, whatever their tactics, the discrepancy between their impact on the Presidency and on the

Congress has been enormous. In 1936 the Wisconsin and Minnesota state minor parties polled over 900,000 votes for their congressional tickets. In the same election, no Farmer-Labor or Progressive party presidential votes were reported.

In the mythology of American politics much is made of the virtues of being an independent. Yet in the contests for President and for Congressman in individual House districts, independents almost never win. As has already been noted, fundamentally the independent or unpledged presidential electors slates that have been on the ballot in some southern states in recent elections appear to resemble the secessionist minor-party movements that have erupted periodically in the past. For the most part they have been spearheaded by political leaders who run as Democrats at the state and local level but who are unwilling to support the national Democratic presidential nominee.[18] The maximum number of House districts they have carried is three, in 1960. Would-be independent Congressmen, on the other hand, have an easier time getting on the ballot in many states, and every presidential year a few of them make the race. Most of them, however, poll a negligible vote. In the 12 presidential election years between 1920 and 1964, only two such candidacies were successful (Table 5.3).

In 1938, Joseph W. Byrns, Jr., was elected Representative from the 5th District in Tennessee, an overwhelmingly Democratic constituency which included the city of Nashville. To win, however, Mr. Byrns first had to enter the Democratic primary to defeat the man who had been elected shortly before to fill the vacancy

18. Conceivably this could change, if the G.O.P. succeeds in establishing a base of support in national elections in southern districts where traditionally preoccupation with the race issue has been strongest. In an election in which neither the Democratic nor the Republican presidential nominee espoused views on race relations that were satisfactory to southern segregationists, support might be generated for third-party or unpledged presidential electors in those areas that would siphon off votes from both the Republican and the Democratic parties. Such a development would be basically an expression of dissatisfaction with both national parties, not solely a temporary secession from the Democratic party. Yet in future years, as a growing number of Negroes, backed by the sanction of federal law, are able to vote in those areas, a powerful counterforce will be introduced that may tend to pull them back into the orbit of the major parties.

caused by the death of Mr. Byrns' father, a former Speaker of the House. Some onlookers at the time were unkind enough to suggest that the younger Byrns won in 1938 largely because he bore his father's name.

During his first term in office, the new Congressman's popularity suffered a jolt when he made a widely quoted remark that the King and Queen of England, who paid a state visit to Washington in June, 1939, were "just a couple of flat tires." Some observers felt that the undignified offhand statement alienated a considerable number of voters, while others pointed to a general feeling in the district that young Byrns would never be able to fill his father's shoes. In any event, the freshman Congressman faced determined opposition in the 1940 Democratic primary. Fortunately for him, however, his detractors' votes were divided between two fairly strong opponents, and once again he won the Democratic party nomination which in his section of Tennessee should have been tantamount to election.

At this point a new issue was injected into the campaign. After the primary, but well before the general election, Byrns voted to delay the application of the Selective Service Act, a move that brought a new outburst of protest among his constituents. Among his strongest critics was J. Percy Priest, an editorial writer for the *Nashville Tennessean,* the most influential newspaper in the district. Shortly thereafter, the editor of one of the smaller papers in the county persuaded Priest, who had not previously been active in politics and who was not even a registered voter, to stand as an independent candidate for the House.

There followed a lively contest. Priest, who had powerful newspaper backing, also turned out to be an effective campaigner. Although he was new to politics he was not unknown. For years he had been a reporter of religious events, and in that lay capacity he had prayed eloquently in practically every church in the district. Although Byrns' two primary opponents professed to support the official party nominee, some observers felt that they threw what strength they could to Priest. Throughout the campaign, the activity of the southern district's few Republicans was of little consequence. On election day, Priest, the independent, won with 3,600 votes to spare.[19] By the next election, however, he saw fit to call himself a Democrat, and eventually he became one of the party's Whips in the House.

Representative Priest won in an overwhelmingly one-party district. In 1952, Frazier Reams, an independent Congressman from the Ohio 9th, won reelection in a constituency where the two major parties normally battled on fairly even terms, although the Democrats usually had the edge. Reams was first elected in 1950, when he charged that the incumbent Democratic representative was a "tool" of Robert T. Grosser, a vice-president of the C.I.O. United Automobile Workers and said to be a "controversial figure" in the Toledo area. But Reams also attacked his Republican opponent, who he asserted had been "nothing more than a cipher" when he was in the House in 1947 and 1948.[20]

In days gone by, Reams had been at least a nominal Democrat. He was the Ohio campaign director for Franklin Roosevelt in 1936 and the State Welfare Director in Governor Frank J. Lausche's Democratic Administration. Both in 1950 and in 1952, he endeavored to present himself to the Toledo electorate as something between a Republican and a left-wing Democrat. But his "main advantage," according to a reporter who covered one of his campaigns, was the voters' memories of him as a courageous and independent Public Prosecutor who had opposed a threat of gang rule in Toledo in the 1930's. As Public Prosecutor, Reams played a major role in sending four gangsters to the electric chair and sending the leader of the movement to the penitentiary for life.[21] In any event, through some combination of personal or policy appeals Reams was able to win again in 1952. In defeating both his Democratic and Republican opponents he polled 40.9 per cent of the district's total House vote. Two years later, however, a new and reportedly strong Democratic nominee defeated him in a three-way race.

---

19. The 1940 congressional vote in the Tennessee 5th was: J. Percy Priest, Independent 24,565; Joseph W. Byrns, Jr., Democratic 20,933; and Julian H. Campbell, Republican 3,459. This account of the 1940 campaign in the Tennessee 5th District is based largely on materials contained in Professor V. O. Key's Election Files.
20. *The Cleveland Plain Dealer*, November 9, 1950, p. 1.
21. *The New York Times*, October 17, 1954, p. 63.

Mr. Reams and Mr. Priest were both successful independent nominees. Yet every presidential year other independents who do not get elected poll at least a few popular votes. In their general impact on the Presidency and on the Congress, independent candidacies differ from secessionist and economic protest parties in two important respects. Independents occasionally win districts for Congressman but seldom for President. Moreover, while their vote totals in individual districts become important only sporadically, they persistently enter some of the House contests in every election year. This persistence is reflected in Figure 5.4: the share of the total vote going to independent House nominees has fluctuated less than the popular vote for any other type of minor-party candidates since World War I.

Figure 5.4—Percentage of the total congressional vote polled by Socialist, Independent, and State Minor Party congressional candidates, 1920–1964

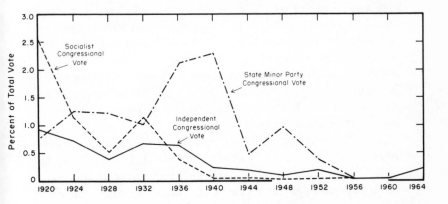

Independent nominees thus resemble the candidates of state minor parties in that their greatest impact on national elections is at the congressional level; but they differ from them in important respects. Their electoral strength, which manifests itself almost exclusively in the elections for Congressman, is concentrated even more completely at the congressional level than is that of the state minor parties. Their influence on House elections is also more dispersed than that of the state minor parties. Over the years, an occasional independent candidate has polled a respectable vote in most major sections of the country. And, although an unusual independent candidate may have a strong personal following and even the rudiments of a personal organization in his district, independent candidacies lack the ongoing organizational base that the important state minor-party movements have had.

Victories of state minor-party House candidates reflect nuances of local sentiment backed by strong local organizational resources. The success of independent House nominees, on the other hand, points to an outpouring of local feeling so strong that even an organization of the moment is sufficient to catapult the independent to victory. The convergence of the right issues and the right personalities is essential. But in a one-party district, such as the Tennessee 5th, the voters' extraordinary recourse to electing an independent may be fundamentally a temporary escape from one-partyism.

In a two-party district, like the Ohio 9th, an independent House victory is something else. It may be the electoral equivalent of the statement "A plague on both your houses" to the major parties. Sometimes the advent of an independent may even serve to give a district's voters a set of policy alternatives more like those offered in other parts of the country. Or it may denote support for a popular individual whose personal appeal is localized within an individual House district.

An escape from one-partyism, rejection of the policy alternatives offered by the major parties, the personal appeal of the independent, and, sometimes, the unattractiveness of the major-party nominees—all these can be the animating force underlying a successful independent candidacy. The point here, however, is that the determinants of cleavage in House contests where the independent vote is large are different from those in the rest of the country. The voters in such districts usually divide differently for Congressman than for the presidential contest. At rock bottom, the election of an independent House member is a ringing assertion of the particularism of an individual congressional district. Perhaps the most important point of all is that there are so few of them.

Minor Parties, Split-Ticket Voting, and the Party System

THE FOREGOING DISCUSSION HAS rested on the assumption that minor-party movements in the United States have been of five broad types: parties of economic protest, secessionist parties, doctrinal parties, state minor parties, and independent candidacies for national office. Most of these political movements have the name "minor party" in common. Yet in many respects the characteristics that divide them are greater than those that unite them. Some third-party movements are regional or national in scope, while the electoral activity of others is confined to an individual state or district. Some possess an elaborate organizational substructure with strong roots at the precinct level; others have a party organization in name only. Some contest elections year in and year out, while others may enter a candidate in the presidential sweepstakes amid great fanfare and then never be heard from again. In addition, American third-party movements differ profoundly in their impact on the elections for President and for Representative. In Table 5.5 the principal characteristics and differences among minor-party movements are summarized.

This variation among third-party movements suggests that different types of minor parties play fundamentally different roles in the American party system. The doctrinal parties that poll votes for President and for Congress is almost equal measure, as has been noted, exist outside the party system. They will therefore be excluded from the subsequent discussion. Significantly, however, it is the dissident party movements which are but crosscurrents in the main stream of American political life that differ so markedly in their impact on the Presidency and the Congress.

A number of questions are prompted by this state of affairs. Why are not the periodic eruptions of substantial minor-party presidential strength paralleled by third-party House victories in the districts where the minor-party presidential tide is strongest? Why are state minor-party and independent movements unable to convert their demonstrated strength at the state and local level into votes for President? Why, in short, do third-party movements have a differential impact on the elections for President and on the contests for Representative? Fundamentally, the answers to

Table 5.5—Salient Characteristics of Minor-Party Movements in the United States and their Impact on the Presidency and the Congress, 1920–1964

Parties of Economic Protest	Episodic Regional or National Weak Organizational Substructure May Carry Districts for President Win No Congressional Seats Poll Many More Popular Votes for President than for Congressman
Secessionist Parties[a]	Episodic Regional or National Weak Organizational Substructure May Carry Districts for President Win No Congressional Seats Poll Many More Popular Votes for President than for Congressman
Doctrinal Parties	Persistent National Fairly Well Developed Organizational Substructure in Some Areas Seldom Carry Districts for President Rarely Win Congressional Seats Sometimes Poll as Many Popular Votes for Congressman as for President, although the Ratio between the Two Vote Totals Varies
State Minor Parties	Persistent Activity Confined to Individual States Well Developed Organizational Substructure Carry No Districts for President May Win Congressional Seats Poll Many More Popular Votes for Congressman than for President
Independent Candidacies	Persistent, although They Assume Importance in Individual Districts Only Sporadically Localized in Individual Districts Usually Weak Organizational Substructure Carry No Districts for President May Win Congressional Seats Poll Virtually All their Popular Votes for Congressman

[a] Secessionist parties include the unpledged presidential electors movements that have appeared in the South since World War II.

these queries seem to lie in the difference between the Presidency and the Congress, and between the nature of the presidential and congressional wings of the major parties which seek to control them.

The American Presidency is a unitary, not a plural, executive office. Individual presidential candidates, of course, sometimes try to straddle the fence on divisive issues. Yet, at bottom, each party's presidential ticket must present the same face in all sections of the country. The programs, policy statements, and the personality of each presidential nominee are the same everywhere—regardless of whether they are popular or unpopular in individual parts of the country. Moreover, each presidential candidate is nominated by his party's national convention, a body where the final decision is usually dominated by two fundamental aims: to select a man who will be a strong vote-getter; and to nominate a candidate who will maintain as much unity within the party as possible as he leads it into the fray.[22]

The ticket put into the field by each major party's congressional wing, by contrast, is of a fundamentally different order. In terms of the personal and policy appeals which each major-party House ticket may make to the electorate, the American Congress is the legislative equivalent of a plural executive. If the duties of legislating, like those of the executive, were to be formally entrusted to one person selected from the country at large, the electorate's response to the congressional campaign might come to resemble its response to the presidential contest. But manifestly they are not. A major-party congressional slate is composed of several hundred House candidates most of whom are nominated in local primaries in up to 435 individual districts. It can and does contain within it the widest variety of programs, policy stands, and personalities. A party's congressional ticket may thus take on a special political coloration in regions where the national presidential nominee is unappealing, as the local House candidates attune themselves more closely to the sentiment in their areas. Moreover, not only can a party's congressional ticket disagree with itself; once its members get to Washington some of them will fight even a President of their own party every day of the legislative session.

22. One must say that these objectives usually predominate in national conventions, but not always, after the Republican National Convention of 1964.

The expression of these differences between the major-party presidential and congressional tickets is facilitated by the fundamentally different ways in which candidates for the Presidency and the House are nominated. It is well known that in the national presidential nominating conventions the big-city states have a powerful, perhaps even a disproportionately powerful, voice. In the local primaries in individual districts which select the nation's House candidates, by contrast, a different coalition of political groups may be dominant. And it is also well known that for many years before the Supreme Court's ruling that House district boundary lines should, if necessary, be redrawn to make the districts substantially equal in population, the interests of the more populous and industrialized areas in the country tended to be underrepresented in the national legislature. In short, the selection of a presidential ticket by a national convention and the local determination of House candidates in a multiplicity of individual districts have been dominated by fundamentally different political forces.

Different political groups control part of a major party's presidential and congressional tickets. It follows that many voters who bolt one part of the national ticket will not be repelled by the other part of the national ticket. Samuel Lubell, when thinking primarily of the national presidential coalitions, compared the major party that controls the Presidency to a sun that is continually threatened with flying apart in response to the attractions of external bodies. Actually, the presidential and the congressional wing of which each major party is composed could be likened to two celestial bodies. Each struggles to maintain itself intact. And each may lose part of its substance through political fission generated by the attraction of external minor-party movements.

Usually the external elements that threaten to pull parts of the two suns away exert a greater strain on one of the celestial bodies than on the other. More than that, the substances which are broken away are usually different. Yet, because the two suns which together constitute the major-party ticket for President and Congressman are, withal, closely interconnected, strains on the viability of one elicit sympathetic tensions in the other. But now let us put this theory to the test of the facts by examining both the presidential and the congressional suns in turn.

The presidential candidate of a major party is the same throughout the country. Moreover, a coalition politics, which reconciles and balances interests in order to generate support for the party's presidential nominee in most regions of the country is necessary to elect him. At times, the two great coalitions that are fashioned together by the major-party nominating conventions contain such a broad general appeal that, between them, they embrace almost all segments of the electorate. In 1940 and in 1952, more than 99.5 per cent of all votes cast for President went to the regular Democratic and Republican presidential nominees.

At other times, however, political conditions change, and the coalitions upon which the major-party presidential wings are founded seem to be on the verge of flying apart. Perhaps new issues arise that are so intractable that they make the coalition no longer viable. Or perhaps one segment of the party struggling for control of its presidential wing may gain too complete a victory and drives other elements of the party away—at least temporarily. In any event, important segments of the party can, and sometimes do, become disaffected from its national presidential nominee.

The precise form which these presidential protest movements take may vary. But the objective of securing a President more congenial to the dissident voters' interests than are the regular major-party nominees remains the same. Some protest movements, like the States' Rights movement in 1948, may be motivated by the hope that by forcing the election of the President into the House they may secure the selection of a Chief Executive under more satisfactory conditions. Others, like the Wallace Progressive movement, may be supported by voters who wish to demonstrate to the leadership of the major party to which they normally adhere just how strong their dissatisfaction with the current course of party affairs is. Indeed, both motives—along with simple, uncalculating dislike of the major-party presidential selections—may play a role in the activity of third-party presidential movements. A few, like the Theodore Roosevelt campaign in 1912 and La Follette's candidacy in 1924, may even reflect a genuine effort to win control of the White House.

Whatever their objective, the support generated for these third-party presidential movements touches off a sympathetic reaction in those parts of the legislative ticket of the major party that are affected most directly, especially among House candidates who must run in districts where the dissident presidential movement is particularly strong. Major-party congressional candidates whose constituents are deserting their presidential running mate in droves to support a third-party presidential nominee can follow one of several courses of action. They can support the third-party presidential nominee who appeals so strongly to the voters in their district.[23] They can maintain a statesmanlike silence on the presidential contest, although before they sit on their hands they may endeavor to remain in the good graces of the national party leadership by going through the formality of endorsing their presidential running mate. Or they can work hard to persuade the voters in their district to support the party's entire national ticket.

A House candidate's appeals for party loyalty are likely to be loudest if the supporters of the third-party presidential movement also run a candidate against him. But, although individual third-party presidential movements differ considerably in the extent to which they are accompanied by nominees for Congress, the great majority of the nation's 435 congressional seats are left uncontested by the episodic minor parties that poll a sizable vote for President. In 1924, only 124 candidates associated with La Follette's presidential candidacy made the race for the national legislature. In 1948, the Progressives ran only 113 congressional candidates; and the States' Righters ran none.

The question that immediately arises, of course, is why. Doubtless the superiority of the organizational resources enjoyed by the major-party House nominees is one factor which limits the success of episodic third-party movements at the congressional level. The fact that 23 of the 25 successful minor-party House candidates analyzed earlier were nominees of state minor parties with strong local roots suggests something of the need for a firm organizational base in order to win contests for the House. Then, too, the major-party congressional candidates are likely to argue that in a House controlled by the major parties, they alone can get the choice

23. In 1948 a number of southern Democratic Congressmen supported Thurmond's States' Rights presidential bid. See Alexander Heard, *A Two-Party South?* (Chapel Hill: University of North Carolina Press, 1952), p. 24.

committee assignments and the full advantages of seniority that will benefit their district. But the success of the Minnesota and Wisconsin third-party candidates suggests that when third-party Congressmen have an organization on which they can rely at the next election, this argument need not be decisive. Organizational and electoral strength that is localized and persistent, in short, is exceedingly important in order for a candidate to win a House contest.

There may, however, be an even more fundamental reason why minor-party House candidates usually are not elected in districts carried by a third-party presidential nominee. The problem is most acute, of course, for the major party that is hardest hit by the dissident presidential candidate's appeal. Yet perhaps the local nominating process by which the party's House candidates are

Table 5.6—*Thurmond Strength in Southern Congressional Districts in 1948 and the Amount of Support for President Truman's Program Given in 1949 by Democratic Representatives Elected in those Districts*

Thurmond's District Percentage[a]	Number of Districts	Percentage Truman Support on 1949 Domestic Issues[b]
0.0–9.9%	28	51.9%
10.0–19.9	29	40.0
20.0–44.9	15	46.2
Over 45.0	30	24.1

[a] In districts where Thurmond polled over 45 per cent of the presidential vote, the South Carolina Governor was listed as the Democratic presidential nominee. While this undoubtedly gave Thurmond an advantage in those districts, it is equally true that in most of those districts sentiment for the States' Rights movement was stronger than anywhere else in the South.
[b] The index of Truman support used in this table is identical to that in Table 4.5.

selected works to ensure that they will be more representative of the sentiment in their districts than their presidential running mate. In districts where the third-party presidential nominee is particularly strong, the major-party congressional ticket may take on the political coloration of the minor-party presidential nominee. Indeed, the views of the major party's House aspirants in such districts may be closer to the views of the minor-party presidential nominee than they are to the policy pronouncements of their own party's presidential standard-bearer.

The election returns from the period of the States' Rights revolt in the South illustrate this tendency. In Table 5.6, southern congressional districts are grouped according to the percentage of the total presidential vote polled in them by Governor Thurmond in 1948. The bulk of the Thurmond strength came from voters who had normally supported the Democratic presidential nominee in earlier elections. By a glance at the table's second column, it is possible to determine the relative amount of support that Democratic Congressmen who were elected from House districts with varying degrees of Thurmond strength gave President Truman's program during the first session of the 81st Congress in 1949. The index of Truman support employed is the percentage of "correct" roll-call votes recorded by Representatives on domestic legislation in 1949, as seen by Americans for Democratic Action. In each instance a "correct" vote coincided with the stand taken by the Truman Administration.

There are irregularities in these data that point to the importance of other factors as well. But the broad outline of the pattern revealed by Table 5.6 is plain. Democratic Congressmen who represented southern districts where Thurmond's third-party presidential movement was weakest tended to support the program of the regular Democratic presidential nominee most frequently. The Democratic Representatives who were elected in the districts where the sentiment for Thurmond was strongest, by contrast, gave Truman by far the least support of the southern delegations to the House.

In sections of the country where greater competition between the two major parties prevails, the variation among the policies espoused by the different House nominees who make up a major-party congressional ticket is likely to be less pronounced. Nevertheless, the Democratic Congressmen who came from districts where Wallace ran well in 1948 were probably well to the left side of their party's representation in the House. The odds are, too, that most of the Republicans who were nominated in local congressional primaries in districts carried by La Follette in 1924 were sympathetic with the Wisconsin Senator's general aims and objectives. In districts where a minor-party presidential nominee and a major-party House candidate both win, the formal partisan cleavage may mask an identity in the policy objectives to which the two candidates subscribe. The interests of voters who bolt a major-party presidential ticket often find expression in the legislature through the party's regular congressional nominee. As a consequence, there is little motive force for a minor-party candidate for the House.

The ideological and personal components of the major-party congressional slates are thus usually broad enough to encompass the fissiparous tendencies which sometimes cause elements of the major-party presidential coalitions to break apart. But if so, why do voters ever desert the major-party House tickets? As has been noted, the dissident candidates who have been most effective in elections at the congressional level have been of two types. Some are nominees of minor parties with pronounced strength in individual states. Others are independent congressional candidates whose appeal is localized within the confines of an individual district. Perhaps here lies the clue to our puzzle. Successful minor-party candidates seem to be the expression of the peculiarities of the political situation in individual states and districts. They are not the result of political movements that are regional or national in scope. But just why the peculiarities of some states and districts, and not of others, should foster successful dissident House candidacies is by no means readily apparent.

The political activity of the state minor parties in New York, which usually have not run House candidates in most districts in the state, has already been described. Eventually the American Labor party began to run presidential candidates on its own. But by then it had undergone a metamorphosis into something like a doctrinal party, a body outside the fundamentally two-party American political system. Before that happened, significantly, both the ALP and the Liberal party always endorsed one of the major-party presidential nominees. Indeed, the ideological kinship between the ALP and the Democratic presidential nominee in 1936 and between the Liberal party and the Democratic presidential nominee in more recent elections were as close, if not closer, than the ties binding the Democratic party's presidential aspirant to the party's regular state political organization.

The activity of the Minnesota Farmer-Labor party and the Wisconsin Progressive party, which together polled hundreds of thousands of votes for minor-party Congressmen, also reflected the peculiarities of the local political situation in those states. In both states, the local Democrats were woefully weak. Yet through the social structure of both states ran a strong strand of dissent from the more conservative brand of Republicanism. In reality, minor-party House candidates represented the major policy alternative to the Republican party in those states in the days when the state parties were strongest.

Nevertheless, the electoral votes of these two states alone could not begin to elect a President, and virtually no votes for President were cast on the Farmer-Labor and Progressive lines in 1936. But if the argument thus far is valid, voters who were repelled by the major-party House candidates should tend to support the major-party presidential nominee whose views most closely paralleled those of their minor-party Congressmen. With this hunch in mind, the 1936 presidential and congressional returns in Minnesota should be examined. The relevant data appear in Table 5.7.

Table 5.7—Popular Votes for the Democratic Presidential Nominee and the Party Affiliation of the Winner of the House Contest in Individual Districts in Minnesota in 1936

District	District's Democratic Presidential Percentage	Party of Winning House Nominee	Farmer-Labor Party Share of Total House Vote[a]
Minn. 8	75.6%	F–L	56.4%
Minn. 4	73.9	R	38.8
Minn. 9	69.2	F–L	48.4
Minn. 7	65.4	F–L	49.7
Minn. 2	64.5	D	32.5
Minn. 6	64.1	R	39.6
Minn. 1	59.1	R	27.6

[a] The Farmer-Labor candidate in the 8th District had a straight fight with a Republican. The other percentages in this column denote the Farmer-Labor party candidate's share of the three-party congressional vote.

The relationship between the 1936 presidential and congressional balloting in Minnesota was exceedingly complicated. In some districts the Democratic congressional organization was a force to be reckoned with. In other districts the votes cast for Democratic House candidates were of distinctly subsidiary importance. The chances are, moreover, that most congressional votes that went to

Democrats in 1936 would have gone to the Farmer-Laborite in a straight fight with a Republican. The variation in the Democratic House strength thus strongly influenced the number of votes polled by the Farmer-Labor nominee.

Despite these complexities, however, the general pattern revealed by Table 5.7 is suggestive. Farmer-Labor House candidates won in districts where Franklin Roosevelt made his best showing in 1936. The three minor-party candidates who were elected all ran in one of Roosevelt's four top districts in Minnesota. On the other hand, in the two districts where the Democratic President's margin was the smallest, Republican Congressmen were elected. The one Republican to win in a banner Roosevelt district, the Minnesota 4th (Saint Paul), was a well-entrenched incumbent. The Republican there also may have benefited from the second largest Democratic House vote in the state—22.8 per cent. This fairly strong showing by the Democrat in a three way race probably cost the Farmer-Laborite a substantial number of votes. As it was, the third-party nominee lost by only 350 votes out of 126,327 cast.

If the votes polled for state minor-party House candidates reflect the peculiarities of the state political situation, the victories of independent congressional nominees signify the triumph of factors unique to an individual district. Sometimes, tickets which are split to support an independent nominee and a major-party presidential candidate point to a partisan divergence which masks an ideological convergence. More often, however, they denote the saliency of an issue or a personality in a district which is so important that it divides the electorate in a way fundamentally different from the presidential contest. House elections won by independents, in short, are the most extreme type of localism in congressional elections. Perforce, they attract voters from a major-party House ticket who remain steadfast in their loyalty to the party's presidential ticket.

By now, however, the reason why most American minor-party movements have a differential impact on the Presidency and Congress should be clear. Perhaps the greatest cause for wonder is that the major-party suns hold together as well as they do. At bottom, the presidential wing of a major party usually maintains itself intact because in most presidential years the national nominating convention selects a candidate who will hold as much of the party together as possible. The national party congressional ticket, on the other hand, maintains its viability because it contains within it all the differences and conflicts which the presidential nominating convention seeks to reconcile and to bring into balance.

Precisely how many third-party supporters have split their ticket at the national level will never be known. Nevertheless, the difference between each minor party's presidential and congressional

Table 5.8—Split-Ticket Votes Cast for President and Congressman Where a Third-Party Candidate Was Involved: An Estimate for the Elections Held between 1920 and 1964

Year	Total Number of Votes for President	Estimated Number of Split-Ticket Voters Who Supported a Third-Party Candidate[a]	Per Cent
1920	26,746,878	781,479	2.9%
1924	29,090,926	4,002,859	13.8
1928	36,772,922	541,554	1.5
1932	39,747,349	1,264,542	3.2
1936	45,647,117	2,108,209	4.6
1940	49,815,312	1,299,021	2.6
1944	47,974,868	630,672	1.3
1948	48,794,009	1,863,707	3.8
1952	61,551,919	672,008	1.1
1956	62,027,040	452,528	0.7
1960	68,836,385	690,701	1.0
1964	70,642,496	575,804	0.8
Total	587,647,221	14,883,084	2.5

[a] Estimates of the number of third-party voters who split their ticket for President and Representative were made by finding the difference between the number of votes cast for presidential and House candidates of the same minor party within each state. Thus, if there were 10,000 Socialist presidential votes in a state and 5,000 Socialist House votes in that state, the estimated number of split-ticket voters in the state who supported a third-party candidate would be 5,000. These estimates are only approximate: no effort has been made to account for voters who may have voted for President but not for Congressman, and *vice versa*; and no attempt has been made to measure the discrepancy between the minor-party presidential and House vote totals within individual House districts (largely because detailed presidential figures for minor parties within each House district are not available before 1952). Compared with the estimates that appear in this table, comparisons of the minor-party vote totals within individual House districts would lead to somewhat larger estimates of the amount of ticket-splitting associated with third-party candidacies.

popular-vote totals in individual elections affords a rough indication of the amount of split-ticket voting associated with minor-party candidacies. This method of estimating the total number of minor-party votes that have been split-ticket votes is a crude one. It assumes that when a minor party ran a candidate both for President and for the House, every voter who supported the minor-party nominee who polled the smaller vote in a district also voted for his running mate. It also fails to make allowance for citizens who voted for President, and not for Congressman, or *vice versa*. Yet even an estimate based on assumptions as crude as these helps to bring into perspective the amount of ticket-splitting associated with third-party candidacies.

As the data in Table 5.8 suggest, split-ticket voting of this type fluctuated widely between 1920 and 1964. In 1924, between an eighth and a seventh of the electorate split their ticket to support a minor-party nominee. In 1956, fewer than one voter in 100 did. Nevertheless, in the 44-year period as a whole, roughly 2.5 per cent of the people voting have split their ballot to support a minor-party candidate for national office. Such is the substantial contribution made by third-party movements to split-ticket voting in the United States.

CHAPTER 6

The Impact of the Electoral System on the Presidency and Congress

Among people who concern themselves with the nature of political systems as a whole, the relationship between formal institutional arrangements and the way citizens behave in political situations has long been a topic for speculation and analysis. Yet probably few American voters realize the extent to which their electoral system affects subtly but pervasively the way in which they express their preferences at the polls. The various formal arrangements for the conduct of elections that prevail in different states are so easily taken for granted that their consequences for the nation's political life may well be overlooked. Nevertheless, these consequences can be profoundly important. In the pages that follow, attention will be focused on two institutional factors that may affect the outcome of congressional elections: the form of the ballot, and the type of constituencies in which House candidates are selected.

The Form of the Ballot and Contests for President and Congressman

THE AMERICAN STATES DIFFER significantly in the extent to which the form of the ballot employed within their jurisdiction facilitates straight-ticket voting. In some states, a single mark of the ballot paper or one tug of a voting machine's party lever is all that is required for a citizen to cast a straight-ticket vote for every office up for consideration. In other states, where no party circle or party lever is available, the voter must register his choice of candidates for each office separately.

Politicians often operate on the assumption that the form of the ballot makes a difference in the ratio between straight-ticket and split-ticket voting in their constituency. In Ohio in 1949, for example, friends of Republican Senator Robert A. Taft spent over $85,000 in successfully backing an initiated proposal to substitute a multiple-choice ballot for the single-choice form. Otherwise, it was feared, Governor Frank Lausche, a popular Democratic candidate, would have strengthened his party's entire ticket by inducing some voters who wished to support him to take a short cut by voting straight Democratic. After his 1950 victory, Senator Taft guessed that the new ballot was responsible "for something between 100,000 and 200,000" of his total majority of 430,000.[1]

Senator Taft's friends were anxious to insulate the Ohio senatorial campaign from the outcome of the gubernatorial contest. The question of interest here is whether the fate of House candidates is more closely linked to the outcome of the presidential battle in districts where the form of the ballot facilitates straight-ticket voting than it is in multiple-choice districts. To be sure, a host of other factors may have a greater bearing than the form of the ballot on the amount of ticket-splitting in a House district. Sometimes the party regularity of citizens who vote for President and for Congressman in districts where a multiple-choice ballot form is used appears to be very strong indeed. In Nebraska in 1952, for example, the discrepancy, or spread, between the percentage of the two-party vote going to the congressional and presidential candidates of the same party was 2.2 per cent or smaller in all of the state's four districts. In two of the districts, less than one percentage point separated the presidential and House candidates of the same party.

On the other hand, in some states which have consistently used

1. V. O. Key, Jr., *Politics, Parties, and Pressure Groups*, Fifth Edition (New York: Thomas Y. Crowell Company, 1964), pp. 642–644.

ballots and voting machines with a party circle or a party lever, there has sometimes been extensive split-ticket voting. Even so, there still may be a general tendency for a larger proportion of the electorate to split their ballot in districts where no provision for voting a straight ticket with one motion has been made. By using data drawn from the nine presidential elections between 1932 and 1964, this conjecture can be tested against the facts.[2]

Split-ticket voting is sometimes reflected in districts with split election results—where the voters' selectivity has its maximum

Table 6.1—House Districts in the North with Split Election Results and the Form of the Ballot, 1932–1964[a]

| | SINGLE-CHOICE DISTRICTS | | | MULTIPLE-CHOICE DISTRICTS | | |
	No. of Districts	No. of Split Election Results	Per Cent	No. of Districts	No. of Split Election Results	Per Cent
1932	166	23	13.9	86	25	29.1
1936	173	24	13.9	85	26	30.6
1940	155	24	15.5	104	25	24.0
1944	152	19	12.5	109	21	19.3
1948	159	25	15.7	155	33	21.3
1952	135	20	14.8	191	31	16.2
1956	155	41	26.5	171	41	24.0
1960	125	28	22.4	194	49	25.2
1964	121	34	28.1	199	75	37.7
Total	1341	238	17.7	1294	326	25.2

[a] Between 1932 and 1964, a single-choice ballot form was used in House districts in the following states: Arizona, Connecticut, Illinois, Indiana, Iowa, Kentucky, Missouri, New Hampshire, New Mexico, Oklahoma, Pennsylvania, Rhode Island, Utah, Vermont, West Virginia, and Wisconsin. But in Indiana, Oklahoma, Vermont, and Wisconsin during part or all of this period, voters had a separate ballot or voting machine section to vote for President, even though they could vote for all other offices with a single "X" or lever. Results from these states when the separate presidential ballot or voting machine section was used were therefore included with the multiple-choice state results. Throughout the 1932–1964 period, a multiple-choice ballot form was used in California, Colorado, Kansas, Maryland, Massachusetts, Minnesota, Montana, Nebraska, Nevada, New Jersey, New York, North Dakota, Oregon, and Wyoming. In six northern states, the form of the ballot was changed at some point between 1932 and 1964. These states were: Delaware, Idaho, Michigan, Ohio, South Dakota, and Washington. Primary Source: Book of the States, Vols. 4–12 (Chicago: Council of State Governments, 1941–1958); and Congressional Quarterly Weekly Report, September 18, 1964, pp. 2173–2175. Districts in Maine for elections when the presidential and House elections were not held concurrently, and districts where one of the major parties failed to run a House candidate are excluded from the analysis.

2. The Republicans' weakness in most parts of the South during much of this period limits the usefulness of comparisons between the presidential and congressional returns from that region. Consequently in the analyses in Table 6.1 and 6.2, all southern districts are excluded. For the rest of the country, all districts for which presidential figures are available are included, save for the relatively few districts where one of the major parties failed to run a House candidate. The total number of district results analyzed is 2,635.

practical effect on relations between the President and Congress. Between 1932 and 1964 the proportion of nonsouthern House districts carried by presidential and House candidates of opposite parties was larger in multiple-choice districts than in single-choice districts in every presidential election year except 1956 (Table 6.1). Individual elections vary markedly, however, in the number of split election results in the two types of constituencies. In some elections, such as 1932 and 1936, the multiple-choice districts were more than twice as likely to return a mixed verdict than were districts where the electorate could vote a straight ticket with one motion. In other elections, however, the discrepancy between the proportion of split election results in the two groups of districts was not nearly so large. And in 1952 and 1956 split results were almost equally common in both types of districts.

During the 32-year period covered in Table 6.1 as a whole, however, split results were more common in the multiple-choice districts than in the single-choice districts. Between 1932 and 1964, about one in every six of the single-choice districts had split election results. In the multiple-choice districts, by contrast, a quarter of the election returns resulted in a partisan cleavage at the national level.

House districts with split election results indicate that some voters in those constituencies have split their ticket. But they afford only a very rough indication of the total amount of ticket-splitting that may have taken place among the electorate as a whole. In a district where the Republican House candidate polled 52 per cent of the vote while his presidential running mate received 68 per cent of the presidential poll, no split result would be recorded. Yet clearly a sizable proportion of the district's voters split their ticket.

A more precise indication of the amount of split-ticket voting in different presidential years between 1932 and 1964 is provided by Table 6.2. The data in this new table are based upon calculations of the discrepancy, or spread, between the percentage of the two-party presidential vote and the percentage of the two-party House vote polled by candidates of the same party in nonsouthern districts where there was a House contest between 1932 and 1964. The data are presented in terms of the proportion of districts in any given election year in which the spread was under 2.5 per cent, under 5 per cent, or over 10 per cent. In contests where the presidential and the

House percentages were similar in many districts, there still may have been ticket-splitting in both directions that was masked by the aggregate election statistics. But where the spread between a party's presidential and congressional percentage is wide, there is unmistakable evidence of split-ticket voting.

Table 6.2—Split-Ticket Voting and the Form of the Ballot in the North: A Comparison of the Spread between the Percentage of the Two-Party Vote Polled by Presidential and House Candidates of the Same Party, 1932–1964[a]

	SINGLE-CHOICE DISTRICTS			MULTIPLE-CHOICE DISTRICTS		
YEAR	Spread Under 2.5%	Spread Under 5.0%	Spread Over 10.0%	Spread Under 2.5%	Spread Under 5.0%	Spread Over 10.0%
1932	61.9	80.7	6.3	38.6	56.6	25.3
1936	57.3	84.8	3.6	31.3	58.9	22.6
1940	57.2	77.6	9.9	36.1	60.9	20.7
1944	58.8	84.5	4.8	27.0	53.0	19.3
1948	57.2	80.0	4.4	39.5	58.9	13.3
1952	57.5	79.9	5.2	34.7	65.9	11.6
1956	18.4	45.4	15.1	24.1	40.3	33.7
1960	44.0	63.2	7.2	20.1	49.0	24.7
1964	23.1	45.4	33.0	18.6	35.7	40.2
All Years	48.8	72.1	9.4	28.7	51.8	24.3

[a] The number of districts analyzed is identical to that in Table 6.1.

In Table 6.2 the marked discrepancy between the probable incidence of split-ticket voting in single-choice and in multiple-choice districts emerges clearly. In 1932, for example, the presidential and the House nominees of the same party ran within 2.5 percentage points of each other in more than six of every ten single-choice districts. In multiple-choice constituencies, by contrast, the presidential and the congressional ticket of the same party were that evenly matched just over a third of the time.

The contrast between the incidence of widespread ticket-splitting in the two groups of districts was even more marked in 1936. When extensive split-ticket voting takes place, it will be reflected in spreads which are larger than 10 per cent. In 1936 only one in every 28 of the single-choice districts had spreads that exceeded 10 per cent. Of the multiple-choice districts, between one in four and one in five had very wide gaps between the share of the vote going to presidential and House candidates of the same party.

The figures for 1952 and 1956 are of particular interest. These were the elections in which there was little difference in the proportion of districts with split results in single-choice and multiple-choice constituencies. As the new data in Table 6.2 make plain, however, there was a marked difference between the proportion of voters who split their ticket in the two types of districts. In 1952, the spread was under 2.5 percentage points in 57.5 per cent of the single-choice districts, compared with only 34.7 per cent of the multiple-choice constituencies.

The 1956 election statistics in Table 6.2, however, present a somewhat different pattern. In that extraordinary electoral contest, President Eisenhower became the first presidential nominee since Zachary Taylor to win four years in the White House while his party failed to gain control of the House of Representatives. The election returns for that contest, in which there was an unusual amount of ticket-splitting generally, must therefore be interpreted with special care. In most districts in the country, General Eisenhower ran well ahead of his G.O.P. congressional running mate. As a result, the average spread in the nation's House districts was substantially higher than it was in other elections in our sample.

This tendency is reflected by the data in Table 6.2. Single-choice districts were only slightly more prone to have spreads of under 5 per cent than were multiple-choice districts. In fact, the multiple-choice districts were actually the more likely of the two groups of constituencies to have spreads of less than 2.5 per cent. Nevertheless, very large spreads (those exceeding 10 per cent) were still more than twice as frequent in districts where the voters could not vote a straight ticket with one motion than they were in single-choice districts. Apparently the form of the ballot still had an effect on the amount of ticket-splitting in 1956, but this showed up most clearly only among districts where the discrepancy between the major-party presidential and House tickets was exceptionally large.

Other evidence also indicates that the fortunes of Republican House aspirants were more closely linked to President Eisenhower's showing in their district in single-choice constituencies than in multiple-choice constituencies in 1956. House candidates who actually run ahead of their presidential running mate in their own district clearly have sources of support which they do not owe to the head of the ticket. In 1956, only six of the 152 Republican congressional candidates in northern districts where the single-choice ballot form was used ran ahead of President Eisenhower. In multiple-choice districts in the North, by contrast, 31 out of 166 G.O.P. House candidates actually made a better showing than Eisenhower.

Figure 6.1—Presidential and congressional elections and the form of the ballot: The spread between the winning President's percentage of the two-party presidential vote and his House running mate's percentage of the two-party congressional vote, single-choice districts and multiple-choice districts compared, 1932–1964

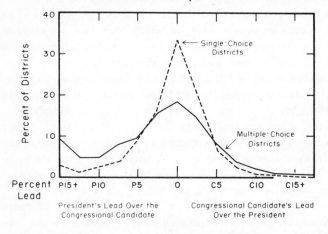

The odds are that the importance of the ballot form as a determinant of voters' behavior varies in response to the special characteristics of individual election campaigns. And the form of the ballot will neither prevent ticket-splitting in single-choice districts or insure split-ticket voting in the multiple-choice districts. Nevertheless, the general tendency is for a party's presidential and congressional nominees to run closely together in single-choice districts and for the House contests to exhibit a greater independence of the outcome of the presidential battle in districts where a multiple-choice ballot form is used. This assertion is underpinned by the data in Figure 6.1. In it the percentage of single-choice and multiple-choice districts which had spreads of varying sizes between 1932 and 1964 is compared. Note how the single-choice districts are bunched toward the center of the graph. In most of them the spread between the presidential and the congressional candidates of the same party was under 5 per cent. And note also how much more variable the relationship was between presidential and House contests in multiple-choice districts. A victorious candidate for President was both more likely to lead his House running mate by more than 5 per cent or to trail him by over 5 per cent in districts where the electorate could not vote a straight ticket with one motion.

The Electorate and the Form of the Ballot

THE PRECEDING DISCUSSION SUGGESTS that the ease of casting a straight-ticket vote in single-choice jurisdictions probably causes some voters to do so who might have been inclined to pick and choose among the candidates offered by the parties if they had had to vote for each office individually. Nevertheless, the odds are that some voters are more likely to be influenced by the form of the ballot than others. Although the social survey data necessary to test this assumption over an extended series of elections are lacking, information collected by the Survey Research Center of the University of Michigan provides an indication of the kinds of voters on whom the ballot form is likely to have its greatest effect.

In interviews with a nationwide sample of the American electorate in 1956, the Survey Research Center sought to determine for each respondent his party identification, whether he preferred one of the major-party presidential candidates, and whether he preferred the stands on issues he associated with one party to the issue positions he associated with the other party. The Center's interviewers also ascertained how each person intended to vote for President. These findings then made it possible to determine how many motives the voter may have had in support of his final vote decision.[3] Thus, if a person who supported President Eisenhower considered himself a strong Republican, also preferred the General's personality to that of Mr. Stevenson, and expressed general agreement with the policy pronouncements of the G.O.P., he had the maximum number of three major political motives in support of his presidential vote determination. A Stevenson voter, on the other hand, who considered himself a strong Democrat, but who preferred Mr. Eisenhower personally to the Democratic presidential nominee, and who expressed no preference for the policy stands of the Democratic party, would have had but one motive in support of his vote for President.

Table 6.3—Relation of Straight-Ticket Voting to Number of Motives Supporting the Vote for President in Single-Choice and in Multiple-Choice Districts in the North in 1956[a]

Number of Supporting Motives	Percentage of Voters Who Were Straight-Ticket Voters in Single-Choice Districts	Percentage of Voters Who Were Straight-Ticket Voters in Multiple-Choice Districts	Ratio Between Straight-Ticket Voting in Single-Choice and in Multiple-Choice Districts
3	77	65	1.18 to 1.00
2	65	53	1.23 to 1.00
1	49	36	1.36 to 1.00
0	45	27	1.67 to 1.00

[a] The data in the first three columns of this table are taken from Angus Campbell and Warren E. Miller, "The Motivational Basis of Straight and Split Ticket Voting," *American Political Science Review*, Vol. 51, No. 2, June, 1957, p. 304.

In Table 6.3 voters are grouped according to the number of motives which they had in support of their presidential vote decision. Each of these groups is then subdivided so that the votes of people who lived in single-choice districts can be compared with the way citizens in multiple-choice districts cast their ballots in 1956. In 1956, even voters who had three major motives which reinforced their vote for President were slightly more likely to vote a straight ticket if they lived in districts where the form of the ballot facilitated straight-ticket voting than if they lived in a multiple-choice district. The point of interest here, however, is that

3. Angus Campbell and Warren E. Miller, "The Motivational Basis of Straight and Split Ticket Voting," *American Political Science Review*, Vol. 51, No. 2, June, 1957, pp. 293–312.

the less motivated voters were much more likely to cast a straight ticket if they could do the job with one motion when they entered the polling booth. This finding is underpinned by the ratios in the fourth column of Table 6.3. In 1956, at least, it was the votes of people who did not have strong views on the parties, candidates, and the issues of the campaign that were more likely to be influenced by the form of the ballot employed in their constituency.

Voters whose sense of identification with one of the major parties was tenuous were also much more likely to be influenced by the form of the ballot than were persons who considered themselves strong party men in 1956. This tendency is brought out by the data in Table 6.4. In this analysis, voters in single-choice and multiple-choice districts are grouped according to whether they regarded themselves as strong party identifiers, weak party identifiers, or as independents.

Table 6.4—Relation of Party Identification to Straight- and Split-Ticket Voting in Single-Choice and in Multiple-Choice Districts in the North in 1956[a]

TYPE OF VOTER	PERCENTAGE OF STRAIGHT-TICKET VOTES CAST BY VOTERS IN:		RATIO BETWEEN STRAIGHT-TICKET VOTING IN SINGLE-CHOICE AND IN MULTIPLE-CHOICE DISTRICTS
	Single-Choice Districts	Multiple-Choice Districts	
Strong Party Identifiers	77	77	1.00 to 1.00
Weak Party Identifiers	70	55	1.27 to 1.00
Independents	48	30	1.60 to 1.00

[a] The data in the first three columns of this table are taken from Angus Campbell and Warren E. Miller, "The Motivational Basis of Straight and Split Ticket Voting," *American Political Science Review*, Vol. 51, No. 2, June, 1957, pp. 307–308.

Voters who considered themselves strong Democrats or strong Republicans were just as likely to support the party of their choice with a straight-ticket vote in multiple-choice districts as in single-choice districts. Other voters, however, whose allegiance to one of the parties was less strongly felt, were more prone to vote a straight ticket in the districts where it was easier to do so. The form of the ballot appears to have had the greatest impact on the votes of people who claimed to be independents without an habitual preference for either major party.

The foregoing data indicate that it was those voters who were least interested in politics and whose sense of party loyalty was most tenuous who were influenced most by the form of the ballot in 1956. Data on other elections would be required to determine whether the less motivated voters and those less committed to a given party are always more likely to be influenced by the ballot form. Yet even if they are, the relevance of these relationships for the political system is probably different in different elections. It is possible, for example, that the ratio of highly motivated voters to unmotivated voters and of strong party identifiers to independents in the electorate varies from election to election. In times of great political crisis, a larger than average proportion of the voters may feel a strong determination to support one of the political parties. The elections of 1932 and 1936, fought under the shadow of the Great Depression, were marked by widespread straight-ticket voting in most parts of the country. Many people may have felt that their welfare really depended upon the outcome of the political battle in those years. In more placid times, however, the electorate's feeling of commitment to one of the parties may be less wholehearted.

Elections probably vary, too, in the intensity and the importance of different types of political motivations. In some years, neither presidential nominee may particularly excite the voters, and traditional party loyalties may be the most important factor governing the outcome of the campaign. In other election years, new issues of burning importance, or candidates who excite strong feelings of admiration or dislike may convert the electorate's apathy into intense concern. Consider, for example, the large number of Democrats who were moved to split their ticket in order to vote for General Eisenhower in 1952 and 1956. A different Republican nominee for the White House might well have resulted in a different pattern of voting. The proportion of the highly motivated voters who decide to split their ticket, whatever the form of the ballot is in their constituency, also may change from year to year.

The effect which an institutional arrangement such as the form of the ballot may have on an electoral contest varies with the issues, the personalities, and the parties which animate the political system. Yet, in a general way, the influence the ballot form has upon the extent to which different groups of voters indulge in split-ticket voting can be delineated. Although the precise nature and the magnitude of its effect varies, the ballot form which individual states adopt can have a direct bearing on the functioning of the political system. The multiple-choice ballot form tends to separate the fortunes of House candidates from the fate of the presidential nominee of their party. It thus may foster a politics of personalities, rather than of parties. When a multiple-choice ballot is used, House members, even those of the President's party, may feel that their survival in their own constituency is less dependent upon the fate of their national party ticket. The net effect of the single-choice ballot, on the other hand, is probably to accentuate the interdependence of presidential and House candidates of the same party.

In most presidential years the ballot form probably has another effect on executive-legislative relations at the national level. As noted earlier, the bulk of the congressional districts with split-election results are constituencies that are carried by the winning President but are lost by his House running mate. Between 1932 and 1964, 17.7 per cent of the single-choice districts had split election results, compared with 25.2 per cent of the multiple-choice districts. Multiple-choice districts thus elect more than their share of opposition Congressmen to harass the victorious presidential nominee. As a consequence, in most elections the multiple-choice ballot widens the cleavage between the legislative and the executive branches of government.

Congressmen Elected At Large

ALTHOUGH MOST FEDERAL HOUSE members are elected in single-member districts into which the appropriate state legislature has subdivided their state, a few would-be Representatives must curry the favor of the electorate of an entire state. Since 1920 these Congressmen elected At Large have represented four major types of constituencies. Some come from states whose total population is so small that it entitles them to only one member of the House. Congressmen from these one-Representative states may thus find themselves called upon to speak for a wide variety of interests. In this respect, their job is perhaps harder than that of their colleagues who are elected in smaller districts whose social and economic structure is more homogeneous. But their task is a relatively easy one, if it can be measured in terms of the number of voters whose wishes they must take into consideration when they survey their prospects for the next election. The number of constituents represented by the At-Large Congressman from states such as Nevada, Vermont, or Alaska is well below the average for the House.

A second group of At-Large Congressmen represent states whose population entitles them to just two House members. Some two-Representative states, like Montana, have been carved into separate districts for the purpose of electing their Congressmen. In others, however, the candidates for both of the House seats must face all of the voters in the state. A special politics of compromise and balance may be fostered in congressional campaigns in states where two candidates for the House appear on the same party ticket. Thus, in New Mexico, where a large group of voters of Mexican descent is counterbalanced by an even larger "Anglo" population, the dominant Democratic party has often run both a Spanish American and an "Anglo" candidate for the state's two At-Large House seats.

Obviously these At-Large Congressmen from the two-Representative states represent more constituents than their colleagues from one-Representative states. Nevertheless, the electorates in the two-Representatives states are still sufficiently small that a conscientious Congressman elected At-Large should be able to cultivate special personal ties with a significant proportion of his voters. In terms of the number of people in the constituency, the size of the district, and the prominence which the races for Congressmen are likely to gain in relation to the rest of the contests settled on a general election day, the one-Representative and the two-Representative At-Large constituencies appear to be fundamentally similar.

A quite different set of circumstances accompany the election of a third group of At-Large Congressmen: those who come from states with large populations where most of the congressional delegation are elected in local House districts, but where one or more Representatives are also elected At Large. Frequently this occurs when a state that has already been subdivided into individual House districts gains a Congressman or two as the result of a new decennial census and the state legislature is unwilling or unable to change the preexisting district boundary lines. The easiest way to resolve the problem is to leave the existing districts as they are and to elect the additional Representatives At Large. In any event, a few At-Large Congressmen are likely to be elected from states with sizable House delegations in every presidential year.

On rare occasions, states with large House delegations also may elect all of their Representatives At Large. Since World War I this has happened only once. But in 1932, four states—Kentucky, Minnesota, Missouri, and Virginia—sent a total of 40 Representatives to Washington who were elected statewide. All four states had

Table 6.5—Representatives Elected At Large in Presidential Years, 1920-1964

Year and Number of Districts		NUMBER OF REPRESENTATIVES ELECTED AT LARGE FROM STATES WITH:				Total Number of House Members Elected At Large	Per Cent of Total House Membership
		One House Member	Two House Members	Some House Members from Local Districts	All House Members Elected At Large		
1920	435	5	—	6	—	11	2.5
1924	435	5	—	2	—	7	1.6
1928	435	5	—	2	—	7	1.6
1932	435	6	2	12	40	60	13.8
1936	435	6	2	8	—	16	3.7
1940	435	6	2	8	—	16	3.7
1944	435	4	6	4	—	14	3.2
1948	435	4	4	2	—	10	2.3
1952	435	4	4	3	—	11	2.5
1956	435	4	4	3	—	11	2.5
1960	437	6	4	3	—	13	3.0
1964	435	5	4	3	—	12	2.8
Total	5222	60	32	56	40	188	3.6

suffered a decrease in the number of Congressmen to which they were entitled after the 1930 Census, and in all four states the legislature failed to draw new district boundary lines before the 1932 general election.

In Table 6.5, the number of At-Large Congressmen of each of these four types who were elected in the 12 presidential years between 1920 and 1964 is indicated. In every election except 1932,

Congressmen who were elected At Large accounted for but a small part of the total membership of the House. Yet, although they are relatively infrequent, perhaps the instances in which Representatives are elected At Large highlight the influence that the type of constituency from which American Congressmen are selected may have on the interrelationship between the balloting for President and for Congressman. At this point our assumptions should be made explicit. The election of the great majority of the nation's lawmakers in individual, local congressional districts with relatively small populations undoubtedly contributes something special to the peculiar character and tone of the American Congress. Perhaps one reason for this is that individual Congressmen, secure in their enclaves of local strength, are better able to withstand a national opposition presidential tide than they would be if they were all subjected to the movement of opinion in their state as a whole. If so, then there should be more ticket-splitting between presidential and House candidates of opposite parties in local congressional districts than in the statewide At-Large contests.[4]

Data which enable us to test this last proposition appear in Table 6.6. This analysis compares the spread between the vote polled by presidential and House candidates of the same party in different types of constituencies. Between 1920 and 1964 the coincidence between the presidential and the congressional vote in the one-Representative states was somewhat greater than in individual local House districts. In the two-Representative states that elected both Congressmen At Large, on the other hand, there was probably somewhat more ticket-splitting than in local House districts. Nevertheless, both in the local House districts into which most of the states have been carved and in the states which elect their one or two Congressmen At Large there was a close parallelism (within 2.5 per cent) between the presidential and the House vote only about a third of the time or less. And in a fifth or more of these differing kinds of districts the spread exceeded 10 per cent.

4. For a general consideration of the impact which the electoral system may have upon a nation's political life, see Maurice Duverger, *L'influence des systèmes électoraux sur la vie politique* (Paris: Libraire Armand Colin, 1950). See also Duverger, *Political Parties, Their Organization and Activity in the Modern State* (London: Methuen & Company, Ltd., 1954), Book II, chs. 1–3.

A quite different set of circumstances attends the election of At-Large Congressmen in some of the larger states which select most of their Representatives in local districts. A few of the House members elected on a statewide basis in these more populous states

Table 6.6—*Split-Ticket Voting Affecting Congressmen Elected At Large and Split-Ticket Voting Affecting Congressmen Elected in Individual Districts: A Comparison of the Spread between the Percentage of the Two-Party Vote Polled by Major-Party Presidential Candidates and House Nominees of the Same Party, 1920–1964*[a]

Type of Congressman	PERCENTAGE OF DISTRICTS IN WHICH THE SPREAD WAS:			Number of Districts
	Under 2.5%	Under 5.0%	Over 10.0%	
House Members Elected in Individual Local Districts	32.6	52.4	29.8	3481
House Members Elected At Large in States with One Representative	35.0	63.3	20.0	60
House Members Elected At Large in States with Two Representatives	20.0	30.0	40.0	30
House Members Elected At Large in States which also Elected Some Representatives from Local Districts	58.3	89.6	4.2	48
House Members Elected At Large in Kentucky, Missouri, and Virginia in 1932 when Entire Congressional Delegation was Elected At Large	92.9	100.0	0.0	28

[a] Districts where one of the major parties failed to run a House candidate and districts for which the presidential returns are not available are excluded from this table.

run far behind or far ahead of their presidential teammate. In Oklahoma in 1940, the Democratic nominee for the At-Large congressional seat, a Mr. Will Rogers, ran 8.5 percentage points ahead of Franklin D. Roosevelt. But there was a fortuitous identity between the House candidate's name and that of the Sooner State's beloved humorist; and in the opinion of many Oklahomans, it paid special dividends at the polls. Other At-Large House candidates may build for themselves impressive statewide, and even national, reputations. In Ohio, both George H. Bender, a Republican, and Stephen M. Young, a Democrat, first occupied At-Large seats in the House and then went on to win election to the Senate.

Despite these individual exploits, however, the fate of most At-Large candidates in states with big electorates has been linked closely to the outcome of the presidential battle in their state. Nearly six of every ten Congressmen elected At Large from states in this category ran within 2.5 per cent of their presidential running mate. And nearly nine of every ten trailed or led their party's presidential ticket by less than 5 percentage points. Of 48 Congressmen elected At Large in these populous states between 1920 and 1964, only two, Don Magnuson, a Democrat who successfully resisted the Eisenhower sweep in Washington state in 1956, and Oliver P. Bolton, a Republican who lost despite making a much stronger showing than Barry Goldwater in Ohio in 1964, ran more than 10 percentage points ahead of their presidential running mate. In most At-Large House contests in larger states, there appears to have been much less ticket-splitting at the national level than in the presidential and House contests held throughout the country in local congressional districts.

These findings suggest that perhaps candidates who run in local and relatively small House districts are better able than At-Large House candidates from the bigger states to develop special personal ties with their constituents that make them less dependent on the outcome of the national presidential contest in their constituency. Yet the data are far from conclusive. New York, Oklahoma, Illinois, Ohio, Connecticut, Washington, Maryland, Texas, and Pennsylvania are the states analyzed that elected part of their House delegation At Large, and this fact alone should prompt the reader to appraise the data in Table 6.6 with special care. In the years when they elected some of their Congressmen At Large, the electorates in several of these states were generally less prone to split their ticket than were voters in many other states. Hence, even though the spreads in these At-Large constituencies were smaller than the spreads in individual districts, the differences may not have been related to the type of constituency from which the Congressmen were elected. Perhaps, however, some meaning can be squeezed from the new data presented in Table 6.7. In this analysis, the divergence between the presidential and House vote in these At-Large constituencies is compared with the spreads at the same elections in local House districts in the same states.

Table 6.7—Split-Ticket Voting for Congressmen Elected At Large and for Congressmen Elected in Local House Districts: A Comparison of the Spread in At-Large House Contests and in House Contests Held in Individual Districts in the Same States in the Same Election Years, 1920–1964[a]

| TYPE OF CONGRESSMAN | PERCENTAGE OF DISTRICTS IN WHICH THE SPREAD WAS: | | | |
	Under 2.5%	Under 5.0%	Over 10.0%	Number of Districts
Elected At Large in States which also Elected Some House Members in Districts	58.3	89.6	4.2	48
Elected in Individual Districts in those Same States in the Same Election Years	48.4	74.2	9.0	399

[a] The states included in this analysis are New York, Oklahoma, Illinois, Ohio, Connecticut, Washington, Maryland, Texas, and Pennsylvania.

The data in Table 6.7 reflect a tendency for the House results to be more closely linked to the outcome of the presidential battle in big-state At-Large constituencies than in local congressional districts. The magnitude of the difference which the type of constituency may make is not large. Nevertheless, in states where direct comparisons are possible, it appears that the presidential and congressional electoral tides were bound together more closely in the statewide House races than in the contests within individual House districts.

In 1932 the legislatures of Kentucky, Minnesota, Missouri, and Virginia failed to redistrict their states before the November general election. As a result, the entire congressional delegation in these four states was elected At Large. In Minnesota, where the Farmer-Labor third party was considerably stronger than the local Democrats at the congressional level, there was an enormous discrepancy between Franklin Roosevelt's presidential total and the Democratic House vote. The spreads in Minnesota were equally wide in 1936 and 1940, however, when the State once again elected its Representatives from local congressional districts.

For the present inquiry, the analysis will be limited to the other three states where the third-party vote was negligible that elected their entire congressional delegation At Large in 1932. The data in the bottom row of Table 6.6 (presented earlier) underscore the extraordinary amount of straight-ticket voting that characterized the contests for President and Congressman in these states when they elected their entire congressional delegation At Large. Roughly 93 per cent of the major-party At-Large House candidates ran within 2.5 per cent of their presidential running mate. All ran within 5 per cent of the share of the presidential vote polled by the head of their party's ticket. In Kentucky it was even closer: there Franklin D. Roosevelt polled 59.5 per cent of the state's two-party vote; and the proportion of the congressional vote received by all nine of the state's Democratic House candidates was exactly the same—59.5 per cent.

The odds are that these figures reflect extensive straight-ticket voting in Missouri, Virginia, and Kentucky in 1932. Still, 1932 was an election in which there was widespread straight-ticket voting in the country generally; and the three states that elected their entire congressional delegation At Large had less of a tradition of ticket-splitting than some other states. Yet perhaps something more of the impact that the election of an entire House slate At Large may have upon the interrelationship between the presidential and the congressional results will emerge if our data are placed in a new light.

In Figure 6.2, the spreads in these 1932 At-Large races are compared with the divergence between the presidential and the House vote in the contests held in individual districts in the same states in 1936 and 1940. In the latter two election years, to be sure, there was somewhat more ticket-splitting in the country as a whole than in 1932. But the increase was scarcely large enough to account for the widening of the spread in individual House districts in Kentucky, Missouri, and Virginia revealed in Figure 6.2.

In 1936 and 1940, several Democratic House candidates in these states were able to pile up a substantial lead over Franklin Roose-velt in their own district. In terms of their electoral support, they were stronger than the President himself in the local constituency on which their chances for reelection depended. When they were

Figure 6.2—*The spread between Democratic presidential and congressional candidates elected in Kentucky, Missouri, and Virginia in 1932, 1936, and 1940: A comparison of the showing made by candidates elected at large in 1932 and by candidates elected in individual districts in 1936 and 1940 (Number of congressmen elected at large in 1932: 28. Number of congressmen elected in districts in 1936 and 1940: 52)*

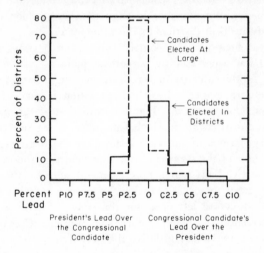

elected At Large, by contrast, the fate of many of these same Congressmen was linked more closely to the outcome of the presidential contest.

Local Congressional Districts and the Party System

KENTUCKY, MISSOURI, AND VIRGINIA elected their entire congressional delegation At Large only once—in 1932. The chances are that if the members of Congress from these states had had the opportunity to run At Large during a number of elections, some of them would have established statewide reputations which might have insulated them somewhat from the vagaries of the presidential battle in their state. Even so, the net import of the data is clear. The election At Large of Representatives from populous states tends to accentuate the interdependence between the fortunes of presidential and congressional candidates of the same party. Congressmen chosen At Large in populous states where the entire House delegation is selected on a statewide basis tend to run closer to the head of their ticket than do Congressmen elected in newly carved local districts in the same states in subsequent elections. And Representatives At Large from states which also elect some of their House members from local districts poll votes which parallel the presidential tide in their constituency more frequently than do Congressmen elected simultaneously in local districts in the same state.

Most House members, of course, run in local congressional districts; and few aspects of the American political system better illustrate the subtle influence of federalism on the nation's political life than the arrangements by which provision is made for the election of its Representatives. The determination of the size and the type of the districts from which Congressmen are selected was left to the legislatures of individual states by the drafters of the Constitution. One of the most vital questions affecting the membership of a legislative body which makes general rules for the nation was thus entrusted to local lawmakers to answer as they wished. The way was therefore left open for the state legislatures, themselves unrepresentative bodies before the Supreme Court intervened,[5] to create national legislative districts that overrepresented some groups in the population while underrepresenting other segments of the electorate.

The consequences of this for the working of the American political system are considerable; and they underscore the enormous potential importance of the 1964 Supreme Court rulings applying the "one-man, one vote" doctrine to the drawing of federal House

5. For an analysis of the degree of inequality in state legislative representation from 1910 to 1960, and the trends concerning the equity of this representation during that period, see Paul T. David and Ralph Eisenberg, *Devaluation of the Urban and Suburban Vote*, Vols. I and II (Charlottesville: Bureau of Public Administration, The University of Virginia, 1961 and 1962).

district boundary lines and to both houses of bicameral state legislatures.[6] If fully implemented, these rulings could bring about a marked change in the kinds of effects the redistricting process has had on U.S. House election results. Nevertheless, the nature of these effects from 1920 to 1964 is still of considerable interest. The most obvious result, of course, is that some groups in the population have had more than their share of Representatives in the House. In elections in which one political party draws the bulk of its support from voters who are underrepresented in the national legislature, the vital business of drawing the nation's congressional district boundary lines may have a very direct bearing on the party struggle.

But it is when the outcome of the House contests are viewed in terms of their relationship to the presidential election that some of the less obvious consequences of the American electoral system during this period may be seen. The President of the United States, as every schoolboy knows, usually attains office by winning a majority in a specially constituted electoral college, where each state's entire electoral vote goes to the presidential nominee who obtains the most popular votes in that state. The arrangements for the election of the President thus give adequate, if not more than adequate, importance to the nation's large population centers. It is even conceivable that a presidential nominee who generally led his

6. The 1964 Supreme Court decisions were the last two of a series of four major decisions concerning legislative districting handed down by the Court between 1962 and 1964. In *Baker v. Carr,* the Tennessee apportionment case decided March 26, 1962, the Court ruled, 6–2, that the courts had authority to review state legislative apportionments which are subjected to legal challenge on the grounds that they violate the equal protection clause of the 14th Amendment. On March 18, 1963, in *Gray v. Sanders,* the court by an 8–1 decision struck down Georgia's county unit system of voting in statewide and congressional primary elections, on the grounds that the system deprived citizens of equal protection of the laws. This decision, for the first time, spelled out the "one man, one vote" principle as official court doctrine. In *Wesberry v. Sanders,* the Georgia congressional districting case decided February 17, 1964, on a 6–3 division, the court ruled that, "As nearly as practicable, one man's vote in a Congressional election must be worth as much as another's." Finally, in a group of cases affecting the legislative apportionments of six states, the court ruled on June 15, 1964, that the apportionment of seats in both houses of a bicameral state legislature must be "based substantially on population." Six of the nine Justices concurred with the basic constitutional reasoning of the majority. *Congressional Quarterly Weekly Report,* June 19, 1964, p. 1218.

party's House ticket but whose strength was concentrated among voters who were underrepresented in the House could have won the Presidency while failing to carry a majority of the congressional districts. After such an election the President's party would have also found itself in a minority in the House. In 1944, an electoral verdict of precisely this type might have occurred, had not the Republicans' strength in small-town and rural districts in the North been counterbalanced by the traditional Democratic strength in the rural South.

It is clear that the drawing of congressional district boundary lines has important consequences for the functioning of the nation's political system. But the type of constituency in which state legislators determine that their national counterparts shall be elected may be of even greater moment. Except when the exigencies of the local political situation prevent a state legislature from redistricting immediately after a new decennial census, it is very unlikely that a populous state's entire congressional delegation will be elected At Large. Most politicians dread the prospect of such winner-take-all arrangements, and they will go to great lengths to avoid it, as the redistricting struggle in Pennsylvania preceding the 1962 election demonstrates.[7] The election in the bigger states of an occasional Representative At Large, while more generally practiced, is still the exception rather than the rule. The election of the nation's Representatives in single-member, local congressional districts is, in fact, so widely accepted as to be virtually a convention of the Constitution. In a sense, it is an institutional embodiment of the localism which colors so pervasively the nature of the American political system, and its consequences for the working of the party system are profound.

Consider, for the moment, the likely consequences, if entire state congressional delegations were elected At Large. Not only would it probably heighten the interdependence between the fortunes of presidential and congressional candidates of the same party. It would also probably deprive voters who were in a minority in an

7. For an analysis of the redistricting battle in Pennsylvania in 1961–1962, see Edward F. Cooke and William J. Keefe, "Pennsylvania: The Limits of Power in a Divided Government," in Malcolm E. Jewell, Editor, *The Politics of Reapportionment* (New York: Atherton Press, 1962), pp. 149–172.

individual state of any representation at all in the national legislature. In 1932, the statewide Democratic tide in Missouri and Kentucky gave the Democratic party every seat in the House from those two states. More than four of every ten voters in those states supported the G.O.P., yet they were left without a single Congressman in the House. Four years later, during the greatest of Franklin Roosevelt's electoral victories, Republicans were able to elect a Congressman in both Missouri and Kentucky in local enclaves of strength which were insulated from the impact of the national presidential tide. In 1940 in Missouri, which was again the scene of a statewide Democratic victory, the Republicans elected three Representatives to the House.

In states where a two-party cleavage is fairly well developed, legislators are more likely to be responsive to the wishes of their own regular supporters than to people whom they know will be in their opponent's camp come the next campaign. The conservative Republican from Minnesota who looked in 1959 at the two Democratic Senators from his state, Hubert Humphrey and Eugene McCarthy, may well have felt that these gentlemen gave scant expression to his views in the Senate. Yet in the House, he could expect a more sympathetic hearing from Representative Walter Judd, as well as from four other Republican members of Congress from Minnesota.

If the election of state congressional delegations At Large would deprive local minorities in individual states of representation in the House, it would also probably greatly weaken the congressional strength of the minority party in the country as a whole. If all Congressmen were to be elected At Large, the verdict in House elections might approach, if it did not equal, the lopsidedness of the outcome of the balloting for President in the electoral college. Changes in the membership of the national legislature would be more violent, and the influence of broad shifts in party sentiment in the country as a whole would tend to be magnified in the House. The odds are that fewer Congressmen would sit in the lower chamber secure in the knowledge that, whatever the outcome of the national presidential campaign, they were certain to be returned to Washington by their own constituents.

Individual Congressmen's prospects for continued employment

may depend in large part upon the local district electoral system. Consider, for example, the career of the orator from the Ozarks, Congressman Dewey Short. Between his first election to the House in 1928 and his defeat in 1956, Short, a Republican, won in Missouri in every presidential year save one. In 1932, after having been narrowly defeated two years before, Short was not even included on his party's slate of House candidates, all of whom ran At Large. Yet even if he had been nominated, it would have been impossible for him to win a statewide victory the year Franklin Roosevelt was first elected President.

By 1934, however, the former Representative was able to win his party's nomination in a newly carved constituency in his home area. Even in 1934 and 1936, he was able to withstand the national Democratic tide and win election to the House. As a result he was able to begin a period of 22 years of consecutive service in the lower chamber. Eventually Congressman Short attained the powerful chairmanship of the House Armed Services Committee. In 1948, he was the only Republican Congressman to survive Harry Truman's decisive victory in his home state during Truman's successful campaign for the Presidency.

Through its impact on the fortunes of individual Congressmen, the election of members of the House in local congressional districts, in conjunction with the seniority system, thus gives a special quality to the legislative process. It probably also fosters the localism of the American Congress. Not only may Congressmen who look first to their own constituency have the opportunity, if they live long enough, to attain positions of great power in the House, but the local district system also makes it possible for voters in the same state to elect Congressmen with the widest variation in their policies and personalities. For years, New York State returned both John Taber and Emanuel Celler to the House. The chances are that if all of the New York Congressmen were elected At Large, their Representatives would not take as consistently clear-cut policy stands as either of these two men.

After most presidential years, the nation's electoral system has still another influence on the role which the Congress plays in the American constitutional system. A victorious presidential candidate, as has been shown, usually carries more districts than his

House running mates. It is even more likely that his portion of the vote in the electoral college will exceed substantially his party's share of the House seats which are filled on the same day. Were all of the nation's Congressmen to be elected At Large, an incoming President would probably find more members of his own party upon whom he could rely for support in the House. The net effect of the election of most Representatives in local congressional districts is thus to widen the cleavage between the executive and the legislative branches of government. Like many other institutional arrangements in the nation's political system, the electoral system gives force to the obstacles to governmental action which are inherent in the American framework of government.

CHAPTER 7

Presidential Elections and the

House of Representatives

It takes a sizable number of analyses to explore some of the major variants of split-ticket voting which occur at the national level in the American party system. And voters who do split their ticket at the national level can have a major impact on the functioning of the party system, on occasion even helping to elect a President who will face an opposition party House majority. Yet this ticket-splitting, dramatic though its consequences may sometimes be, should not obscure one of the central facts about the nation's party system. Most American voters tend to support presidential and congressional candidates of the same party.

The implications of this proposition are of considerable importance. It suggests, for example, that trends affecting a party's strength at the presidential level may also have an impact on the party's congressional nominees—and *vice versa*. It also indicates that the complex interrelationship between a party's presidential and congressional vote contains an important key to the functioning of the party system at the national level. In the pages that follow, the objective will be to subject this relationship between the vote for President and the vote for Congressmen to closer study.

The Relationship Between the Vote for President and the Vote for Congressmen

THE FATE AT THE polls of candidates for President and Congressmen who run on the same ticket has long intrigued analysts of the nation's electoral system. Most inquiries bearing on the topic, however, have had one objective: to determine the effect which the presidential battle has on the contests for Congressmen which are held at the same time. Broadly speaking, there are two ways in which the contest for the White House can influence congressional elections. First, there is the effect which a presidential campaign can have on the number and the type of citizens who go to the polls on election day. Many people who record a choice for President seldom vote on other occasions. When they do get to the polling booth, however, most of these people also vote for a Representative, and the potential impact of this increased turnout on House contests is substantial. In presidential years, the total vote for Congressman is from a third to one half again as large as the comparable turnout at midterm. In times when most of these occasional voters come from segments of the population that have a strong preference for one party, their arrival at the polls can have a major impact on the distribution of party strength in the House. Thus well over half of the occasional voters who turned out in 1936 and 1940 probably came from groups in the population which had Democratic leanings.

The second way in which the presidential battle may influence House elections concerns an even larger portion of the electorate. Potentially, it may involve both the voter who is drawn to the polls by his interest in the presidential contest and the citizen who would have voted for Congressman whether there were a presidential election or not. Both types of voters may support a House nominee primarily because they are attracted to his party ticket by the appeal of his presidential running mate.

Angus Campbell has advanced some general findings that bear on these relationships based on examination of social survey data covering the elections of 1948, 1952, 1956, and 1958. During this period, he found, people who voted in a high-turnout presidential year but not at midterm had markedly lower levels of interest in politics than persons who voted at both elections. The in-and-out voters also included a high proportion of independents or persons with only a weak feeling of loyalty to either of the major parties. Citizens who voted regularly in presidential and midterm contests, by contrast, were likely to have a stronger sense of identification with one of the parties. In presidential years when interest in the contest for the White House was keen, the irregular, independent voters gave the bulk of their votes to the winning presidential nominee.[1] And in most elections of this kind one would expect many of these voters also to support the winning President's congressional running mates, thus helping to elect some House members of his party.

The odds are that the precise nature of the impact of the presidential contest on the battle for control of the House varies from election to election. Campbell notes, for example, that the vote given G.O.P. congressional candidates appears to have been influenced much less by Eisenhower's strength in 1956 than in 1952. Analyses presented earlier in this study also suggest that the ratio between a party's presidential and congressional strength changes markedly from year to year.

In some years a presidential candidate's electoral strength is closely paralleled by support for his party at the congressional level. In other presidential elections, it is not. In Franklin Roosevelt's day, a vote for the Democratic chief executive was likely to be accompanied by a vote for a Democratic House candidate throughout the industrialized portions of the North. In the same constituencies in 1956, President Eisenhower's strength was not accompanied by comparable support for the G.O.P. congressional ticket. In 1956, as Campbell points out, many people who called themselves independents—and a substantial number of Democrats—voted for Eisenhower though declining to support a Republican House nominee.[2]

Some House nominees undoubtedly do receive support from

1. Angus Campbell, "Surge and Decline: A Study of Electoral Change," *Public Opinion Quarterly*, Vol. 24, No. 3, Fall, 1960, pp. 397–418.

2. Ibid., pp. 413–416. For a discussion of the interrelationship between presidential and congressional elections based on a consideration of both aggregate election statistics and voting behavior studies, see Lewis A. Froman, Jr., *Congressmen and Their Constituencies* (Chicago: Rand McNally & Company, 1963), especially pp. 61–64.

citizens who are intent primarily on voting for one of the presidential candidates, and it is possible that in some circumstances House contests may also influence the vote for President. Both types of relationships, however, involve complex questions of voters' motivations; and a fuller picture of how they occur and how the process varies from election to election must await the acquisition of additional social survey data.[3] Yet once this disclaimer about the uses to which our aggregate data can be put has been registered, one can still ask what the district-by-district returns do reveal about the broad interrelationship between the presidential and congressional constituencies.

The analysis can be simplified by focusing attention on the fate of presidential and House candidates of the party that wins the Presidency. As we have seen, successful presidential candidates usually poll a larger percentage of the two-party vote than the majority of their congressional running mates in individual House districts. In recent presidential elections, only Truman and Kennedy failed to lead their congressional ticket in well over half of the House districts. On the other hand, every victorious presidential candidate since 1924, including Eisenhower and Johnson, has trailed his congressional teammate in at least some House districts. Between 1924 and 1964, the winning President led or ran even with his party's House nominee in 2,606 of 4,318 districts analyzed. In the remaining 1,712 constituencies, however, it was the House candidate who led—even though his party's presidential standard-bearer was sent to the White House.[4]

These districts where a winning President trailed his House ticket varied enormously—both in their location and in their social struc-

3. For two studies bearing on the interrelationship between the presidential and congressional vote which do draw on social survey data, see: Warren E. Miller, "Presidential Coattails: A Study in Political Myth and Methodology," *Public Opinion Quarterly*, Vol. 19, No. 4, Winter, 1955–1956, pp. 353–368; and Angus Campbell and Warren E. Miller, "The Motivational Basis of Straight and Split Ticket Voting," *American Political Science Review*, Vol. 51, No. 2, June, 1957, pp. 293–312. See also William A. Glaser, "Fluctuations in Turnout," in William N. McPhee and William A. Glaser, eds., *Public Opinion and Congressional Elections* (New York: The Free Press, 1962), pp. 19–52.

4. In this analysis, districts where the winning presidential nominee led his House running mate are those districts where the presidential candidate's percentage of the two-party presidential vote exceeded his House running

Table 7.1—The Relationship between the Vote for President and the Vote for Congressman: Districts where the Winning Presidential Candidate Polled a Larger Percentage of the Vote than His Party's House Ticket and Districts Where He Polled a Smaller Percentage of the Vote than His Party's House Ticket; and the Percentage of the Two-Party Vote Polled by His House Running Mates in those Districts, 1924–1964[a]

District's Percentage of House Vote Polled by Nominees of Winning President's Party	No of Districts	NO. OF DISTRICTS WHERE:		% OF DISTRICTS WHERE:	
		House Nominee Led His Winning Presidential Running Mate	Winning Presidential Nominee Led His House Running Mate[b]	House Nominee Led His Winning Presidential Running Mate	Winning Presidential Nominee Led His House Running Mate[b]
95–100	491	480	11	97.8	2.2
70–94.9	497	351	146	70.6	29.4
65–69.9	282	155	127	55.0	45.0
60–64.9	399	174	225	43.6	56.4
55–59.9	455	191	264	42.0	58.0
52.5–54.9	249	75	174	30.1	69.9
50–52.4	238	65	173	27.3	72.7
47.5–49.9	248	61	187	24.6	75.4
45–47.4	216	42	174	19.4	80.6
40–44.9	390	57	333	14.6	85.4
35–39.9	261	42	219	16.1	83.9
30–34.9	141	14	127	9.9	90.1
5–29.9	144	5	139	3.5	96.5
0–4.9	307	0	307	0.0	100.0
Total	4318	1712	2606	39.6	60.4

[a] Districts for which no presidential figures are available are excluded from this table.
[b] The 33 districts where the winning presidential candidate polled the same percentage of the vote as his House running mate are also listed in this column. All percentages have been computed to the nearest tenth of one per cent.

ture. Some were urban big-city constituencies. Others were rural farming areas. Some were in the North; others were in the South. Nor can any common ethnic or religious strand be found that might provide a key to why the House nominees in these districts led their victorious presidential running mate. These findings are equally

mate's percentage of the two-party congressional vote. The winning presidential nominee trailed his party's House ticket in those districts where his percentage of the two-party presidential vote was smaller than his House running mate's percentage of the two-party congressional vote. In 33 of the districts analyzed for the period 1924–1964, the two percentages were identical. All percentages were computed to the nearest tenth of one per cent.

true, it should be added, when the analysis is limited to the individual election years which make up our sample.

Yet one factor was common to most of these districts where a winning President trailed his House running mate. Most of the districts were banner congressional strongholds of the winning President's party. This relationship is brought out by the data in Table 7.1. Between 1924 and 1964, the larger a party's House vote in a district was, the greater the chances were that the local House candidate would lead his party's presidential nominee. Close to two thirds of the House contestants who ran ahead of a President from their party garnered more than 60 per cent of their district's congressional vote. About seven of every eight (87.4 per cent) of the congressional aspirants who led their party's winning presidential candidate were sent to Washington.

The actual number of House nominees who run ahead of a victorious presidential nominee on their party ticket varies from election to election. But the basic pattern revealed in Table 7.1—a pattern which affects the Democratic and Republican parties alike—remains the same. House candidates often run ahead of their presidential teammate in their party's traditional strongholds. Winning presidential nominees, on the other hand, lead their congressional running mate in nearly all of the constituencies where their party is relatively weak.

The probable consequences of this for the ongoing struggle between the executive and legislative branches of government invite reflection. Although many Congressmen from banner Democratic strongholds in the big cities of the North have been among the staunchest supporters of Presidents Roosevelt, Truman, Kennedy, and Johnson, these recent Democratic Presidents have also run behind certain other Democrats with whom they had to tangle more than once on Capitol Hill—men such as Edward E. Cox of Georgia and Howard W. Smith of Virginia. Republican Presidents, too, have encountered stout opposition from Congressmen of their own party who were stronger than the President was in their own local district. Fundamentally, the data in Table 7.1 suggest that many of the House candidates whom even a popular President can help most are those whose chances of victory are marginal, or worse. Conversely, many Congressmen from the

President's own party who exercise· great power in the House because they are returned to Washington year after year not only come from safe districts but are stronger in those districts than the President himself.

It is worth speculating on what is happening in districts where a House aspirant leads a successful presidential candidate of his party. Some voters who support the congressional nominee are either abstaining from voting for President, or are supporting the opposition's presidential candidate. At the same time, in constituencies where the winning President's House running mate makes a relatively poor showing, the President is able to appeal to voters who decline to support the congressional wing of his party. Fundamentally, then, the relationship between a party's presidential and congressional vote in a district turns on two things: the appeal which its presidential hopeful has relative to the opposition's presidential choice; and the attraction of the party's local House nominee relative to his congressional opponent.

Many of the House nominees from the strongholds controlled by their own party who lead their presidential running mate are incumbents—veteran Congressmen with assured tenure, who come from one-party districts and enjoy seniority and extensive contacts on the Hill. Some of these men, with a shrewd eye to the next election, have earned a reputation for being able to "get things done" for their district. Some House nominees may also run ahead of their presidential standard-bearer because some of their constituents find their views on questions of public policy more congenial than those of the party's presidential nominee. Thus, in a number of Democratic congressional strongholds in the South, some supporters of conservative Democratic Congressmen may prefer the G.O.P. presidential nominee to the choice of a Democratic national convention controlled by that party's more liberal elements.

Both the policy preferences of the candidates and an incumbent's strength at the polls may color the returns in districts where a winning President trails his House teammate. But incumbency can hardly account for the numerous House nominees making their first race for Congress in strongholds of their party who also outrun a President of their partisan affiliation. And an incumbent Congressman's decision to run again probably has a less important bearing on the outcome of a subsequent House contest in his district than the fact that his party already controls the constituency at the congressional level.[5] Consider the respective states of the local parties in a one-party district. Over a period of time the dominant party probably obtains more than its share of the abler leaders, money, and other sources of strength which count in a local political contest. And when one party is strong in a constituency, the other party frequently is pitifully weak. Often it is stretching a point to speak of a second party organization in the area at all. Yet from the supporters of the party which finds itself in a local minority must come a House candidate—if the district's seat in Congress is to be contested at all.

To a talented young man with political ambitions, the nomination of a party that is usually defeated by two to one is likely to appear decidedly uninviting. It should therefore hardly occasion surprise when a party that finds itself in a virtually permanent minority in a district nominates a House candidate who has little that would encourage the perceptive voter to support him. Yet even an able candidate in such a district is likely to be hindered by lack of organizational support, by insufficient funds, and by a host of other obstacles that make it difficult for him to take his case with effectiveness to the electorate. In most situations it is extremely difficult for a party to muster the full potential support for its national party viewpoint at the congressional level in strongholds of the opposition party.

The fate of the party's national presidential candidate in such areas, by contrast, may be somewhat better. The choice of the party's national nominating convention is likely to be a man of at least some competence. In most cases, he will be a stronger candidate than the party's local congressional hopeful. The national candidate also benefits from extensive coverage by the mass media. This widespread publicity may enable him to appeal more effectively to wavering voters than the party's local congressional nominee without upsetting delicate local arrangements that may be contingent upon continued one-party domination of their local area. The urge of politicians not to compete seems to be stronger at lower levels of government than in the balloting for President.

5. This is the core of the argument in Chapter 3.

If these notions are correct, they help to indicate why presidential candidates frequently are more successful in breaking into opposition party strongholds than are their party's candidates for lesser offices. In this light, too, the vote for a party's congressional ticket and its relation to the party's presidential vote becomes more clear. For it is in elections at the congressional level that influences on the voting that stem from the national presidential contest and influences stemming primarily from the peculiarities of the local political situation collide and merge.

The Presidency and the Congress: The Erosion of Sectionalism in the South

THE PRIMARY EMPHASIS OF the preceding discussion has been on the differences between the presidential and congressional constituencies. Yet in the country as a whole, there is a broad overlap between the vote which each major party polls for President and for Congressman. In areas where one party is strong, the dominant party usually obtains generous margins for its candidates at both the presidential and the congressional level. And when the opposition breaks into a party's traditional stronghold at one level in the selection of national officers, it may be time to watch its impact at the other level as well.

Although Barry Goldwater's presidential nomination evoked a pronounced sectional response in parts of the South in 1964, in recent years the more general tendency has been for the impact of sectionalism on the balloting for President to decline. In the 1930's and 1940's, Franklin Roosevelt and Harry Truman broke into erstwhile G.O.P. strongholds in the Midwest and in New England. They also polled a heavy vote in other parts of the country where previous Democratic presidential nominees in this century had been notably unsuccessful. In the 1950's the most politically cohesive region of all, the once solidly Democratic South, was cracked at the presidential level by the Republicans' Dwight D. Eisenhower.

For a hundred years, the South has been the prime demonstration of the sectionalism of the American political system. Yet it is well to remember that the South has not always been dominated by one political party. In the 1830's and 1840's, there was spirited competition between two major parties in the South. And this competition reflected profound social and economic differences within the population of the region. "The economic and political interests of the southern Whigs were the 'special interests' of the slavocracy. During the early 1840's the Whig party was frequently denounced as the aristocratic party of the slaveholders." The Democrats, by contrast, drew on "the opposite side of the social scale—especially upon the small farmer of the back hill-country who could always be reached by the party's appeal to the agrarian spirit."[6] At the national level, southern electoral votes were cast for Whig as well as for Democratic presidential candidates, and Whig Congressmen, as well as Democratic Representatives, were sent to Washington by the voters of the South.[7]

Then came The War. Except in a few isolated enclaves of Republican strength in the Appalachian Mountains, where Unionist sentiment was strong during the Civil War, southern white electors coalesced with extraordinary unanimity behind candidates of the Democratic party in opposition to the party of Lincoln and Grant. From Richmond, Virginia to Brownsville, Texas, from Tallahassee, Florida to Little Rock, Arkansas, two common factors peculiar to southern society—the Negro and memories of a losing Civil War and the Reconstruction that ensued—combined to produce a superficial picture of political unanimity. In the vernacular of American politics, the "Solid South" became a commonplace.

It was the southern whites in the black belt—areas where the Negro population was largest—for whom this sectional solidarity was of crucial importance. And their determination to preserve a one-party system was made plain when the Populists attempted to provide an alternative to the Democratic party in the South in the 1890's. As V. O. Key declared: "In the fight against Populism and in the subsequent agitation about the place of the Negro, the black belts strengthened their position by reenforcing the South's attachment to the Democratic party. The raising of a fearful specter

6. Arthur C. Cole, *The Whig Party in the South* (Washington: American Historical Association, 1914), pp. 69–72.
7. For a discussion of the relatively even balance of power between the Whigs and the Democrats in the South in the 1830's and 1840's, see Charles Grier Sellers, Jr., "Who Were the Southern Whigs?" *American Historical Review*, Vol. 59, No. 2, January, 1954, pp. 335–346.

of Negro rule and the ruthless application of social pressures against those who treasonably fused with the Republicans under Populist leadership put down for decades the threat of the revival of two-party competition.

"Two-party competition would have been fatal to the status of blackbelt whites. It would have meant in the 'nineties an appeal to the Negro vote and it would have meant (and did for a time) Negro rule in some black-belt counties. From another standpoint, two-party competition would have meant the destruction of southern solidarity in national politics—in presidential elections and in the halls of Congress. Unity on the national scene was essential in order that the largest possible bloc could be mobilized to resist any national move toward interference with southern authority to deal with the race question as was desired locally."[8]

For several decades after Reconstruction, this remarkable sectional solidarity was reflected in full at the presidential level. In the 1920 Republican landslide, Harding carried Tennessee; but it was not until the Democrats nominated Al Smith—a wet, a Roman Catholic, and a New Yorker—that a Republican was able to poll a heavy vote for President in the South. In 1928, Herbert Hoover ran ahead of Smith in five of the region's eleven states. The Republican's share of the total presidential vote in the area was 47.3 per cent. Within a year, however, the Great Depression had begun, and in 1932 the southern states were once again solidly Democratic. As late as 1944, Franklin Roosevelt received more than seven of every ten votes cast for President in the South.[9]

By 1948, however, the political climate below the Mason-Dixon line had changed considerably. A hastily constructed States' Rights presidential ticket, headed by South Carolina's J. Strom Thurmond, gave a third choice to southerners who were dissatisfied with the national Democratic Administration of Harry Truman. The results of the balloting must be interpreted with some care, because it was

8. V. O. Key, Jr., *Southern Politics in State and Nation* (New York: Alfred A. Knopf, 1949), pp. 8–9.
9. Roosevelt drew 71.5 per cent of the South's total presidential vote in 1944. The Republican presidential nominee, Thomas E. Dewey, polled 25 per cent, while other candidates received 3.5 per cent of the total. *The World Almanac and Book of Facts for 1957* (New York: *The New York World-Telegram and The Sun*, 1957), pp. 52–77.

in the four states where Thurmond ran as the Democratic nominee that the South Carolinian made his best showing.[10] Nevertheless, when the votes polled by the G.O.P. candidate and by Thurmond were subtracted, the national Democratic presidential nominee was left with barely half of the southern popular vote. The Republican share of this turnout, however, was still a meager 26.6 per cent of the total.[11]

In 1952 it was different. Republican national leaders decided to make a determined bid for southern votes. In a precedent-shattering move, the new G.O.P. presidential nominee, General Eisenhower, began his campaign in Atlanta, deep in the heart of the Southland. Even the most optimistic Republican strategists must have been gratified by the region's response. Between 1948 and 1952, the number of southerners who voted for President increased by two thirds. Nearly half of this record number of votes—4.1 million out of 8.5 million—went to General Eisenhower, a showing which enabled the G.O.P. to carry four states with 56 of the region's electoral votes.[12] Four years later, Eisenhower solidified his strength in the South. For the first time since Reconstruction, a Republican presidential nominee polled more votes than his Democratic opponent in the eleven states of the former Confederacy. The 1956 popular vote in the South was:

Eisenhower (Republican)	4,211,461	48.9 per cent
Stevenson (Democrat)	4,122,778	47.8 per cent
Andrews (Independent)	152,336	1.8 per cent
Byrd (Independent)	131,471	1.5 per cent
Others	2,152	— [13]

10. Thurmond appeared on the ballot as the Democratic presidential nominee in Louisiana, Mississippi, Alabama, and South Carolina.

11. The 1948 presidential percentages in the South were: Truman 50 per cent; Dewey 26.6 per cent; Thurmond 22.6 per cent; Wallace (Progressive) 0.6 per cent; and others 0.2 per cent. *The World Almanac and Book of Facts for 1957, op. cit., loc. cit.*

12. The 1952 popular vote figures in the South were: Eisenhower 4,113,525; Stevenson 4,428,163; and other candidates 12,023. The percentages of the total vote were: Eisenhower 48.1 per cent; Stevenson 51.8 per cent; and others 0.1 per cent. Richard M. Scammon, Editor, *America Votes* (New York: Macmillan Company, 1956).

13. *The World Almanac and Book of Facts for 1957, op. cit., loc. cit.*

In 1960, when Richard Nixon was undoubtedly helped in the region by his opponent's Roman Catholicism, and in 1964, when Barry Goldwater espoused views on the race question that many southern whites found congenial, the Republican presidential nominee also polled a large vote in the South.

The potential appeal in the South of a G.O.P. presidential ticket is now taken seriously by managers of both parties. But until recently discussions of the electoral prospects of southern Republican House candidates were frequently greeted with chilling

Figure 7.1—Southern popular votes for Republican presidential and congressional candidates, 1944-1964

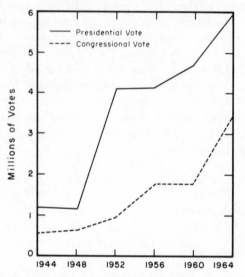

skepticism. Yet here again, a close look at the recent voting trends in the region is in order. In a growing minority of the House districts of the South, G.O.P. congressional aspirants are becoming a real threat to their Democratic adversaries.

Nineteen-fifty-two was the year of the first great Republican breakthrough in southern presidential voting since the New Deal. It was in 1956, however, that the largest gains up to that time were registered by G.O.P. House candidates in the South. This upsurge of the popular vote for Republican congressional nominees is under-scored by the data in Figure 7.1. Between 1944 and 1952 the vote polled by would-be southern Republican Congressmen increased substantially. On the other hand, between 1948 and 1952 alone, the G.O.P. presidential vote in the South more than trebled. In 1956 President Eisenhower received about the same number of southern popular votes as he polled four years earlier. But between 1952 and 1956, the vote cast for Republican House candidates in the region increased by two thirds.

This narrowing of the gap between the southern Republican vote for President and for Congressman took place even though President Eisenhower was on the ballot in all of the region's 106 House districts while southern electors could vote for a G.O.P.

Figure 7.2—Republican percentage of the two-party vote for Representative in the South, 1948–1964

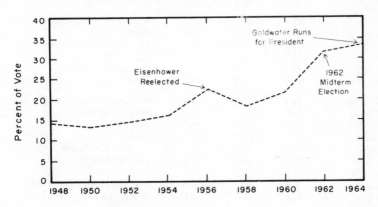

congressional candidate in only 42 districts. In part, the increased House vote reflected greater organizational activity by the G.O.P. In 1956 the party contested ten more seats than it had four years before. But the respectable showing made by Republicans in several of the newly contested districts also indicates that increasing areas of the South were becoming receptive to active two-party competi-tion at the congressional level. Even in districts which had been contested earlier, however, G.O.P. House nominees reduced the gap separating their own vote tallies from those of President Eisenhower between 1952 and 1956.

The Republicans' percentage of the total House vote in the South in the elections between 1948 and 1964 is indicated in Figure 7.2. In

Table 7.2—Southern House Districts in which Republican Congressional Candidates Polled 40 Per Cent or More of the Two-Party Vote in 1962

District	Rep. % House Vote	% Population Urban	% Population Negro	District's Location in State
Tenn. 2	70.6	51.5	6.0	E. Central–Knoxville
Va. 6	65.4	60.1	13.5	W. Central–Roanoke
Fla. 12	64.5	91.1	8.8	W. Central–St. Petersburg
Tex. 5	56.3	97.5	14.5	Dallas
N.C. 8	56.0	53.5	25.2	S. Central–Charlotte
Va. 10	55.4	88.8	6.1	Wash. D.C. suburbs
Tenn. 1	55.1	32.1	2.6	Northeast
Tex. 16	53.8	84.9	3.9	West–El Paso
Fla. 11	51.9	68.9	15.8	E. Central–Orlando
Tenn. 3	51.1	56.1	13.2	Southeast–Chattanooga
N.C. 9	50.5	34.9	12.1	N.W. Central
Va. 3	49.7	82.8	25.7	Richmond and environs
Tenn. 9	49.4	87.8	36.3	Memphis
Va. 7	49.4	29.4	8.1	N. Central–Winchester
Tex. 3	48.0	48.0	24.7	East–Tyler
S.C. 2	47.2	47.7	37.2	Central–Columbia
Tex. 22	46.5	98.1	14.7	Houston—South and suburbs
N.C. 10	44.9	42.3	12.2	W. Central–Gastonia
N.C. 11	44.8	26.0	6.0	West–Asheville
Ga. 5	44.4	90.0	26.5	Atlanta
Tex. A. L.	43.9	75.0	12.4	Texas
Fla. 3	42.4	98.8	17.8	N. Dade Co.–Miami
N.C. 4	41.9	40.8	22.6	Central–Raleigh
Tex. 18	41.2	69.2	3.9	N. Panhandle–Amarillo
N.C. 5	40.8	40.9	22.4	N. Central–Winston-Salem
N.C. 6	40.1	67.5	23.0	N. Central–Durham

Source: U.S. Bureau of the Census, *Congressional District Data Book* (*Districts of the 88th Congress*) (Washington: U.S. Government Printing Office, 1963).

the midterm Democratic landslide of 1958, the Republicans' share of the House vote dropped in the South, as it did elsewhere in the country. The party scored a defensive victory in the region, however, by retaining control of all seven of its southern House seats, including the five it had captured since 1950. In 1960, the party's share of the southern House vote again moved upward; and in 1962, the party made its best showing up to that point in the

South while polling nearly 32 per cent of the region's vote. At the same time, four more southern Republican House seats were added to the seven that the party had previously controlled.

There were 26 districts in the region where Republican House candidates polled 40 per cent or more of the two-party vote in 1962. By study of these, the two major sources of strength for the Republican party in southern House contests before 1964 can be traced. Data which bear on these constituencies appear in Table 7.2. The great majority of the southern districts where the G.O.P. made a respectable showing in 1962 were located either in the Appalachian Plateau region embracing western Virginia, central and western North Carolina, and eastern Tennessee, or in rapidly growing industrial and urban enclaves scattered from Richmond, Virginia to Miami, Florida and Dallas, Texas. The existence of some Republican strength in the uplands of the South has a long history, although since World War II it has been increasing. The emergence of Republicanism with mass support among the professional and middle classes of the region's economically expanding urban centers, on the other hand, is a more recent phenomenon. And it has profound implications for the future of southern politics.

In many respects, the land which in popular lore is ascribed to the "hillbilly," and the respectable urban neighborhoods of an emergent middle class are worlds apart. But nearly all of these districts representing the twin strands of persistent southern Republicanism have one factor in common: a smaller Negro population than average for the South. In only two of the 26 districts did the number of Negroes in the population substantially exceed one in four. In nearly two thirds of the districts, it varied from one in five to one in 40. As the proportion of Negroes in southern districts increased, by contrast, the number of respectable Republican vote tallies and even candidates became few and far between.

This association between the black-belt districts and continuing Republican weakness at the congressional level in 1962 is brought out by the data in Table 7.3. In all of the nine southern districts where the 1960 Negro population exceeded 40 per cent, the G.O.P. did not even run a House candidate.[14] In the 1960 presidential ballot-

14. For the record, perhaps it should be noted that in most black-belt House districts relatively few Negroes voted in 1962.

ing, five of these districts were carried by the Democratic presidential ticket, two went Republican, and two supported an unpledged presidential electors ticket. Where an unpledged or states' rights ticket alternative was available, the voters in these black-belt districts gave it considerable support, but up until 1964 these dissident presidential protests did not affect the voting for Congressmen, in part, no doubt, because the black-belt voters' views on racial issues were already forcefully represented by their incumbent Democratic Congressmen.

Table 7.3—1962 Republican House Vote in Southern Districts Where the Negro Percentage of the Total Population Exceeded 40 Per Cent in 1960

District	% Population Negro	Rep. % House Vote	% Population Urban	District's Location in State
Miss. 2	59.1	0	28.0	Northwest
N.C. 2	48.4	0	31.9	Northeast
Va. 4	47.9	0	27.4	Southeast
S.C. 6	46.5	0	27.8	East
Miss. 3	46.4	0	53.8	Southwest
S.C. 1	43.8	0	44.5	South–Charleston
Ga. 6	41.3	0	53.8	Central–Macon
La. 5	40.4	0	44.8	Northeast
Miss. 4	40.3	0	25.8	Central

In 1952 President Eisenhower drew upon three major sources of support in the South: traditionally Republican areas in the Appalachian Plateau; urban voters registering a protest against the economic policies of the Fair Deal; and black-belt electors expressing their disapproval of the national Democratic party's stand on racial issues.[15] In 1956 President Eisenhower had lost the support of many in this last group, but his gains in the cities and in the uplands more than made up for their defection. The significant fact

15. Samuel Lubell, *The Revolt of the Moderates* (New York: Harper Brothers, 1956), pp. 179–180. Donald Strong has pointed out that in 1952 the black-belt counties swung to Eisenhower in South Carolina, Mississippi, Louisiana, and Alabama, while supporting Stevenson in North Carolina, Tennessee, Texas, and Virginia. Stevenson did well in the black belt in the latter states, Strong suggests, because some Negroes voted in these areas, and because the white voters' attachment to the Democratic party was reinforced by the presence of a relatively strong Republican opposition within the state. See Donald S. Strong, "The Presidential Election in the South, 1952," *Journal of Politics*, Vol. 17, No. 3, August, 1955, pp. 343–389.

about the southern Republican House strength is that from 1945 through the 1962 midterm elections it never stemmed from the black belt. With but few exceptions, its base lay primarily in the Appalachian Plateau and the cities.

As the preceding discussion indicates, until 1964 southern Republicanism had no history of gradual, steady growth in the black belt—either at the presidential or the congressional level. But in the Appalachian Plateau and the cities, the evolution of Republican strength for President and Congressmen deserves treatment in somewhat greater detail. As early in 1944, there were 22 districts in the South where Thomas E. Dewey was able to poll more than four votes of every ten for the Republican presidential ticket. Most

Table 7.4—House Districts Where Dewey Polled the Heaviest Presidential Vote for the Republican Party in the South in 1944 and the Republican Percentage of the Congressional Vote in Those Districts in 1948 and 1956[a]

DISTRICT'S REPUBLICAN PERCENTAGE FOR PRESIDENT IN 1944	NO. OF DISTRICTS	DISTRICTS WHERE REP. HOUSE NOMINEES POLLED OVER 45% OF THE VOTE IN 1948		DISTRICTS WHERE REP. HOUSE NOMINEES POLLED OVER 45% OF THE VOTE IN 1956		DISTRICTS CARRIED BY REP. HOUSE NOMINEES IN 1956	
		No.	Per Cent	No.	Per cent	No.	Per Cent
55–65	2	2	100.0	2	100.0	2	100.0
50–54.9	5	0	0.0	4	80.0	3	60.0
45–49.9	6	1	16.7	4	66.7	1	16.7
40–44.9	9	0	0.0	3	33.3	1	11.2
Total	22	3		13		7	

[a] Slightly under a third of the districts analyzed in this table lost one or more counties between 1944 and 1956 as a result of redistricting. In every case, however, the changed districts retained the same major population centers.

of these constituencies were scattered throughout the Appalachian Plateau. But there also were harbingers of the Republicans' growing urban strength in the South. Dewey did fairly well in the less rural districts of Florida, and in scattered constituencies which included the cities of Chattanooga, Tennessee and Dallas, Texas. In nearly all of these districts, however, the vote received by G.O.P. House nominees lagged well behind the Republican presidential poll.

In Table 7.4, an analysis is presented which makes it possible to follow the fortunes of subsequent G.O.P. House candidates in these southern districts where Dewey did best in 1944. By 1948, only three

Republican congressional nominees polled over 45 per cent of the vote in these constituencies. And the only ones who were elected came from the two longtime Republican strongholds of eastern Tennessee. By 1956, however, the fortunes of Republican House nominees in the southern districts where Dewey had made his best showing in 1944 had improved markedly. In 13 of the districts, the G.O.P. House vote exceeded 45 per cent. In seven of the constituencies, a Republican Congressman was elected. All but one of the 1956 Republican House seats listed in Table 7.4 remained Republican at the congressional level in 1960 and 1964.

Every southern Republican Representative who was sent to Washington in 1956 was elected in a district where Dewey had polled over 40 per cent of the presidential vote in 1944. Moreover, the larger Dewey's vote had been earlier, the better a Republican House candidate was likely to do in the district in 1956. In the Appalachian uplands and the cities of the South, lines of cleavage that were etched by the presidential battle of 1944 were being paralleled in the contests for Representative more than a decade later. The G.O.P. House vote still lagged behind the party's presidential poll, but the Republicans' congressional gains in the South followed in the wake of G.O.P. successes at the presidential level.

With the nomination of Barry Goldwater by the Republicans in 1964 this basic pattern of Republican weakness in the black belt and growing Republican strength in urban areas and the Appalachian Plateau that had prevailed in southern House contests since World War II was radically altered. But the 1964 returns also gave another demonstration of the impact that the direction of the presidential vote can have on the vote for the House. In the six southern states that rim the Deep South (Virginia, North Carolina, Florida, Tennessee, Arkansas, and Texas), the predominant swing of the presidential tide compared with 1960 was to the Democratic party. The number of House districts in these states where the Democratic presidential percentage increased between 1960 and 1964, and the number where it decreased, were as follows:

Dem. % Up in 1964	Dem. % Down in 1964
57	12

In the five Deep South states of South Carolina, Georgia, Alabama, Mississippi, and Louisiana, on the other hand, there was a swing to the Republican presidential ticket in every House district except the two in the Atlanta, Georgia area.[16] The number of House districts in these states moving in each direction in the presidential voting were as follows:

Dem. % Up in 1964	*Dem. % Down in 1964*
2	35

The shifts in the 1964 House results tended to parallel this trend in the presidential voting. In the rim of the South, Republicans actually lost two of the eleven southern House seats they had won in 1962; and in another southern Republican district in the area, the Virginia 10th, the Republican came closer to losing his seat than at any other time since his first election in 1952. On the other hand, in the Deep South, where the Republicans held no House seats before 1964, the party elected seven Congressmen—five in Alabama, and one each in Georgia and Mississippi; and the odds are that they missed an opportunity to win even more. In 1964, the Republicans failed to contest four House seats in each of four Deep South states —Louisiana, Mississippi, South Carolina, and Georgia. They also left two seats uncontested in Alabama. Had the Republicans run more House candidates in the Deep South in 1964, their gains in the area might well have been larger.

Table 7.5 provides a listing of some salient characteristics of the southern House districts where the Republican party did best in 1964. The Republican congressional strength in certain urban areas and the Appalachian uplands remains; but to it has been added

16. Georgia was redistricted shortly before the 1964 election, and Atlanta was the only area of the South where there was some doubt concerning the net movement of the presidential vote between 1960 and 1964 where it was not feasible to obtain the 1960 presidential vote within the new 1964 district boundary lines. If the two Atlanta area districts are lumped together, the 1960 Democratic presidential vote in them was 51.0 per cent. In 1964 it was 51.8 per cent. Data sources for the presidential vote in southern House districts in 1960 and 1964 were: U.S. Bureau of the Census, *Congressional District Data Book (Districts of the 88th Congress)* (Washington: U.S. Government Printing Office, 1963); special supplements to the *Congressional District Data Book* for states redistricted in 1963–64; and *Congressional Quarterly Weekly Report*, "Complete Returns of the 1964 Elections by Congressional District," March 26, 1965.

Table 7.5—Southern House Districts Where Republican House Candidates Polled 40 Per Cent or More of the Two-Party Vote in 1964

District	Republican Percentage of Two-Party House Vote	Per Cent of Population Urban	Per Cent of Population Negro	District's Location in State
Tenn. 1	71.7	32.1	2.6	Northeast
Ala. 2	62.8	55.7	35.8	S. Central (Montgomery)
Fla. 12	60.6	91.1	8.8	W. Central (St. Petersburg)
Fla. 11	60.6	68.9	15.8	E. Central (Orlando)
Ala. 6	60.6	86.5	31.7	N. Jefferson Co. (Birmingham)
Ala. 1	59.9	68.2	37.0	Southwest (Mobile)
Ala. 7	59.6	34.8	7.7	N. Central (Gadsden)
Ala. 4	59.1	40.5	30.5	E. Central (Selma)
Ga. 3	57.4	51.9	36.9	S. W. Central (Columbus)
Va. 6	56.2	60.1	13.5	W. Central (Roanoke)
Miss. 4	55.7	25.8	40.3	Central
N.C. 9	55.2	34.9	12.1	Northwest
Tenn. 2	54.8	51.5	6.0	East (Knoxville)
Tenn. 3	54.6	56.1	13.2	Southeast (Chattanooga)
N.C. 8	54.3	53.5	25.2	S. Central (Charlotte)
Va. 10	50.7	88.8	6.1	Wash. D.C. suburbs
Va. 3	49.6[a]	82.8	25.7	Richmond and environs
N.C. 5	48.4	40.9	22.4	N. Central (Winston-Salem)
N.C. 4	48.2	40.8	22.6	Central (Raleigh)
Tenn. 9	47.4	87.8	36.3	West (Memphis)
Ala. 5	47.0	49.3	42.5	W. Central (Bessemer)
Ga. 5	46.0	91.4	33.4	Atlanta
La. 8	45.5	36.7	28.9	Central (Alexandria)
Ga. 7	45.3	39.4	8.8	Northwest
Ark. 3	45.3	38.6	2.2	Northwest
Tex. 18	45.0	69.2	3.9	N. Panhandle (Amarillo)
La. 2	45.0	79.3	30.8	W. New Orleans and suburbs
Tex. 16	44.3	84.9	3.9	West (El Paso)
Ga. 4	43.1	88.7	19.8	Atlanta suburbs
Tex. 5	42.5	97.5	14.5	Dallas
Tex. 22	41.9	98.1	14.7	Southern Houston
Va. 9	41.8	19.3	2.7	Southwest
N.C. 10	41.4	42.3	12.2	West Central
Tex. 3	40.7	48.0	24.7	East (Tyler)
Tenn. 5	40.2	87.7	19.1	Nashville

[a] The Republican House nominee polled 49.6 per cent of the major-party vote in Virginia's 3rd District, but there was also a large vote (31.5 per cent of the total) cast for independent nominees in the district. The Republican's share of the total House vote was 34.0 per cent.

Sources: U.S. Bureau of the Census, *Congressional District Data Book* (*Districts of the 88th Congress*) (Washington: U.S. Government Printing Office, 1963), and special supplements to the *Congressional District Data Book* for states redistricted in 1963–64.

Republican strength in the black belt. In June 1965 the victory as a Republican of South Carolina's former Democratic Representative, Albert W. Watson, in a special election added one more district with a heavy element of black-belt counties to the Republican total.

This establishment of a congressional beachhead in the black-belt districts of the South may be one of the most important legacies of the 1964 election to the Republican party, although members of that party will differ as to whether its effects on the G.O.P. in other areas of the country are an advantage or a liability. The base of support for the Republican congressional ticket in some of the urban districts and the Appalachian Plateau region of the South seems sufficiently well established that it is likely to endure and in all probability will grow. The prospects for the Republicans in the black-belt, however, are less certain, and, in the short run at least, turn on the queston whether, once Goldwater is off the Republican ticket, these districts will support conservative Democratic or conservative Republican candidates for Representative.

The stakes involved are high. For if there is enduring Republican House strength in these districts, the areas in the South that will be opened up for an effective Republican challenge to traditional Democratic control will be substantially increased.[17] Over a period of time, too, such a trend could sharply reduce the size of the dissident conservative wing of the Democratic congressional party, while increasing the number of conservatives in the congressional ranks of the G.O.P.[18] Yet even if the black-belt House districts that elected Republican Representatives in 1964 were to return to the

17. The number of southern House districts where the Republican House candidate polled 35 per cent or more of the vote may give a rough indication of the districts in the South where the Republicans must be taken seriously in a congressional race. Of districts of this type, there were nine in 1944. In 1954 there were 17. In 1964, after the Republican breakthrough in the black belt, there were 44.

18. These speculations, it should be added, may apply only to a relatively short "short run." They are essentially an extrapolation of black-belt trends during a period when many Negroes in these areas were deprived of the vote. If Negroes begin to vote in large numbers in these districts, some of the districts might actually switch from sending opponents of federal welfare and civil rights legislation to sending supporters of such measures to Washington. The emergence of large numbers of Negro voters in the black belt could also constitute a powerful additional force laying a basis for two-party competition in black-belt House districts.

Democratic party, the basis for active two-party competition at the congressional level already exists in close to a third of the House districts of the South. In the years ahead, the region is likely to become an important battleground in Republican party bids for control of the House of Representatives.

The Presidency and the Congress: The Erosion of Sectionalism Outside the South

A MAJOR PROCESS OF partisan realignment at the congressional level is underway in the South. The shift since 1945 in the southern states' House vote has not always been steady. But the long-term trend has clearly been toward increased southern Republican congressional strength and a breakdown of one-party Democratic domination of the region's House contests. Yet in other regions of the country, where Republican rather than Democratic House candidates have been dominant throughout most of the 20th century, there are signs of a partisan realignment that is moving in the opposite direction. In recent years there has been increasing Democratic strength in several long-time congressional strongholds of the Republican party.

If the Civil War left a one-party South that has had a profound impact on American politics for a century, the sectional cast that congressional voting patterns outside the South assumed in the aftermath of the Civil War and the election of 1896 have been scarcely less important. Except for the Progressive Era when Woodrow Wilson won the Presidency—a victory made possible by divisions in the Republicans' ranks—the Republicans dominated the House contests in most regions of the country outside the South and Border States from the turn of the century until the Great Depression. The House returns for the 1924 election that are summarized in Table 7.6 provide a sample of the sectional character of the House vote during most elections from 1900 through 1930. In 1924 Democrats won every seat but two in the South and three fifths of the seats from the Border States. Outside these areas the Republicans had an enormous lead. The Democrats were particularly weak in New England, the Midwestern and Pacific Coast states, and the Plains states. Even in 1930, after the Depression had

Table 7.6—Democratic and Republican House Members, by Region, Elected in Selected Years Between 1924 and 1964

Region[a]	1924 D	1924 R	1930 D	1930 R	1936 D	1936 R	1942 D	1942 R
South	102	2	101	3	100	2	102	2
Border States	28	19	36	11	41	2	28	14
All Others	52	227	80	203	193	84	85	190
New England	4	28	8	24	14	15	7	21
Mid-Atlantic	24	67	28	64	64	30	41	52
Midwest	14	71	31	55	65	18	21	64
Plains States	5	33	6	34	13	16	0	30
Rocky Mountain	3	11	4	10	14	0	11	5
Pacific Coast	2	17	3	16	23	5	15	18

Region[a]	1948 D	1948 R	1954 D	1954 R	1960 D	1960 R	1962 D	1962 R	1964 D	1964 R
South	103	2	99	7	99	7	95	11	90	16
Border States	37	5	30	8	32	6	28	8	29	7
All Others	123	163	103	188	132	161	136	157	176	117
New England	11	17	10	18	14	14	15	10	17	8
Mid-Atlantic	45	46	38	50	43	45	41	43	54	30
Midwest	38	49	30	57	36	51	34	54	46	42
Plain States	5	26	5	26	6	25	5	22	12	15
Rocky Mountain	12	4	7	9	11	5	10	7	13	4
Pacific Coast	12	21	13	28	22	21	31	21	34	18

[a] The following states are contained in the regions as defined for this table: South—Ala., Ark., Fla., Ga., La., Miss., N.C., S.C., Tenn., Tex., and Va.; Border States—Kent., Md., Mo., Okla., and W.Va.; New England—Conn., Me., Mass., N.H., R.I., and Vt. ; Mid-Atlantic—Del., N.J., N.Y., and Pa.; Midwest—Ill., Ind., Mich., Ohio, and Wisc.; Plains Sates—Iowa, Ks., Minn., Nebr., N.D., and S.D.; Rocky Mountain—Ariz., Colo., Ida., Mont., Nevada, N.M., Utah, and Wyo.; Pacific Coast—Cal., Ore., and Wash., and, beginning in 1958–1959, Alaska ahd Hawaii. The total number of seats accounted for in each region may vary slightly from election to election, both because the total number of seats allocated to a given region may have changed following a decennial census, and because occasionally a House seat may have been won by a minor-party or independent congressional nominee.

begun, the Republicans had an advantage over the Democrats in every region of the country except the South and Border States.[19]

19. The Democrats were able to organize the new House after the 1930 elections, but it was not because they were strong that year in regions north of the Mason-Dixon Line. Compared with 1924, the Democratic House gains outside the South and Border States in 1930 were relatively moderate, and the Democrats still trailed the Republicans outside those two regions by 123 House seats. The Democrats' gains in 1930 were sufficient to enable them to gain control of the House only because of the enormous lead the Democrats piled up in the South and the Border States. For an analysis of regional patterns in congressional voting for the period 1896–1944, see Cortez A. M. Ewing, *Congressional Elections, 1896–1944* (Norman, Okla.: University of Oklahoma Press, 1947), especially Chapter 6.

Then came the full impact of the Depression. From 1932-1948 the Democratic presidential ticket demonstrated strength in virtually all major regions of the country. At the peak of the New Deal's strength, Democratic House candidates also did well in all areas, as the House returns for 1936 in Table 7.6 indicate. In several regions, however, Democratic House strength receded sharply following 1936; and by the early 1940's the pattern of House strength outside the South had once again assumed a fairly marked sectional character. New England, the Midwest, the Plains states, and the Pacific Coast area were predominantly Republican at the congressional level. In good Democratic years the Democratic presidential ticket was able to poll a sizable vote in some of these areas, as Harry Truman demonstrated in 1948. But this Democratic presidential strength was strength the local Democrats were not able to match at the congressional level.

The figures in the final six columns of Table 7.6 indicate the number of House seats won by each party over several elections between 1942 and 1964. Because of the extraordinary size of the Democratic congressional sweep in 1964, the 1962 figures probably give a better indication of more normal levels of Democratic congressional strength in recent years. (The Democrats' House strength roughly equalled or exceeded the 1962 Democratic showing in 1958 and 1960, as well as in 1964.) Nevertheless, even comparisons of the House results since 1942 that omit 1964 reveal a sizable increase in Democratic congressional strength in several regions outside the South.

The distribution of House seats in the Mid-Atlantic states has been fairly evenly balanced since 1942, and the Democrats have held a lead in the relatively small number of districts in the Rocky Mountain states in most elections since the 1930's. But in New England, the Plains states, and the states along the Pacific Coast, all areas where the Republicans tended to have a lead in House contests in the 1940's and early 1950's, there has been greater Democratic House strength in most recent elections. New England did not elect a majority of Democratic Congressmen even at the high tide of the New Deal in 1936, and in 1954 the New England House delegation contained 18 Republicans and 10 Democrats. But in 1962 the Democrats held a margin in the region of 15 House seats to 10. In 1954 Republican Congressmen from the Pacific Coast states outnumbered the West Coast Democrats by 28 to 13. In 1962 there were 10 more Democrats than Republicans in the area.

The growth of Democratic strength in the Plains states has been more spotty. In several recent elections the Democrats have elected only 5 or 6 congressmen from the area (compared with no Plains states Democrats in 1942). But these figures on seats won conceal a considerable improvement in the popular vote for Democratic congressional candidates in most recent elections in the area.[20] They also conceal the fact that the Democrats have been giving Republicans hard fights in a number of the region's House seats, compared with the situation in the 1940's and early 1950's, when most of these seats were safely Republican. Republicans still tend to be favored to win in most districts in the Plains states, and the House results in the area have been highly volatile over the past 10 years. Nevertheless, as the Democratic successes in the area in 1964 demonstrate, in some elections Democrats can now capture a significant share of the Plains states' House seats, and a sizable part of the area is now potentially competitive at the congressional level.

Partisan Realignment and the Nationalization of House Elections

The over-all House results outside the South and Border States indicate what has been happening in recent elections to the Republicans' traditional sources of congressional strength. Between 1954 and 1962, the Republicans' net lead over the Democrats in the number of Congressmen elected from all areas outside the South and the Border States dropped from 85 to 21. These figures call attention to the peculiar dilemma which the Republican party faces in its bids for control of the House of Representatives in the 1960's. Areas outside the South that were once heavily Republican (aside from the peak years of the New Deal) are now sending substantially more Democratic Congressmen to Washington than they

20. From the end of World War II to 1964, the Democratic percentages of the two-party vote for the House in the Plains states were as follows: 1946, 38.2%; 1948, 44.7%; 1950, 40.7%; 1952, 37.7%; 1954, 44.9%; 1956, 46.9%; 1958, 51.6%; 1960, 47.0%; 1962, 44.8%; and 1964, 51.0%.

did in the 1920's or even in the early 1950's. This erosion of sectional-ism in the North has gone far to deprive the Republican party of its domination of its traditional regional strongholds above the Mason-Dixon Line.

The result is that the Republicans have lost their top-heavy margin of House seats in their former northern sectional strong-holds. But they have not yet registered some countervailing gains in the South that would be theirs if the tempo of partisan realign-ment were the same throughout the country. Until the G.O.P. adds substantially to its strength for the House in the South—as it al-ready has for President—the party faces formidable obstacles in its bid for control of the House of Representatives. Yet if the portents of recent election returns are fulfilled, in time these gains by south-ern Republican House candidates will come.

It remains only to restate the basic argument of this chapter. The sectional cast which the American national party system assumed between the end of the Civil War and the turn of the present cen-tury is gradually wearing away. New lines of cleavage were first riven through each major party's regional strongholds by the voting for President. In time, however, those cleavages have tended to appear in the form of enduring strength at the congres-sional level as well. In some areas, this second phase in the process of partisan realignment is now fairly well advanced. In other areas, the process is still in its initial stages.

Predictions concerning the course which the American party system is likely to follow in the future are hazardous in the extreme. To an extent that is probably inadequately appreciated, this de-pends on the relationship of the United States to the rest of the world. It also is contingent upon the evolving nature of the American domestic political struggle. If present trends continue, however, there will in years to come be a greater parity of con-gressional strength between two national parties in most of the great regions of the country which were dominated by one party before the New Deal. In fact, in this sense, a nationalization of American politics is already taking place.

A Note on
Data Sources

Unless it is expressly indicated otherwise in the text or in the relevant footnotes, the following are the data sources used throughout the book for all presidential and congressional election returns analyzed.

House Election Figures:
For 1964: *Congressional Quarterly Weekly Report,* March 26, 1965.
For 1952–1962: Richard M. Scammon, Editor, *America Votes,* Vols. 1–5.
For 1920–1950: Biennial Reports of the Clerk of the United States House of Representatives, "Statistics of the Presidential and Congressional Election of [date] ," or "Statistics of the Congressional Election of [date] ," 1920–1950 (Washington: United States Government Printing Office, 1921–1951); except that for those states where House returns for 1946–1950 were reported in *America Votes,* Vol. 1, the *America Votes* volume was used as the data source.

Presidential Election Returns, by House Districts:
For 1952–1964: Tabulations that appeared in the *Congressional Quarterly Weekly Report* in the late winter or early spring following the November general election.

For 1920–1948: Original data collection compiled by Dr. Ruth C. Silva, of The Pennsylvania State University. These data cover all but the 13 Cook County, Illinois congressional districts for 1948. For the 1920–1944 period, between 68 and 90 districts (out of a possible 435), mostly northern big-city constituencies, were missing for individual election years. The precise number of districts analyzed for each year may vary slightly from table to table, because of the differing ground rules for excluding House districts that applied to different analyses. However, the maximum or very close to the maximum number of districts that could be analyzed for presidential-congressional vote comparisons for each election year are indicated in the lefthand column of Table 1.1 on p. 10.

In a number of instances the data are analyzed or discussed by region. Most frequently, the returns from the South may be broken out from the returns from the rest of the country. But other discussions of the data from individual regions are also included. Unless expressly indicated otherwise, for purposes of analysis the regions were defined as consisting of the following states: *South* — Ala., Ark., Fla., Georgia, La., Miss., N. C., S. C., Tenn., Tex., and Va.; *Border States* — Kent., Md., Mo, Okla., and W. Va.; *New England* — Conn., Me., Mass., N. H., R. I., and Vt.; *Mid-Atlantic* — Del., N. J., N. Y., and Pa.; *Midwest* — Ill., Ind., Mich., Ohio, and Wisc.; *Plain States* — Iowa, Ks., Minn., Nebr., N. D., and S. D.; *Rocky Mountain* — Ariz., Colo., Ida., Mont., Nevada, N. M., Utah, and Wyo.; *Pacific Coast* — Cal., Ore., and Wash., and, beginning in 1958–1959, Alaska and Hawaii.

Index